PREFACES

WRITING SAMPLE

KIERKEGAARD'S WRITINGS, IX

PREFACES

WRITING SAMPLER

by Søren Kierkegaard

Edited and Translated
with Introduction and Notes by

Todd W. Nichol

PRINCETON UNIVERSITY PRESS
PRINCETON, NEW JERSEY

Library of Congress Cataloging-in-Publication Data

Kierkegaard, Søren, 1813–1855.
[Forord, Skrift-Prøver. English]
Prefaces : writing sampler / by Søren Kierkegaard ;
edited and translated with introduction and notes by Todd W. Nichol.
p. cm. — (Kierkegaard's writings ; 9)
Translation of: Forord, Skrift-Prøver
Includes bibliographical references and index.
ISBN 0-691-04827-4 (alk. paper)
I. Nichol, Todd W., 1951– . II. Kierkegaard, Søren, 1813–1855.
Skrift-Prøver. English. III. Title. IV. Title: Skrift-Prøver.
V. Series: Kierkegaard, Søren, 1813–1855. Works. English. 1978 ; 9.
PT8142.F57F6713 1997
198'.9—dc21   97-8631

Preparation of the volume has been made possible in part by a grant from
the Division of Research Programs of the National Endowment
for the Humanities, an independent federal agency

CONTENTS

Writing Sampler
69

HISTORICAL INTRODUCTION

During two weeks in June of 1844, Søren Kierkegaard published four books. The first of these works, *Three Upbuilding Discourses*, appeared on June 8. Signed by Kierkegaard in his own name, this collection epitomizes the religious works that regularly accompanied the pseudonymous writings of this period. Five days later came *Philosophical Fragments, or a Fragment of Philosophy*, by Johannes Climacus and edited by S. Kierkegaard, a compressed work on philosophical and Christian themes central to Kierkegaard's authorship. This was followed on June 17 by *The Concept of Anxiety*, a book unique among the pseudonymous writings for its direct pedagogical style. Attributed to the pseudonym Vigilius Haufniensis, this work on anthropology in relation to Christian dogmatics was in Kierkegaard's judgment essentially different from the other pseudonymous writings. Furthermore, although it had a signed counterpart among the upbuilding discourses, it also had a mate of a different sort, published simultaneously with *Anxiety* on June 17, the satirical *Prefaces* by Nicolaus Notabene. In the account of his authorship included in *Concluding Unscientific Postscript to* Philosophical Fragments, Kierkegaard emphasized the simultaneity as well as the intentional pairing of the serious and the satirical in this conjunction of works.[1]

The Concept of Anxiety and *Prefaces* were indeed written and readied for publication during the same period. The seventh section of *Prefaces* seems originally to have been intended to introduce *The Concept of Anxiety*, but it was transferred to its present position when Kierkegaard decided that it did not comport with the purpose and style of the completed larger work. Kierkegaard, however, still wished to make public what he had intended to say in the original preface. With this and other

---

[1] See *Postscript*, pp. 268–71, *KW* XII.1 (*SV* VII 228–29). A similar pairing occurs with *Christian Discourses* and *The Crisis and a Crisis in the Life of an Actress* (*KW* XVII; *SV* X), published on April 26, 1848, and July 24–27, 1848, respectively.

purposes in mind, he worked on several polemical projects during the period 1843–47.[2]

The drafts of these efforts are undated but located within specified periods by the Danish editors of Kierkegaard's papers. While the chronology cannot be precisely determined, the sequence is evident on the basis of internal evidence. The earliest of the polemical writings specifically related to *Prefaces* was "New Year's Gift" by Nicolaus Notabene.[3] The use of this pseudonym for the projected work and the inclusion in it of some material originally written in 1843–44 as portions of a response to a review of *Repetition*[4] by the literary arbiter Johan Ludvig Heiberg (1791–1860) indicate that "New Year's Gift" preceded the more fully developed *Prefaces*. Although skeletal, "New Year's Gift" reveals the development of a satirical attack on Heiberg, the evolution of a humorous approach to themes developed in *The Concept of Anxiety*, and the origins of Kierkegaard's parody in *Prefaces* of the lavish New Year's books produced in nineteenth-century Denmark for presentation as Christmas gifts.

Kierkegaard integrated elements of "New Year's Gift" into *Prefaces* along with some materials prepared even earlier. A portion of an early version of "Preface IV," satirizing New Year's books, was originally appended to an unpublished response to Heiberg's criticism of *Repetition*.[5] This focus on New Year's literature was later carried over into the preparation of "New Year's Gift" and from there into *Prefaces*. Other passages initially

---

[2] See, for example, Supplement, pp. 127–28 (*Pap.* VI A 146).

[3] See Supplement, pp. 100–08 (*Pap.* IV B 125–39).

[4] See J. L. Heiberg, *Urania: Aarbog for 1844* (Copenhagen: 1843; *ASKB U* 57), pp. 94–102, in which the author discusses for his own purposes passages and concepts from Kierkegaard's *Repetition*. Kierkegaard wrote replies to Heiberg but did not publish them. See *Repetition*, Supplement, pp. 283–319, *KW* VI (*Pap.* IV B 110–17), and pp. 379–83, note 14. Heiberg had also commented rather critically on *Either/Or* in "*Litteraire Vintersæd*" (Literary Winter Grain), *Intelligensblade*, 24, March 1, 1843. Kierkegaard replied in *Fædrelandet*, 1168, March 5, 1843. See "A Word of Thanks to Professor Heiberg," *The Corsair Affair*, pp. 17–21, *KW* XIII (*SV* XIII 411–15). See also *Either/Or* II, Supplement, pp. 406–07, *KW* IV (*Pap.* IV B 54).

[5] See Supplement, p. 99 (*Pap.* IV B 117). See also *Repetition*, Supplement, p. 301, *KW* VI (*Pap.* IV B 117).

included in Kierkegaard's unpublished response to Heiberg were also eventually incorporated into *Prefaces*.[6] Originally prepared to introduce *The Concept of Anxiety*, "Preface VII" in its present location is both a comment on that work as well as an element of its comic counterpart. The remaining sections of *Prefaces* were prepared specifically for the published work. In its final form, *Prefaces* is a result of Kierkegaard's practice of working on several projects at various desks at the same time, of "multiple writing," as the editors of *Søren Kierkegaard's Journals and Papers* have aptly termed it.[7]

The decision to make the published volume a collection of prefaces without a book to follow them, and yet to introduce the whole with a preface of its own, signals Kierkegaard's satirical intent. The curious form of *Prefaces* invites the interested reader to wonder whether there is not more of a book here than might be expected. The position of the work in Kierkegaard's authorship is, of course, a hint of this, and the text is strewn with clues to the author's intention. In form and substance, *Prefaces* exemplifies satire etymologically defined as *satura*, as a "mixed dish" or medley of comic irony.

In its immediate context, *Prefaces* is Kierkegaard's satirical response to critics of his pseudonymous works, particularly J. L. Heiberg. In Kierkegaard's view, Heiberg and other critics had neither read nor discussed these books with care. In response, Kierkegaard wrote in the ironic guise of an author who could not get his works published and took the conventional scholar's marginal note, *NB* or *Notabene* [Note well!] as his pseudonym.[8]

Although the work is addressed to readers and critics in general and against all facile writing and reading, Kierkegaard keeps

---

[6] See, for example, *Repetition*, Supplement, p. 285, *KW* VI (*Pap.* IV B 110, p. 260), and p. 299 (*Pap.* IV B 116, p. 278). Cf. p. 24 below.

[7] See *JP* V 5726 (*Pap.* V B 47:13), note 1099.

[8] In the year prior to the publication of *Prefaces*, Kierkegaard considered the pseudonym Nicolaus Notabene for another project labeled simply "Idea," but did not develop this idea further. See Supplement, p. 100 (*JP* V 5671; *Pap.* IV A 119). Kierkegaard also considered Nicolaus Notabene as a pseudonym for the unfinished *New Year's Gift* and the unpublished "Writing Sampler." See Supplement, pp. 100–08 (*Pap.* IV B 125–39) and p. 127 (*Pap.* V A 99).

J. L. Heiberg particularly in view throughout *Prefaces*, a fact not lost on contemporary readers. "Preface III" and "Preface IV" are, among other things, comic attacks on Heiberg's remarks on *Either/Or* and his comments on *Repetition* in his luxuriously printed New Year's book, *Urania: Aarbog for 1844*.[9] Heiberg himself never responded publicly to *Prefaces*, but readers of the day knew that the lance had struck its mark. Kierkegaard's antagonist of a few years later, Peder Ludvig Møller (1814–1865), for example, said of *Prefaces* that it was "not only some of the wittiest but unconditionally the most elegant of what has been written against Heiberg; . . . I do not remember any polemical writing in Danish as excellent."[10] Although *Prefaces* received comparatively little public attention when it was published, perhaps in part because of Heiberg's decision not to comment directly on it and so to doom it to insignificance among Copenhagen's cultural elite, what mention it did receive in the contemporary press quickly focused on the polemic against him.[11] "We have spoken," a contemporary reviewer reported, "with various people who immediately seemed to betray a certain acquaintance with Nicolaus Notabene's *Prefaces* as well as with Vigilius Haufniensis's book *The Concept of Anxiety* and S. Kierkegaard's *Philosophical Fragments* and his new *Upbuilding Discourses*. But, strangely enough, every time we wanted to go into one or another of these works a little, they always reverted to the comments about Prof. Heiberg in *The Preface* [sic]."[12] A few years later the press returned the favor to Kierkegaard when a sentence from *Prefaces* was revived as a caption to a malicious cartoon caricaturing him as an equestrian.[13]

Kierkegaard's desire to respond to J. L. Heiberg's criticism of the earlier pseudonymous works was, however, only the imme-

[9] (Copenhagen, 1843; *ASKB U* 57), pp. 94–102.

[10] See Corsair *Affair*, p. 99, *KW* XIII, for this comment by P. L. Møller in "A Visit in Sorø."

[11] See *Stages on Life's Way*, p. 748, note 136, *KW* XI.

[12] *Ny Portefeuille*, pub. Georg Johan Bernhard Christensen, ed. Jørgen Christian Scythe, II, 13, June 30, 1844, col. 309. See also *Stages*, Supplement, p. 648, *KW* XI (*Pap.* VI B 184, p. 256), and p. 748, note 136.

[13] See p. 5, note 7. See Corsair *Affair*, Supplement, pp. 120–21, *KW* XIII, for this article in *Corsaren* 278, January 16, 1846, col. 2–8.

diate occasion for the publishing of *Prefaces*. Nor did a desire to comment on reading and literary criticism exhaust Kierkegaard's intentions for this work. *Prefaces* is also a more general reckoning with Danish Hegelianism, represented in literature by J. L. Heiberg and in theology by Hans Lassen Martensen (1808–1884), then a professor in the theological faculty at Copenhagen and later to become Bishop of Sjælland.

Prefaces continues in comic mode the attack on Danish Hegelianism initiated in earlier works and soon to be more fully developed in *Stages* and *Postscript*. Satirical comment on speculative idealism in Danish dress surfaces early in *Prefaces* when Nicolaus Notabene mocks those who promise a philosophical system but never write it and later when he makes a burlesque of J. L. Heiberg's promises to develop a philosophical system comprehensive enough to include an astonishing array of arcane studies including, among other things, astrology. The final two prefaces are an extended lampoon of Danish Hegelianism. Here, in comic form, are some of the themes from earlier works, particularly the unpublished "Johannes Climacus, or De Omnibus Dubitandum Est" and topics that will occupy Kierkegaard in major works to come: epigones who claim originality for themselves, the philosophical system as a grandiose illusion, mediation as intellectual sleight of hand, pretentious scholarly language, scholarship that claims to understand everything but the self, and falsely heroic doubt that cannot doubt all things and that does not direct itself to that which is most important. Wondering in print about how to address confusions in these matters, Nicolaus Notabene speculates at length on what a proper philosophical periodical might look like, and thereby introduces into this little book, ironically presented as if it had no proper genre of its own, satirical treatment of yet another literary form, intellectual journalism. Kierkegaard appears in this period actually to have considered publication of such a periodical.[14]

Just as *Prefaces* encapsulates Kierkegaard's confrontation with Danish Hegelianism, it also prefigures Kierkegaard's final collision with Danish Christendom. In what is certainly a direct

---

[14] For a preliminary sketch for such a journal, see Supplement, p. 100 (*Pap.* V A 100).

reference to H. L. Martensen, Kierkegaard attacks theologians who claim to have become philosophers in response to the demands of the times and who incorporate Christian theology in a system like Hegel's, while claiming to have gone beyond him. This broadside against the Danish dogmatician and ecclesiastic is preceded by ironic but respectful comment on Jakob Peter Mynster (1775–1854), Bishop of Sjælland and religious mentor to cultured Danes. These remarks are an indirect contribution to a controversy between Mynster and an Odense schoolmaster later to become an admirer of Kierkegaard, Hans Peter Kofoed-Hansen (1813–1893). Kofoed-Hansen had argued in an inflammatory article that the Danish Church, through want of philosophical sophistication, had alienated the cultured.[15] In a sharp and extended reply, Mynster repudiated the claim that Christianity needed a "philosophical bath" to make it respectable, citing Kierkegaard's *Fear and Trembling* and *Upbuilding Discourses* as the work of a cultivated person of faith.[16] Entering this debate, Nicolaus Notabene ironically proposes the publication of a suitable devotional book for the cultured and takes the occasion to display an up-to-date intellectual's contempt for a collection of sermons by Mynster, *Prædikener paa alle Søn- og Hellig-dage i Aaret*, a work Kierkegaard knew as a youth and continued to use in later years.[17] In disparaging these sermons, Nicolaus Notabene points out that they are uncorrupted by any systematic tendency, are suitable in form for daily devotional reading, are ever timely by virtue of their neglect of current events, and directed to the interests of the self alone. The pseudonymous deprecation of these works is an ironic expression of gratitude on the part of Søren Kierkegaard. These appreciative comments on Mynster are indeed Kierkegaard's first published mention of the pastor who confirmed him and who later became the leading cleric of Denmark. This reference to Mynster also points toward the con-

---

[15] Kofoed-Hansen's article, a review of *Either/Or*, appeared in *Fyenske Fierdingsaarsskrivt for Literatur og Kritik* (Odense), IV, 1843, pp. 384–85.

[16] See Kts, "*Kirkelig Polemik*," *Intelligensblade*, ed. J. L. Heiberg, IV, 41–42, January 1, 1844, pp. 97–114. "Kts" was Mynster's pseudonym, formed from the initial consonant of the second syllable of each name (Ja*k*ob Pe*t*er Myn*s*ter).

[17] I–II (Copenhagen, 1837; *ASKB* 229–30).

clusion of the authorship. Appearing as it does in a book containing remarks critical of H. L. Martensen, this portion of *Prefaces* anticipates Kierkegaard's attack on Martensen for his designation of Mynster in a funeral oration as a "truth-witness" and the polemical battle that followed, ending with Kierkegaard's death in 1855.

This, however, lay in the unknown future when Kierkegaard wrote *Prefaces*. In their proximate context, Nicolaus Notabene's comments on Mynster's devotional work reveal something of Kierkegaard's immediate intent. The frequent use of the phrase "the cultured [*de Dannede*]" in this context signifies an engagement not only with Mynster's critic, Kofoed-Hansen, but with the social transition underway in Denmark in the tumultuous years just before the revolution of 1848. The phrase "the cultured" was claimed both by advocates of liberal reform, among them Peter Martin Orla Lehmann (1810–1870), against whom Kierkegaard had written as a youth,[18] and by the conservative guardians of Denmark's retrospective high culture, including J. L. Heiberg and J. P. Mynster. The satire in *Prefaces* is directed against both factions when Kierkegaard presents "culture [*Dannelse*]" as a collective, socializing experience that, misconstrued and abused, can lead individuals into abandoning their proper responsibility for themselves. As Kierkegaard employs it, the satire in *Prefaces* thus functions at more than one level. In the specific instance of Kierkegaard's satirical treatment of Nicolaus's satire of Mynster as minister to cultured Christians, negative criticism is converted into constructive proposals for devotional literature actually appropriate to the times. *Christian Discourses*, signed by Søren Kierkegaard and published in the revolutionary year 1848, was intended to be and is an example of such.[19]

[18] See "To Mr. Orla Lehmann," *Early Polemical Writings*, pp. 24–34, *KW* I (*SV* XIII 28–39).

[19] That Part IV of *Christian Discourses* was not dedicated to J. P. Mynster, as Kierkegaard originally intended, is not a repudiation of Mynster's devotional writings but rather an early sign of Kierkegaard's impending clash with established Christendom in Denmark. For an evaluation of *Christian Discourses* as a devotional work, see "*Geschichtliche Einleitung zur zwanzigsten Abteilung*," in Sören Kierkegaard, *Christliche Reden*, ed. and tr. Emanuel Hirsch (Düsseldorf, Cologne: Eugen Diedrichs Verlag, 1959), pp. viii-ix.

None of this, of course, will surprise the alert reader. In the opening pages of *Prefaces*, Nicolaus Notabene advises the reader to consider that this farrago of occasional pieces may conceal a fundamental argument: "The incommensurable, which in an earlier period was placed in the preface to a book, can now find its place in a preface that is not the preface to any book."[20] *Prefaces* is, in fact, essentially of a piece with the major constructive works of this period of Kierkegaard's authorship. The satire regularly implies sounder alternatives, often explicated in trenchant, apothegmatic passages threaded through the work. A noteworthy example of this inversion of the satirical, intertwining arguments specific to *Prefaces*, as well as to the authorship as a whole, occurs in the context of Nicolaus Notabene's comments on the relation of author and reader. "Each being is assigned only to himself, and the one who takes care to remain here has a solid foundation to walk on that will not shame him."[21] It would be difficult to find a more concise summary of Kierkegaard's project and aim in the pseudonymous works.

Kierkegaard did not expect a favorable reception for *Prefaces*. "Such an idiosyncratic and his opinion," as Nicolaus Notabene puts it, "are usually not well liked, because those concerned surely notice that, consciously or unconsciously, it contains a satire on their opinion."[22] Kierkegaard himself, however, appears to have been sufficiently satisfied with *Prefaces* to have twice drafted a sequel, titled "Writing Sampler,"[23] although this work from the period 1844–47 remained unpublished during his lifetime. Considering a variety of pseudonyms before settling on "A.B.C.D.E.F. Godthaab,"[24] Kierkegaard first turned to this work shortly after the publication of *Prefaces*. Apparently seriously considering publication,[25] he prepared a substantially altered fair copy sometime in the period 1845–1847.[26] Kierke-

---

[20] P. 4.   [21] P. 42.   [22] P. 18.

[23] See Supplement, pp. 127, 129–45, 148–50, the first draft of *Skrift-Prøver* (*Pap.* VI B 194–235), undated but from the years 1844–45, and pp. 69–90, the final version (*Pap.* VII² B 274:1–24), likewise undated but from the period 1845–47.

[24] Literally "A.B.C.D.E.F. Goodhope."

[25] See *JP* V 5754 (*Pap.* V A 99).

[26] See pp. 69–90 (*Pap.* VII² B 274:1–24).

gaard's journals indicate that as late as 1847 he thought of publishing a version of this work along with other pieces as a fourpart "mystification" to be called "The Writings of a Young Man" and to appear under the ebullient pseudonym Felix de St. Vincent.[27]

The reader who wishes to study *Writing Sampler* in the context of this projected but unpublished work is invited to read in the following order: (1) *The Crisis and a Crisis in the Life of an Actress*;[28] (2) "A Eulogy on Autumn";[29] (3) "Rosenkilde as 'Hummer'";[30] (4) "Writing Sampler."[31] Situated in "The Writings of a Young Man," "Writing Sampler" would have centered on esthetic considerations and been an example of the compatibility of esthetic and religious interests in the stages of an individual's life.[32] Standing by itself, "Writing Sampler" is a polemical miscellany like *Prefaces*, although Kierkegaard intended to emphasize the satirical and ironical elements in the sequel even more than he had in *Prefaces*.[33]

"Writing Sampler" remained among Kierkegaard's unpublished papers during his lifetime, and *Prefaces* itself was little noticed in the months after its publication. Only two contemporary reviews appeared in the Danish press, and, like most of Kierkegaard's works, the greater number of the 525 copies of *Prefaces* printed in 1844 remained unsold after a few years and were purchased as remainders by C. A. Reitzel in 1847.[34] *Prefaces* was not reprinted during Kierkegaard's lifetime and did not again appear

---

[27] See Supplement, p. 156 (*Pap.* VIII^1 339). The pseudonym might be literally translated as "The lucky one from St. Victor."

[28] See *KW* XVII, pp. 301–25 (*SV* X 319–44).

[29] See Supplement, pp. 156–60 (*Pap.* VII^1 B 205–10).

[30] See Supplement, pp. 160–62 (*Pap.* VIII^2 B 172–74). This is a brief sketch for an essay on the performance of a Danish actor, Christen Niemann Rosenkilde (1786–1861), in the part of Hummer in J. L. Heiberg, *De Uadskillige, Skuespil af J. L. Heiberg*, I-VII (Copenhagen: 1833–41; *ASKB* 1553–59), IV, pp. 223–348.

[31] See Addendum, pp. 69–70 (*Pap.* VII^2 B 274:1–24).

[32] See *Crisis, KW* XVII (*SV* X).

[33] See Supplement, p. 127 (*Pap.* V A 99).

[34] By July of 1847, 208 copies had been sold. See Frithiof Brandt and Else Rammel, *Søren Kierkegaard og Pengene* (Copenhagen: Levin & Munksgaard, 1935), pp. 18–19.

in print until the publication of the first critical edition of the works, *Søren Kierkegaards samlede Værker,*[35] in 1901–06. "Writing Sampler" was first printed in 1914 and 1916 in volumes VI and VII[2] of *Søren Kierkegaards Papirer.*[36] With a few noteworthy exceptions, scholars have paid little attention to either work.[37] *Prefaces* is rarely mentioned in secondary studies, and even one of Kierkegaard's most sympathetic American biographers suggested that it would never be translated into English. It was, Walter Lowrie said, "an amusing book only for those who are familiar with Copenhagen in that age."[38] After rendering *Prefaces* into German, Emanuel Hirsch temperately observed that a wealth of contemporary allusion and compact wit make it a work difficult to translate.[39] The same may be said of its sequel, "Writing Sampler." Like *Prefaces* it is a work constructed of the historical particular.

These are, indeed, Kierkegaard's Copenhagen books, unmistakably linked to the city, an era, and specific individuals.[40] They are the creations of a writer with Copenhagen in his marrow, and to read them is to walk down the streets of that city in the middle of the nineteenth century, to meet its inhabitants, and to enter their lives. If only for this, *Prefaces* and "Writing Sampler" make

[35] I-XIV, ed. A. B. Drachmann, J. L. Heiberg, and H. O. Lange (1 ed., Copenhagen: Gyldendal, 1901–06).

[36] I-XI[3], ed. P. A. Heiberg, V. Kuhr, and E. Torsting (1 ed., Copenhagen: Gyldendal, 1909–48).

[37] In addition to the unsigned review in *Ny Portefeuille,* II, 13, June 30, 1844, col. 305–312, another unsigned review was "*En Bemærkning, foranlediget ved Nicolaus Notabenes 'Forord,'*" *Den Frisindede,* 75, July 2, 1844, pp. 299–300.

Niels Thulstrup is among the comparatively few scholars who have given *Prefaces* much attention. See, for example, *Kierkegaard's Relation to Hegel,* tr. George L. Stengren (Princeton: Princeton University Press, 1980), pp. 365–69.

[38] Walter Lowrie, *A Short Life of Kierkegaard* (Princeton, New Jersey: Princeton University Press, 1942), p. 261.

[39] See "*Geschichtliche Einleitung zur elften und zwölften Abteilung,*" in Sören Kierkegaard, *Der Begriff Angst; Vorworte, Gesammelte Werke,* ed. and tr. Emanuel Hirsch (Düsseldorf: Eugen Diederichs Verlag, 1952), p. x.

[40] Niels Thulstrup called *Prefaces* Kierkegaard's "arch-Copenhagen" book. See *The Copenhagen of Kierkegaard, Bibliotheca Kierkegaardiana,* I-XVI (Copenhagen: C. A. Reitzels Forlag, 1978–1988), XI, p. 131.

enjoyable and historically informative reading. Yet Kierkegaard did not write only to amuse and inform. His intent in these works is to grasp the crucial through the customary, to approach the enduring through the ephemeral, and above all to engage the individual through the illustrative. Of this strategy Nicolaus Notabene observes: "Even an author who in his work defies the times may nevertheless in the preface accommodate himself to custom in trivial matters and is thereby put to the test in many a collision—very droll for the observer—with regard to how far and how."[41]

Aristotle in his *Rhetoric*, a treatise carefully studied by Kierkegaard, borrows a question from Euripides: "Why all this preface?"[42] One answer to the question is: to catch the reader unaware. "If you wish to distract his attention, you should imply that the subject does not affect him, or is trivial or disagreeable, But observe, all this has nothing to do with the speech itself."[43] Perusing the prefaces of the happy but hapless unpublished writer in little Denmark, Nicolaus Notabene, the contemporary reader may be tempted to think this volume a literary lark through a time and place vanished, a pastiche that never was and still is not a book, at most no more than a satire on small town pretensions. Yet at this point a troubling thought may invade the reader's mind. "Everyone sees material for parody in small-town life," Kierkegaard once remarked, but few recognize the large type represented by the small.[44] Who is the object of the fun in such a parody? Only the properly self-interested will recognize themselves as the people parodied and thus reckon with the argument animating this curious work. If, as Nicolaus Notabene says, "Writing a preface is like ringing someone's doorbell to trick him,"[45] the reader of this work can expect to meet only himself or herself on the doorstep.

[41] P. 3.

[42] Aristotle, *Rhetoric* (III.14.1415b), in *The Complete Works of Aristotle: The Revised Oxford Translation*, I-II, ed. Jonathan Barnes (Princeton: Princeton University Press, 1984), II, p. 2260.

[43] Ibid.

[44] *JP* V 5246 (*Pap.* II A 126).

[45] P. 5.

What Kierkegaard once said about his own life in Copenhagen may well serve to introduce *Prefaces* to the contemporary
reader. "The only person I can say I envy is he, when he comes,
whom I call my reader, who in peace and quiet will be able to sit
and purely intellectually enjoy the comic drama I have allowed
Copenhagen to perform just by living here."[46] At the same time,
however, Kierkegaard warns the reader that this is humor with a
more than esthetic intent. It stretches the limits of the esthetic, it
intimates the possibility of ethical striving, and it portends an
invitation to Christian faith. "From a poetic point of view it is
not at all interesting . . . poetically it must be abbreviated. So it
will be for my reader. But in and with the dailiness begins the
religious . . .."[47] While resisting the temptations of the genetic
fallacy, the interested individual may find these observations a
guide to locating *Prefaces* and "Writing Sampler" in Kierkegaard's authorship and a key to reading them.

[46] *JP* VI 6288 (*Pap.* IX A 471).
[47] Ibid.

PREFACES

*LIGHT READING FOR PEOPLE IN VARIOUS
ESTATES ACCORDING TO TIME
AND OPPORTUNITY*

by Nicolaus Notabene

PREFACE[1]

It is a frequently corroborated experience that a triviality, a little thing, a careless utterance, an unguarded exclamation, a casual glance, an involuntary gesture have provided the opportunity to slip into a person and discover something that had escaped more careful observation. Lest, however, this insignificant remark be distorted and become pompous, I shall for the moment forego further pursuit of it and get on with my project. [2]In relation to a book a prologue is a triviality, and yet by means of a more careful comparison of prologues, would one not gain an opportunity for observation at a bargain price! In the scholarly world much is made of classifying literature and assigning the writing of each individual author to its proper place in the age and the writing of the age in that of the human race. Yet no one thinks about what might be gained if one or another *literatus* [literary type] could be trained to read only prologues, but to do it so thoroughly that he would begin with the earliest times and advance through all the centuries down to our own day. Prologues are characterized by the accidental, like dialects, idioms, colloquialisms; they are dominated by fashion in a way entirely different from the way works are—they change like clothing. Now they are long, now short; now bold, now shy; now stiffly formal, now slapdash; now worried and almost repentant, now self-confident and almost brash; now not entirely without an eye for the weaknesses of the book, now stricken with blindness, now perceiving these better than anyone else; now the preface is the first distillation of the product, now an aftertaste of it. And all of this is purely ceremonial. Even an author who in his work defies the times may nevertheless in the preface accommodate himself to custom in trivial matters and is thereby put to the test in many a collision—very droll for the observer—with regard to how far and how. Indeed, the more I think of this, the richer the yield promised by such a study seems to me. Just think of the contrast: the Greek naïveté

that would furnish a superb basis for the presentation of the results. But I halt this flight of thought, which would probably lead
me astray since I lack the equipment.

The preface has received its deathblow in recent scholarship.
Looked at from its point of view, an older author easily becomes
a pitiful figure over whom one does not know whether to laugh
or to cry, because his halting manner in getting to the point
makes him comic, and his naïveté, as if there were anyone who
cared about him, makes him pathetic. Nowadays a situation like
this cannot be repeated, because when one begins the book with
the subject and the system with nothing[3] there apparently is
nothing left over to say in a prologue. This state of affairs has
given me occasion to become aware that the preface is an altogether unique kind of literary production, and since it is el-
bowed aside it is high time for it to liberate itself like everything else. In this way it can still come to be something good.
The incommensurable, which in an earlier period was placed in
the preface to a book, can now find its place in a preface that is
not the preface to any book. I believe that in this way the conflict
will be settled to mutual satisfaction and benefit; if the preface
and the book cannot be hitched up together, then let the one
give the other a decree of divorce.

[4]The most recent scholarly method has made me aware that it
would have to come to a break. My merit will be this, to make
the break in earnest; now there is only a phenomenon that points
to the deeper reason. Every esthetically cultivated author surely
has had moments when he did not care to write a book but when
he really wanted to write a preface to a book, no matter whether
it was by himself or by someone else. This indicates that a preface
is essentially different from a book and that to write a preface is
something entirely different from writing a book; if not, this
need would express itself only when one had written a book, or
when one imagined that one would write it just as one superfi-
cially imagines it, and thus raises the question of whether one
should write the preface first or last. Nonetheless, as soon as a
person is in one of these situations, he either has had a subject or
imagines having it. But now when lacking also this he desires to
write a preface, it is easy to perceive that this must not deal with

a subject, because in that case the preface itself would become a book, and the question of the preface and the book would be pushed aside. The preface as such, the liberated preface, must then have no subject to treat but must deal with nothing, and insofar as it seems to discuss something and deal with something, this must nevertheless be an illusion and a fictitious motion.

The preface is thereby defined purely lyrically and defined according to its concept, while in the popular and traditional sense the preface is a ceremony according to period and custom. A preface is a mood. Writing a preface is like sharpening a scythe, like tuning a guitar, like talking with a child, like spitting out of the window. One does not know how it comes about; the desire comes upon one, the desire to throb fancifully in a productive mood, the desire to write a preface, the desire to do these things *leves sub noctem susurri* [in a low whisper as night falls].[5] Writing a preface is like ringing someone's doorbell to trick him, like walking by a young lady's window and gazing at the paving stones; it is like swinging one's cane in the air to hit the wind, like doffing one's hat although one is greeting nobody.[6] Writing a preface is like having done something that justifies claiming a certain attention, like having something on one's conscience that tempts confidentiality, like bowing invitingly in the dance although one does not move, like pressing hard with the left leg, pulling the reins to the right,[7] hearing the steed say "Pst," and oneself not caring a straw for the whole world; it is like being along without having the slightest inconvenience of being along, like standing on Valdby Hill[8] and gazing at the wild geese.[9] Writing a preface is like arriving by stagecoach at the first station, stopping in the dark shed, having a presentiment of what will appear, seeing the gate and then the open sky, gazing at the continually receding road beyond, catching a glimmer of the pregnant mystery of the forest, the alluring fading away of the footpath; it is like hearing the sound of the posthorn and the beckoning invitation of the echo, like hearing the powerful crack of the coachman's whip and the forest's perplexed repetition and the jovial conversation of the travelers. Writing a preface is like having arrived, standing in a comfortable parlor, greeting longing's desired object, sitting in an easy chair, filling a pipe, lighting it—and then

V
8

having endlessly much to converse about. Writing a preface is like being aware that one is beginning to fall in love—the soul sweetly restless, the riddle abandoned, every event an intimation of the transfiguration. Writing a preface is like bending aside a branch in a bower of jasmine and seeing her who sits there in secret: my beloved. Oh, this is how it is, this is how it is to write a preface; and the one who writes it, what is he like? He moves in and out among people like a dupe in winter and a fool in summer;[10] he is hello and good-bye in one person, always joyful and nonchalant, contented with himself, really a light-minded ne'er-do-well, indeed an immoral person, since he does not go to the stock exchange to feather his nest but only strolls through it; he does not speak at public meetings, because the atmosphere is too confined; he does not propose toasts in any society, because this requires notice several days in advance; he does not run errands on behalf of the system; he does not pay installments on the national debt and in fact does not even take it seriously; he goes through life the way a shoemaker's apprentice walks whistling down the street, even though the one who is to use the boots stands and waits—then he must wait so long as there remains a single place left for sliding or the slightest object of interest to see. This, yes this is what one who writes prefaces is like.

See, everyone can ponder all this as he wishes, just as it crosses his mind and when it crosses his mind. With me it is different because a promise and an obligation bind me to busy myself only and solely with this kind of writing. I will without delay tell the reader how all this hangs together, since it is in exactly the right place here, and just as defamation belongs at a coffee party, this is something that very properly belongs in a preface.

[11]Although happily married as only few are and also thankful for my happiness as perhaps only few are, I have nevertheless run up against difficulties in my marriage, the discovery of which is due to my wife, because I suspected nothing. Several months had passed by since the wedding. I had gradually become somewhat practiced in the pattern of marital life; then little by little there awakened again in me a desire that I had always nourished and in which I in all innocence thought I might indulge myself: engagement in some literary task. The subject was chosen, books along

this line that I myself owned were set out, particular works were borrowed from the Royal Library, my notes were arranged synoptically and my pen was, so to speak, dipped. Meanwhile, my wife had scarcely conceived a suspicion that some such thing was in the wind before she began watching my movements very carefully. Occasionally she dropped an enigmatic word, vaguely suggested that all my busyness in the study, my longer sojourns there, and my literary ruminations were not altogether to her liking. I did, however, keep all my wits about me and pretended not to understand her, which I actually did not at first. Then one day she catches me off guard and extracts from me the formal confession that I was on the way to wanting to be an author. If until now her conduct had been more a reconnoitering, she now zeroed in more and more definitely, until she finally declared open war, *et quidem* [and this] so openly that she intended to confiscate everything I wrote, in order to use it in a better way as the underlayment of her embroidery, for curlers, etc. An author's situation can hardly be more desperate than mine; even a person under special censorship can still hope to get his work to the point where it "may be printed,"[12] but my writing is always suffocated at birth. How desperate my position was became clearer and clearer to me in another way. I had scarcely discovered that I had become the object of persecution of the press before, as is natural, something became clear to me that previously had not entered my mind at all: that it would be an irretrievable loss to humanity if my writing did not see the light of day. What is now to be done about it? Unlike a censored author, I do not have recourse to the chancery, the provincial estates, the esteemed public, or posterity's memory. I live and die, stand and fall, with my wife. Now, I certainly am considered by my contemporaries to be a good and very experienced debater who can adequately plead my case, but here this proficiency will be of only slight benefit to me, because even if I can debate with the devil himself, I cannot debate with my wife. She has, namely, only one syllogism, or rather none at all. What learned people call sophistry, she, who wants nothing to do with being learned, calls teasing. Now, the procedure is very simple, that is, for the one who knows how to proceed properly. Whenever I say

something that she does not like, whether it is in the form of a
syllogism or not, whether a long speech or a short remark—the
form does not matter—but when she does not like what has been
said, she looks at me with a countenance that is lovable, charming, good-natured, and captivating, yet at the same time is triumphant, devastating, and she says: It is only teasing. The consequence of this is that all my skill in debating becomes a luxury
item for which there is no demand at all in my domestic life. If
I, the experienced dialectician, fairly well exemplify the course
of justice, which according to the poet's dictum is so very long,[13]
my wife is like the royal Danish chancery, *kurz und bündig* [short
and to the point], except that she is very different from that august body in being very lovable. It is precisely this lovableness
that gives her an authority that she knows how to maintain in a
charming way at every moment.

That is how things stand. I have never gone further than an
introductory paragraph. Since this was of a general nature and in
my view so successfully composed that it would be enjoyable to
her if I were not the author, it crossed my mind whether I might
not be able to win her to the enterprise by reading it to her. I was
prepared for her to reject my offer and for her to utilize the
advantage to say, "Now it has even gone so far that not only did
you occupy yourself with writing but I am obliged to listen to
lectures." Not at all. She received my proposal as kindly as possible; she listened, she laughed, she admired. I thought that all was
won. She came over to the table where I was sitting, put her arm
intimately around my neck, and asked me to read a passage again.
I begin to read, holding the manuscript high enough so that she
can see to follow me. Superb! I am beside myself but am not
quite through that passage when the manuscript suddenly bursts
into flames. Without my noticing it, she had pushed the single
candle under the manuscript. The fire won out; there was nothing to save; my introductory paragraph went up in flames—amid
general rejoicing, since my wife rejoiced for both of us. Like an
elated child she clapped her hands and then threw herself about
my neck with a passion as if I had been separated from her, yes,
lost to her. I could not get in a word. She begged my forgiveness
for having fought in this way for her love, begged with an emo-

tion that almost made me believe that I had been on the way to becoming the prodigal husband.[14] She explained that she could not endure my being changed in this way. "Your thought belongs to me," she said, "it must belong to me. Your attentiveness is my daily bread. Your approval, your smile, your jests are my life, my inspiration. Grant me that—oh, do not deny me what is justly due me—for my sake, for the sake of my joy, so that with joy I may be able to do what is my only joy: to think of you and to find all my satisfaction in being able, day in and day out, to continue wooing you as once you wooed me."

Now, what justifies a wife in such conduct, a wife who is lovable not only in the eyes of all who know her but above all is lovable in my eyes, is as delightful as the day is long? Her view is *in contento* [in substance] as follows: a married man who is an author is not much better than a married man who goes to his club every evening, yes, even worse, because the one who goes to his club must himself still admit that it is an infraction, but to be an author is a distinguished unfaithfulness that cannot evoke regret even though the consequences are worse. The one who goes to his club is away only as long as he is away, but an author—"Well, you probably do not know it yourself, but a total change has taken place in you. You are in a cocoon of thoughtfulness from morning til night, and it is especially obvious at the dinner table. There you sit and stare off into space like a ghost or like King Nebuchadnezzar who is reading the invisible writing.[15] Then when I myself have prepared coffee for you, have set it out on the tray, come joyfully to you, stand before you, and curtsy to you—then, then out of fright I almost drop the tray, and above all I have then lost my cheerfulness and my joy and cannot curtsy to you."

Just as my wife on each occasion knows how to get in her Catonian *preterea censeo* [furthermore I am of the opinion] even though she does not do it as tiresomely as Cato,[16] so must everything also serve her for argument. Her argumentation is like an invocation of nature. If in a doctoral dissertation defense I was in the position that an opponent offered similar arguments, I would probably turn my back on him and say about him what the *Magister* [Master of Arts] says in Holberg: An ignoramus who does

V
12

not know how to distinguish between *ubi praedicamentale* [the where predicative] and *ubi transcendentale* [the where transcendental].[17] With my wife it is something else. Her argumentation comes straight from the shoulder—and to the heart, from which it actually comes. In this regard she has taught me to understand how a Roman Catholic can be built up by a service in Latin,[18] because her argumentation, viewed as such, is what Latin is for the one who does not understand it, and yet she always builds me up, moves and affects me.

"To be an author when one is a married man," she says, "is downright unfaithfulness, directly contrary to what the pastor said, since the validity of marriage is in this, that a man is to hold fast to his wife and to no other."[19] She is by no means at a loss for an answer if I reply that one might almost think that she was so neglected that she needs to go to confirmation instruction again, that she perhaps was not really listening to what the pastor said, that marriage is a special duty, a *specific* duty, and that all duties can be divided into the general and the specific and are duties to God, to ourselves, and to the neighbor.[20] Then she will get into no difficulty at all. The whole thing is declared to be teasing, and "moreover, she has not forgotten what is said about marriage in the catechism, that it is the husband's duty in particular." I futilely seek to explain to her that she is in linguistic error, that she is construing these words illogically, ungrammatically, against all principles of exegesis, because this passage is only about the husband's particular duties with regard to marriage, just as the very next paragraph is about the wife's particular duties. It is futile. She takes her stand on the preceding, "that to be an author when one is a married man is the worst kind of unfaithfulness." Now it has even become the "worst" unfaithfulness. If I then remind her that according to all divine and human laws the husband is the ruler, that otherwise my position in life becomes exceedingly low, since I become only an *encliticon*[21] to her, which still is claiming too much, she reproaches me for my unfairness, "since I know very well that she demands nothing, that in relation to me she desires only to be nothing at all." If, however, I protest because, if ultimately I am to be only an *encliticon*, it becomes important to me that she become as much as possible so that I

V
13

will not become even less by being an *encliticon* to nothing, then she looks at me and says: Just teasing.

My wife is consistent, fixed in her idea. I have tried to flatter her: that it would indeed be pleasant to see my, our, name praised, that she is the muse who inspires me. She will hear nothing of it. She regards the former as the greatest disaster and my complete perdition, because she wishes with her whole heart that emphatic criticism would send me home again. She does not believe the latter, wishes it even less, and from the depths of her soul prays God to forbid that she should in this way deserve the loss of her wedded bliss. She is inaccessible, and the *summa summarum* [sum of sums], "when everything has been said,"[22] comes down to this, "Either," she says, "a proper married man—or else . . . . . well, the rest is unimportant."

Now, although the reader will no doubt find, as I do, that her argumentation is rather weak and that she entirely disregards all the issues actually in question, namely, the boundary disputes involving the marital and the individual, which could give a profound and also acute mind enough to work on, she still has an argument *in subsidio* [in reserve], to which the reader will perhaps give more weight. One day after we had threshed through our differences and the conflict as usual had resolved itself in a *redintegratio amoris* [re-establishment of love],[23] she finally took me intimately by the arm, looked as winsomely as possible at me, and said, "My dear, I have not wanted to say this to you so bluntly, because I hoped in another way to get you to give up this project and hoped to be able to save you from humiliation, but since that will not succeed, I will say it to you with all the frankness you can require of your wife: I do not think you are cut out to be an author—but on the other hand, yes, now laugh at me just a little, but on the other hand, you have the genius and talent and extraordinary gift to be my husband in such a way that I would ceaselessly admire you while I myself would happily feel my own lowliness and make my love apparent to you with thanksgiving."[24] She did not, however, embark upon a development of the argument in detail. As soon as I wanted to embark upon a whether, to what extent, and how, she would have another explanation, "that someday I would regret having been unfaithful

v
14

to her by becoming an author, and then I would not be able to disregard this regret but would suffer its bitterness."

And what, then, was the end of this conflict? Who was victorious, my *hostis domesticus* [domestic enemy] or the author? It certainly is not difficult to guess, even though it is momentarily difficult for the reader when he reads this and thus sees that I became an author. The end was that I promised not to insist on being an author. But just as at academic disputations, when the author has disarmed all of one's objections, one comes forward with some linguistic triviality in order nevertheless to turn out to be right about something, and the author politely agrees that one is right in order nevertheless to admit that one is right about something, I thus reserved for myself permission to venture to write "Prefaces." In this connection I appealed to analogies, that husbands who had promised their wives never to use snuff any more had as recompense obtained permission to have as many snuffboxes as they wished. She accepted the proposal, perhaps with the idea that one could not write a preface without writing a book, which I indeed do not dare to do, unless one is a famous author who writes such a thing on request, which, to be sure, could not possibly be the case with me.

So it is with regard to my promise and my obligation. The little or the trifles that I hereby publish I was able to write *salva conscientia* [with good conscience]. Yet I have done so without my wife's knowledge by using a sojourn in the country for this. My request to criticism is that it will go easy on me, because, suppose it found that it was as my wife said, that I was not cut out to be an author, suppose that it unmercifully raked me over the coals, suppose my wife learned of it—then very likely I would in vain seek encouragement and consolation from my companion in life. She would probably exult with joy over carrying her point and over my having been taught a lesson in this way, and she would find her faith in a righteous Governance confirmed and her idea strengthened that to be an author when one is a married man is the worst unfaithfulness.

I

[25]What a pleasure it is indeed to have written a book! It is foolish and infatuated talk—which is therefore also rarely heard and never has the voice of the times in its favor—that the occupation of thinking while the work is underway, that the beating of the heart in the disquiet of deliberation, that the blushing and paling of the inner being in the presentiment and embrace, in the seeking and finding, are supposed to be the most beautiful. No, the beauty, the glory, the reward—and the significance of the book—appear only later. What a pleasure it is to have written a book that does not owe its origin to an inexplicable inner need and therefore is ignorant of whether it fits into the world, indeed, is bashful and ashamed like an ambivalent witness to a sinful love affair—no, a book that is the fruit of a marriage of convenience between publisher and public, written as the publisher wants to have it and as the times demand, a book whose coming into existence would be well known to all because of its timely appearance, a book for which criticism already has a nursemaid at hand, a book that is published at the opportune moment to the benefit of all: to the author, the publisher, the printer, the bookbinder, the reviewer, the reader.

If a person wants to publish a book, he should first consider at what time of year it will appear. The time of year is of enormous importance. On this matter all the wisest and best men agree that New Year's is the moment;[26] what Holophernes says about tapping on the cartridge pouch[27] pertains to the appearance of books around New Year's Day: without this I would not give you a pipeful of tobacco for the whole thing.

If a person wants to publish a book, he should next make sure that it will be of benefit. To that end he asks a publisher or a philosophical fellow or his barber or a passerby what it is that the times demand.[28] Lacking this, he himself comes up with something, about which he does not forget to say that it is what the

times demand. Not everyone, of course, is given the mental ca-
pacity to understand the demand of the times, so much the less
when to the doubtful it may seem that the times' demand is
multifarious and that the times, although one, can have, like
Maren Amme,[29] several voices.

See, I have done all this and am therefore happy to pass on to
the esteemed public my New Year's gift, especially elegant and
dainty[30] in every way. I have neglected nothing in order to dare
to flatter myself that it will appear at an opportune moment for
the reading public and particularly for any family that celebrates
Christmas Eve and New Year's Eve, since it can in every way
serve as a gift in good taste that can even be hung on the Christmas tree itself by means of a silk ribbon that is provided in the
gilded slipcase.

Yet it is true that I had almost forgotten something. So it goes,
and at times even worse, that one forgets the most important
thing. In the literary world it is the custom to make a sacred vow.
The ceremony is not definitely prescribed. In ancient times, as is
well known, one swore by Frey's boar;[31] Hamlet swears on the
fire tongs;[32] the Jews seem to have done it even in an unseemly
manner.[33] The ceremony, however, is unimportant; the vow is
the main thing. Therefore, I vow: as soon as possible to realize a
plan envisaged for thirty years, to publish a logical system, as
soon as possible to fulfill my promise, made ten years ago, of an
esthetic system; furthermore, I promise an ethical and dogmatic
system, and finally the system.[34] As soon as this has appeared,
generations to come will not even need to learn to write, because there will be nothing more to write, but only to read—the
system.[35]

II

To be an author in Denmark is almost as troublesome as having to live in public view[36] and is especially tortuous for a lyrical author who, even though as a person he is the very opposite, yet *qua* author is always a little shy, escapes from all the vociferousness, just as much whether it is praise or blame, and devotes himself in solitude to the refreshing, cozy, sweet infatuation that here or there sits a secret reader who offers a cordial reception, who, speaking purely esthetically, shuts his door and speaks with the author in secret. If anyone finds my first sentence exaggerated, then he will perhaps nevertheless be patient enough to await my next, that to be an author in Denmark is for the most part identical to being an author in Copenhagen, which is just about as problematic as concealing oneself on a plate. The forces of the reading public are concentrated in Copenhagen, and yet this concentration has nothing to do with strength but only with uproar and noise and racket and officious busyness in all external endeavors.

The appearance of a book is, then, an event that promptly sets the reading public in motion. Ordinarily there is an individual who even knows it somewhat in advance. Such a person must be regarded as fortunate. He rushes more swiftly through the streets than that barber who gave his life in order to be the first to bring the news of the victory at Marathon.[37] His shout causes more sensation than when the one who first catches a glint out at sea shouts loudly throughout the whole fishing village: Herring! Such a person is fortune's child, more fortunate than the author, welcome everywhere. By a kind of preemptive move, he collects some of the favor that is destined for the author. The shouter has no further information, knows only something ambiguous about the title of the book and what it deals with, but this is precisely what is most endearing about him in the eyes of the reading public, because a rumor carries away the reading public as the muse's impulse the poet, since like always affects like.

The book has come out. The reading public is gathered in the synagogue for mutual entertainment.[38] "Have you read the book?" No, not yet, but I have heard that it is not great. "Have you read the book?" No, but I paged through it a little at Reitzel's book shop;[39] if only I knew who the author is. "Have you read the book?" No, but I am eager to see it and already have promises in three places for the loan of it. There are variations on these and similar themes while the hubbub and noise increase, because empty barrels make the greatest sound and the synagogue, like the church bell, has—a tongue and an empty head. If one wants to make visible to the eye what here is presented mostly to the ear, then one sees the multitude of the reading public crowded together at the alarm center. All are milling around in total confusion. If one looks more closely, one notices a few characters who are differentiated from the crowd. By their watchful gaze, their restless glances, their outstretched necks, their perked up ears, one easily identifies them—they are the reviewers. Perhaps you think that a reviewer is to be looked upon as a police inspector in the service of good taste. You are mistaken. A reviewer is a conspirator, a worthy member of the Intemperance Association. When he has heard what he wants, he then rushes home, and while the empty chatter is still rattling in his head, he writes a review.

A fortnight later, the visible reading public (there is a distinction, like that between the visible and invisible Church[40]) is gathered again in the synagogue. People begin where they left off. "Have you read the superb review?" No. "Then you must read it. You must be sure to read it; it is exactly as I myself could have written it." —"Strangely enough, what the interesting reviewer says is the same as what I said when I had just paged through the book at Reitzel's." —"I have not read it yet, but I heard from a friend out in the country, who has a damned good head and is a connoisseur, that the book falls short, even though there are some beautiful passages in it." —It is linked together in the following way. That friend out in the country has not read the book but received a letter from a man in the capital who has not read the book either but read the review that in turn was written by a man who had not read the book but heard what that trust-

V
20

worthy man said who had paged through it a little at Reitzel's. *Summa summarum*, it is not at all inconceivable that a book could appear, create a sensation, and occasion a review that was read, whereas the book might just as well have not been written or at best have been as briefly composed as that first courier's announcement. If only the chatter can be set in motion, then all is well. And what if it cannot get underway? Then it must be an odd book. No wind is so bad that it does not blow somebody something good, and no wind is so good that it does not blow somebody something bad.

By paying attention to the opinion of the visible reading public and of the usual reviewers, one falls into the most fatuous confusion. I would like to illustrate the confusion with an incident from daily life. A cellar-dweller wanted to rent a cellar from me. Despite his well-known integrity etc., he was not, on a landlord's gold scales, found to be a full-weight renter.[41] There arose then the question of a guarantee. With all courtesy, I allowed myself to make known my misgivings, but, smiling, he looked at me and said, "Do not worry. I am all right; I myself, damn it, am the guarantor for a cellar-dweller in Strandstræde."[42] I had to steady myself with a chair, because, at the very moment I tried to turn over what he had said, I blacked out. In the same way the usual reviewers guarantee the opinion of the reading public, and if one were to take the reviewer as an individual, he is most often very far from being able to vouch for himself, although he perhaps is willing enough to reassure the troubled person who calls attention to the difficulties in the same way as that cellar-dweller reassured me. —Now, if playing this game can entertain the Copenhageners, I say *Glück zu* [good luck to them], the crazier the better. My fondness for people is beyond measure, especially when they make themselves ludicrous; I am a friend of humanity but an even greater friend of laughter. It is indeed an amusing jest, as one of the seven sages has already pointed out, that in war games it is the connoisseurs of the art who do battle, and those who do not understand the art who judge it.[43]

V
21

The intention in the preceding is certainly not to condemn all subjective opinions. The question is only how they are presented. When a humorous individuality pronounces, with all possible indolence, a non-appealable opinion expressive of personality and mood, he is within his rights. If a man were to speak like this: "I opened the book at only three places and came across the word 'sweet' every time, and for that reason I do not care to read the book." "I looked at only the title page but saw there that he spells the word *Indolents* [indolence] without a *t*.[44] That was enough for me, and I concluded that the author is affected." [45]"Upon opening the book, I read these words: One must doubt everything. For that reason I sent the book back immediately, because this phrase is offensive to me and is an obscenity at which one needs merely to hint." If a man were to express himself like this, he would only assert his individuality in all its accidental character, which is an honorable matter. But such an opinion is altogether different from the opinion of that reading public. Such an idiosyncratic and his opinion are usually not well liked, because those concerned surely notice that, consciously or unconsciously, it contains a satire on their opinion. The opinion of the reading public, although based on just as little as his, is vain and full of pretension. While an author thus has his worst enemies and traitors in those orthodox exclamation marks, he often has in such a humorist a cryptic friend who has read the book in all inwardness but only seeks in this way to save his soul and the book from any connection with such nonsense.

Then finally fate has mercy on the author; a new book comes out and he comes to himself again just as bewildered and giddy as a cat bashed out of the barrel.[46] If the reading public can simply have Shrovetide fun, then forget the author. But Shrovetide fun there must be. If there is no author, then one seizes some suspicious fellow who is "working on a book," throws him into the barrel, and now the merriment begins. What a devil of a thing it is to be an author if one does not know how to get one's private pleasure[47] from such treatment and above all does not know how to trick the reading public so that it does indeed have something in the barrel, but not oneself, not one's deeper personality, but a personality that one oneself puts out like the leg Morten Frederiksen let the authorities keep when he escaped from prison in Roskilde.[48] —Why does no one write a literary *Barselstue*?[49] In such a production one would see people who have an astonish-

V
22

ing resemblance to the ladies in that comedy, people who slay the unfortunate with chatter, envious, malicious people who have worse tongues than those ladies, and to make everything complete there would rarely be lacking a part that could be played best by a woman, just as in Holberg there is a woman's part that is played by a man.[50]

In this scheme of things, those who best hold their own are the reviewers, who, supported in many ways by the public as is natural, have created the misunderstanding that the relation between author and public is as follows: The author is a wretched bungler who knows nothing and understands nothing but with anxiety and horror waits for the rigorous judge, for the wise and insightful judgment of the most esteemed public. That the public should be able to learn something from an author would be as fatuous as the notion that a professor should be able to learn something from the student he is examining. What the author writes is an examination paper, and even if he stood a chance of holding his own well enough, the person who subjects himself to it is still a bit lunatic, because he is already much further ahead by not writing, because he is then an integral part of the most esteemed public. The reviewers, on the other hand, are the highly trusted minions of the most esteemed public, its cupbearers and privy councilors. Thus everything is superb and complete in madness.

One needs only to glance at the writing in newspapers to see what is nowadays regarded as a review. It would indeed be really too bad if the public's gossip were to go to waste. Therefore every newspaper runs a wastewater drain through its territory. The reviewer is the acting water inspector who takes care that the wastewater flows freely and without obstruction. Everything is thereby completed in itself; the water comes from the public and flows back into the public.

That this is so certainly requires no demonstration. If such is demanded, I perhaps would not find it worth the trouble to do it. Even Herr Prof. Heiberg,[51] who was, after all, the public's unquestionable favorite and very far from appearing surly or unreasonable toward it, even he seems to despair, to have abandoned the reading public's prodigal sons as prodigal.[52] What was

the result of this? Who lost thereby? It was the public itself that
lost, and it was especially serious for the innocent who had to
suffer along with the guilty. Prof. H. no longer wanted to be
what he was, what he always could be: an excellent minister of
the interior, a unquestionable talent as a minister of police and
justice *in republica literaria* [in the republic of letters]. The unforgettable editor of *Flyveposten*,[53] who, the last time people began
to play "The Rope Is Burning,"[54] knew how to find the rope
and how to use it, the vaudeville poet, admired as much for his
wit and his humor as for his lyrical-musical fervor, grew weary
and sought to become what is called a new man. And now, now
when he is really needed again, when surely both those who
were contemporary with that exuberant cheerfulness, and the
younger ones, who again and again seek to revive for themselves
the memory of those happy times, long to see again one of his
days of glory—now he himself seems to want to be—well, it is
hard to say what he wants to be now. In *Intelligensblade* his per-
sona as an author actually goes through as many changes as that
cloud before the eyes of Polonius in *Hamlet*,[55] as the awaited
beast in *Recensenten og Dyret* while Herr Klatterup with courteous
obligingness accommodates himself according to the caprices of
the presiding "first gentleman."[56]

   [57]With this I have finished. I have the straw man ready, which
I toss adroitly into the barrel while I myself stand aside and enjoy
the fun. It is not in my power to halt all this violence; at most I
could propose that a committee be set up to take under consideration how the critical proceedings could be discontinued. It
would already amount to something if one could learn what criticism ought to be (which a single honorable exception pre-
scribes, although not adequately), that criticism ought not to be
a robber who attacks a published book, nor a gasbag who clings
tightly to a work in order to have a place and a hearing for his
comments, nor a supercilious beggar king who uses the appearance of a book "to take the occasion" to say something himself.[58]
A reviewer is and ought to be, ought to stake his honor on being,
a ministering spirit. [59]If he is willing to be that, he will be a
benefit to the public, a joy to the author, who cheerfully entrusts
himself into his hands, although nowadays, if one were really to

lend one's personality to this, to be reviewed would be as loathsome as letting a barber's assistant fumble about one's face with
his clammy fingers.[60] A review, then, should be a balm, whereas
now, like a condolence, it is declined because it increases the
pain, or rather causes pain, causes pain to the one who is otherwise happy and contented but still does not wish to be compelled
to lose all illusory faith in the reading public.

III

That a printing of a thousand copies was sold out in two months adequately indicates that my New Year's gift[61] knew how to engage the interest of the times. This happy result flatters and amazes me all the more because from it I may conclude that it was purchased also in the new year and not only prior to New Year's Eve. The author who satisfies the Christmas and New Year's seasons has not lived in vain; the book that is purchased in the Christmas and New Year's seasons has not been written in vain—how much more then the author who satisfies even in January and the book that is purchased in January. Yet I may assure a highly esteemed public that the good will and attention shown have not fallen to the lot of an unworthy person who would venture to arrogate something to himself or venture to be something different from what the public demands. My faith in the New Year's season is unshaken, and for next year I hope to have ready in good time in December a New Year's gift that will leave nothing to be desired in elegance and good taste. I already use the present occasion to notify the esteemed families that they should not go out and purchase some other New Year's gift or some other toy for their Christmas trees.

This second printing is unaltered and is sold for the low price of three marks, or one-eighth of the bookstore price of the first printing.[62]

In conclusion, I would like to thank the very honored reviewer for his most interesting review, to which in large part the speedy sale is no doubt due. When literature and journalism can work hand in hand in such a perfect way—oh, then Denmark's future stands bright before us!

IV

---

[63]As is well known, the literary New Year's rush of the commercial scriveners begins in the month of December. Several very sleek and elegant[64] books intended for children and Christmas trees, but especially useful as gifts in good taste, chase past each other in *Adresseavisen*[65] and other newspapers in order, after creating a *furore* [sensation] for a fortnight, to be assigned by a courteous critic to a place in some anthology[66] as inspiring models for all writers of esthetic literature in fine style. Esthetic fine style—that is the watchword. And esthetic fine style is a deadly earnest matter for which one trains oneself by abandoning idea and thought. Oh you great Chinese god! I would have sworn to it; is not Prof. Heiberg along in the parade this year? Yes, quite right, it is Prof. Heiberg. Yes, when one is decked out in this fashion, one can easily put in an appearance before the astonished crowd. Not even Salomon Goldkalb in all his glory was thus clothed.[67] This is indeed pure gold. Even if no one else buys this book, the museum of art curios will buy it.

At every other time of the year, a person can escape being decked out like a Haiduk and avoid every disturbing collision and misunderstanding. One cannot, unfortunately, be confused with the first-rate, but then, on the other hand, no toasts, announcements, flattery, subscription hawking, repeated assurances that "in another passage" etc., distant cries from an anchorite who is concentrating on greater works, prophecies, promises, revelations—all these things cannot possibly thwart any production or cause confusion but can only in a more subtle way help one come to the attention of the one by whom one wishes to be read.

What, I wonder, will "one" say about this book now?[68] My dear reader, if you are not able to find out in any other way, then our literary telegraph manager, Prof. Heiberg, will probably be kind enough to be a tax collector again and tally the votes, just as he once did in connection with *Either/Or*, and report it in *Intelligensblade*.[69] And what, I wonder, will the Herr Prof. himself say? Yes, who would be capable of reading the riddle of this man, who recently seems to ascend more and more daringly into the enigmatic? Yet one should not shirk work and toil, if only there is a reward that beckons. One should not become weary standing expectantly on tiptoe if only there is the prospect that the hour of transfiguration,[70] which is my hope and yearning, will come soon. Just as at an earlier time, when I dared to believe that I was able to comprehend the professor, after spending the effort to acquire understanding I had the pleasure of relaxing in a festive mood of admiration, so with regard to his later period my admiration is not less but is a different, an inexplicable, an enthusiastic admiration. This I share with various of my contemporaries, who like me with eager expectancy look forward to the result, although they, just as I do, modestly hand over to professionals the judgment of whether the Herr Prof.'s later astronomical, astrological,[71] chiromantical,[72] necromantical, horoscopical, metoscopical, chronological studies will be of benefit to science and humanity; the judgment of whether the Herr Professor will succeed through all these arts and sciences in healing the "depression of the times";[73] the judgment of whether he will have the luck, after having found the congregation, now also to turn its gaze heavenward, since he himself, like that councilor not unfamiliar to those congregations, sets a praiseworthy example.[74]

But let the result be what it may, it is already glorious to envisage Herr Prof. when he stands there and prophetically gazes far away until he catches a glimpse of the system and the realization of long contemplated plans;[75] or when, as in these later days, he fixes his eyes on heavenly things, counts the stars, reckons their courses, and watches for the heavenly inhabitants of those distant planets,[76] forgetting the earth and earthly life, states, kingdoms, lands, associations, and individuals over the matchless discovery[77] that also in the astronomical sense the earth has a very respectable place in the heavens.[78] But let the result be as it may, this last is and remains of extreme importance, that Prof. Heiberg has thrown himself into astronomy. Is this not a piece of good luck, if not for astronomy, then at least for theology? When a few years ago the Herr Prof. brought to light the mysteries of the heavens in his apocalyptic poem and an obliging review and also an officious opinion baldly gave us to understand that Prof. Heiberg had now become Dante,[79] I secretly began to be afraid. The one who then attended a little more carefully to our situation will certainly not deny that sometimes phenomena did occur that seemed to point to the terrible possibility that Prof. H., who had always been also a philosopher, might suddenly undergo a new metamorphosis and step forth as the one who had come to the world in order to solve the riddles of theology.[80] Now, that would have been waggish enough but nonetheless would scarcely be desirable. The Prof. has chosen now, and he has chosen astronomy. There is, then, no danger anymore, since it will be easy to keep him astronomically occupied in the future. The method for this is very simple, similar to the one Pernille uses against Vielgeschrey in Holberg's *Stundesløse*.[81] One arranges to have astronomical inquiries to Herr Prof. be received by some newspaper; then one arranges to have a foreign newspaper request an astronomical *votum* [opinion] etc. from him. If this does not prove to be adequate, then one ventures the ultimate. Two hired waiters are dressed up as emissaries from a distant nation knowledgeable in astronomy, and they come to pay their compliments to the Herr Prof. and to submit an astronomical riddle to him, the solution of which will make manifest that he is the awaited savior of that people. For that purpose the waiters are instructed as follows: as soon as the Herr Professor has replied, no matter what, they are to fall on their knees and worship him. In this position they are to announce the remainder of their mission, that they have come to fetch him—I wager that Prof. H. will never again write vaudevilles but will leave his native land and all of us. See, is this not fortunate for theology, and must not one always be grateful to Herr Prof. H. that he at one time wrote *Julespøg og Nytaarsløier*[82] and that these days he makes jests and jokes at New Year's time and does it so well that he himself believes it is earnestness?

[83]My dear reader, if I were not accustomed to writing a preface to all my books, I could just as well not have written this one, because it does not in any way pertain to the book, which, both with and without a preface, since it is indeed both, entrusts itself completely to you.

V

V
31

Writing is not speaking; sitting at a desk and copying what is said is only baneful toil in comparison with stepping forth in an assembly, looking at a great throng who all are inspired by the same thing and for the same thing, having the stillness enter in like the prayer before battle, having the word break forth like the thunder of combat, being oneself transported by the silence that is the silence of attention, hearing the whisper that is the whisper of approval, sensing the stentoriousness of the Amen of conviction. Yes indeed, only a general assembly inspires. Only the sound of a crowd affects a speaker as martial music does, as the whistle of the bowstring affects the warrior. But the great purpose of the association to which I have the honor of belonging requires that I seek also to circulate in print my address on liquor, for which I certainly require no other reward than the applause that was my lot that evening, that unforgettable evening, which will forever remain unforgettable to me. Yet the interest of the association to which my life belongs with its sole desire to be an effective member, the interest of this association requires that I try to draw attention to our endeavor through the publication of this address, to invite those who stand at a distance to come nearer to us, because truly the person who attends our meeting just once will be eternally faithful to us. The Total Abstinence Association[84] seeks in vain its equal and dares with proud self-confidence to think that this search is in vain. Or what substance is there, after all, in a partial abstinence, which is neither cold nor hot and therefore worthy only to be spewed out?[85] Or what is the point, after all, of the many associations that are founded nowadays, inasmuch as the need, which first finds its fulfillment only in the Total Abstinence Association, is seen in a misunderstood way? People form an association, people want to be active, but the association's activities seem to have no meaning for the individuals. Even if the activities of the Scandinavian Society[86]

V
32

accomplished something astounding, it would take microscopic observation to discover how much benefit would come to the individual from it. Indeed, that kind of social activity is just as fatuous as it is a piece of folly if the individual thinks that in satisfying himself he has sufficient reward for his labor. But what reward is it to lose oneself in the whole or to remain alone by oneself? No, praise be to our association, glorious is its reward. When the individual does what is ordinarily even unimportant to the individual, he thereby becomes, if he joins our association, important for the whole. Is this not something marvelous, is this not evidence of the tremendous significance of our association? That a person, out of regard for his spiritual or physical health, abstains totally from strong drink, that he himself is aware of this, what reward is this—or has it ever occurred to such a person to take pride in this? But if he joins our association, he acquires by this an infinite significance for the whole, something that is known by everyone who is a member. That a person who once was addicted to strong drink conquers the desire through total abstinence, that he himself is aware of this—what glory is there in that? Or has it occurred to such a person to take pride in that, since, on the other hand, even though he conquered, he still did not entirely conquer a certain shame over his having been so weak and indeed was happiest when he succeeded through a long and distressing circuitous way in getting to the point where, like others, he could enjoy, could abstain, without being tempted by feeling a lack or by tasting. If, however, he joins our association, he will become infinitely important for the whole. Perhaps he will serve the association by allowing himself to be exhibited in the market towns and in this way even achieve a distinction beyond any other.

What wonder is it, after all, that the significant is significant? But to make the intrinsically insignificant more significant than the most significant—that surely is still a task. And this task has never before been accomplished in the world, unless it would have been by those morally perfect people, monks and nuns, and will never be accomplished in such a way as when the Total Abstinence Association consistently grows larger and larger. That a husband is faithful to his wife, that he himself knows this and joyfully knows this together with her, what reward is this?[87] But when the Total Abstinence Association takes up this side of life also—then when he joins our association he will become infinitely important, yes, is it not marvelous, infinitely important by doing what every husband ought to do and what the great number do without knowing how infinitely important it is? But outside the Total Abstinence Association, this is the way it is everywhere: there the old saying still holds, that a person, when he does his duty, is an unworthy servant.[88] In the Total Abstinence Association, this saying has been canceled. How would a person's moral power be strengthened and encouraged when he will always be reminded that he cannot do more than his duty; but how far will the moral power be brought beyond the universal, yes, to the point of taking the mighty by force,[89] when one becomes infinitely important just by doing what is unimportant!

Yet however great the reward, I will not conceal what it cannot be the association's intention to conceal, that the danger can also be multiple, precisely because what is unimportant, which has been transmuted into the infinitely important by the association's almighty words, has a continued tendency to rebel. Moreover, the association and each of its members are struggling, struggling against all the rest of imperfect, indeed fallen, humanity. If one then does not want to withdraw completely like the cenobites, does not want to forsake all contact with anyone who drinks a dram or a glass of wine, which one should not do in the hope of saving someone, the collision can be terrible enough. Yet the great thing is to be completely faithful. And if there is some beloved old man who wishes to enhance a festive occasion with the enjoyment of the drink that, as we say, gladdens the heart of man,[90] and if he takes out something that has been stored for many years, saved for this moment, and if he brushes away a tear while he wipes the old rum glass, and if everything is in beautiful and ceremonious accord with the festive enjoyment of the wine, and if all that is required of me is that I should bring the glass to my lips—I would rather disrupt everything than taste the wine. But then the old man would also hear with astonishment, yes, perhaps without properly understanding it, about that marvelous association that has just now been organized and would be amazed at the moral power it knows how to inspire in its adherents. —Or if it is a happy young person, if it is his happiest moment, when he has won everything in life and won joy for his whole life, and if he invites me to visit him, and if his soul and his mood that enhances his countenance crave to see the foaming of the wine, which like youth bursts its bonds when it senses just the slightest air, and if he asks of me only what he himself, intoxicated with happiness, intoxicated with impatient bliss, wishes, to drink himself sober with the meager, yes, disappointing, one-time ration of foam—I would rather disrupt everything than taste what is forbidden. But then that young person would also be overwhelmed with admiration—perhaps out of joy over me, he would even join the Total Abstinence Association.

But here I cut short my preface. The thought of our association and its efforts carries me away immediately, more than Bacchus carried the poet away,[91] since it is fitting for every member of our association to be as intoxicated as a drunken man, but, note well, intoxicated with enthusiasm, which is all the more marvelous the less there is of that which produces intoxication.

VI

Danish literature has not until now had a devotional work for cultured people; the lack, however, has indeed been generally felt among the cultured.[92] May this circumstance contribute to excusing the boldness of the one who here attempts to accomplish this difficult task; may it also contribute toward making way for the book and a lenient appraisal among the cultured to whom it addresses itself.

As for the work itself, the cultured person will readily discover that throughout the twenty-four sermons of which the volume consists there is a striving, a leading theme, a systematic tendency. The individual sermon will not stand by itself or mean anything by itself, but by continually pointing beyond itself it will lead the reader to the totality, by which alone the cultured person can be built up. It is self-evident that it must be read just as it is written, in a way different from the way devotional writings are usually written and read. If by way of comparison one were to take, for example, the most widely distributed devotional work up to now, Bishop Mynster's *Sermons*,[93] one will to no avail look for such a tendency in that collection. It is not our idea to undervalue a work that has had its great and justified merit, which from a subordinate point of view it still has in part. It is not our intention to mislead anyone's opinion of the venerable author who, although advanced in years, still stands preeminent among us as the helmsman and leader of the Danish Church,[94] but the truth is dearest to us, that this work, despite all its excellence, no longer satisfies—the cultured. The collection is very beautifully rounded out by starting with a sermon on the object of the devotional hour and ending with a sermon against offense,[95] but one seeks futilely for anything scholarly in this plan. The venerable author has provided a sermon for every festival day and has particularly had in mind that the single individual would take out his book on the festival days, would gather his

thoughts away from worldly distraction, would remind himself
of the object of a devotional hour, would read the appointed
sermon aloud to himself and perhaps to those close to him,
would be built up by what was read, would not entirely forget it
during the course of the week, but on the other hand, after having read his sermon, he would also cheerfully close the book,
unconcerned about the connection of this sermon to the others,
to the whole, without examining and ascertaining by close examination whether the Herr Bishop had succeeded in constructing a whole or whether it had been the Herr Bishop's intention
to want to construct a whole. It is not our aim to deny that such
a limited reading can have its importance; yes, the claim is even
made that there are many instances of the less cultured who
throughout a long life have continued year in and year out to
reprint,[96] as it were, this book, so that it remained for them and
their family a book that continually comes out "this year"[97] although the binding seems to give different evidence. But what
are the consequences of this for the cultured person? He cannot
read in this way, is not satisfied so easily, is not built up in this
manner; if this is supposed to be the right way, then he would
first have to be reconstituted in order to be built up.

In another way, too, the present devotional work proceeds
from the totality and toward it. We shall here refer again to
Bishop Mynster's collection, which in contrast seems to illustrate
best the higher point of view that the cultured person now holds.
Admittedly that collection will particularly awaken and nourish
in the single individual a more earnest self-examination, a deeper
concern about himself and for himself, his well-being, his salvation, his eternal happiness. The presentation is also designed for
this, which often makes it almost impossible for the reader to
escape the thought that what he is reading pertains to himself.[98]
It must therefore be assumed that it is hereby done adequately
also for the less cultured person. For the cultured person, however, it is truly too little to have to deal with an individual human
being, even though that human being is himself.[99] He does not
want to be disturbed when he is to be built up, does not want
to be reminded of all the trifles, of individuals, of himself, because to forget all this is precisely the upbuilding. The life of the

congregation, the grand definition of the system, the purely human—all of which does not tempt the individual to think about himself or to want to finish something, but builds him up only by his thinking it *over*—are the subject for consideration in the present work. It is again this totality toward which it strives. The cultured person thus seeks the congregation,[100] to call to mind a word of the poet to whom the present devotional work is so very much indebted and whom I do myself the honor of naming as the authority and as the chosen bard of the cultured, the pondering Professor Heiberg.

This devotional work is also Christian, which stands to reason since it addresses itself to the cultured, since the cultured are, of course, Christians. That for which Christianity has striven through eighteen hundred years is specifically to produce the cultured person, who is the fairest flower and richest unfolding of the Christian life. The essentially Christian is not something historically concluded that enviously would be able to judge whether the cultured person is Christian. On the contrary, the cultured person provides the criterion and thereby contributes to the exaltation of the doctrine that admittedly began as a village affair (paganism)[101] but now through the cultured has gained admittance to circles where tone, manners, elegance, wit, intellect are reconciled with their vanquished opposite. But just as the essentially Christian was not concluded in the past, so also it is not concluded in the present moment either but has the future open and can still become what it is to be. Only in this view is the truth infinitized in the infinite, whereas otherwise the truth is construed as finite, as if there were something that stood fixed for all time. No! The cultured person knows that all things move, but he does not therefore cowardly take flight backwards. He plunges boldly into the movement. Every point of view has its importance, even though it is vanquished by a new one. That is the source of this unprecedented magnanimity, the equal of which no past age has known.

Furthermore, the present work is not frightened at the thought that its point of view will perhaps be quickly supplanted by a new point of view. How would it fear something like that and venture to commend itself to the cultured person! No! He

V
38

will quickly surpass this and perhaps himself produce a new work that the author of the present work will then in turn surpass.

Therefore, neither do I present this work quietly, as if I had nothing more to do than to be secretly concerned or pleased if the individual finds rest or guidance in it. It calmly anticipates criticism, with sublime self-denial. Fair and knowledgeable criticism will discover the total tendency in it. Even if it wins no approval, even if it cannot bear the demands of criticism, just to have occasioned a discussion is not an unfruitful work, while the discussion itself will be for the upbuilding of the cultured.

VII[102]

To write a book is the easiest of all things in our time, if, as is customary, one takes ten older works on the same subject and out of them puts together an eleventh on the same subject. In this way one gains the honor of being an author just as easily as one gains, according to Holberg's advice, the rank of being a practicing physician and the possession of his fellow citizens' money, trust, and esteem by getting a new black suit and writing on one's door: "John Doe *praktisirender Arzt* [Physician]."[103] Now, even though such an eleventh book sometimes ought to be considered a work of some merit commensurate with its thoroughness, as in another time it certainly was, yet if its worth cannot be appraised higher and the reward to be harvested is estimated only in relation to that, the competition in writing an eleventh book would not be greater in our time than in any other. Since, however, this is the case, it follows that the consideration must have become something different, because what in itself is something rather subordinate has now become an inspiring goal that beckons every scribbler and promises him that this eleventh book will become more important than everything earlier, more important than the ten preceding, which nevertheless had cost their respective authors considerable brain racking, since they did not plagiarize one another, more important than the ten all together before the marvelous transubstantiation occurred by which the eleventh book saw the light of day. "Is this not like witchcraft? Would perhaps the eleventh book also be a false alarm?" With the deep voice of the times, I will reply to the one who questions in this way: Wretch, you have not comprehended mediation,[104] its significance for scholarship—and for banal minds.

If mediation were really all that it is made out to be, then there is probably only one power that knows how to use it with substance and emphasis; that is the power that governs all things. And there is only one language in which it belongs, the language that is used in that council of divinity to which philosophers send delegates no more than small landholders do, and from which philosophers receive regular couriers no more than small landholders do. Since, however, the authors of the eleventh book are least of all concerned to hear about what may take place in that council, it readily follows that mediation means something else, yes, to speak more definitely, that it means nothing at all, although it still enjoys divine veneration and worship and gives everyone absolute importance. Yes, it has a magical and marvelous power that no other word in any other language in heaven or on earth has or has had or will have or be able to have, so that even in the mouth of the most obtuse person it is and remains the loftiest wisdom, but without the most obtuse person's needing to become even just moderately sagacious with nothing to spare. The eleventh book, which is the mediation, yields no new thought, but the only difference from the earlier ones is this, that the word "mediation" appears several times on each page and that in the introduction to each section the author unctuously goes through the rigmarole that one must not stop with the ten but must mediate. Now, because learning to say this is not judged to be too difficult for even a diligent parrot to learn, the gospel is preached with this word to all banal minds on a scale unparalleled in the world, and this word announces an indulgence such as no pope has ever announced, since at the same time as it announces indulgence from work and the suffering of punishment, it announces the great prize more assuredly than any lottery.

The one who is placed in the greatest predicament by this mediating is naturally the reader, upon whom the author places the heavy burden and duty of thinking something in connection with what he is saying and whom he excludes from the absolute importance and immortal merit achieved by saying: It must be mediated. In the reading of an eleventh book, my experience has been like an experience once out at the Dyrehave carnival.[105] In the company of some other naïve people, I went over to take a peek through the little lens into a peep show in order that my eyes might feast on the sight while my ears caught the showman's unctuous explanation. The author of the eleventh book, or to

V
41

stick with the Dyrehave carnival, the owner of the peep show
and the priceless interpreter of its contents, by the cranking of the
barrel organ, produced a soft quiet music to put the soul into the
mood. By an odd happenstance, however, the picture did not
appear. There was nothing to see in the box except an empty
space, but the showman cranked out his musical piece and his
explanation in a very satisfying manner—if only there had been
something to see. Likewise mediation does not appear, and one
continually hears only the author's melodramatic lecture. This
may be a matter of indifference, of course, to the author of the
eleventh book and to the man with the barrel organ; he will not
read the book or look into the box, but it is not a matter of
indifference to the viewer or to the reader. What then is to be
done to amend this? The reader must try to derive an advantage
by being an author himself. In such a way, then, also this difference between the reader and the author, like all other opposites,
is canceled and raised [*hævet*] in a higher lunacy.[106]

Assisted by mediation, everyone is then able to acquire absolute and immortal importance in relation to bygone world history. Therefore it is strange that in *Adresseavisen* no one offers to
perfect (in less than three hours) everyone, everyone with only
middling preparatory knowledge, in the idea of mediation, by
which anyone becomes the conclusion toward which all of by-
gone world history is tending. If a person is thus assured of the
millennia of the past, what is left is only to perfect himself in the
association-idea by which one captures all of the future; then
anyone in our age becomes more bifrontally important than
Noah was.[107] To fulfill even a simple rule of life requires some
time and diligence and in no way earns for the individual an
importance for the whole or for the most recent generations. But
to found an association, yes, what is an even more inspiring great
deed, to set up a committee—that is easy, and an immortal merit.
To participate in a festive banquet is not difficult—and yet is an
opus operatum [act done][108] for the universal and the future.
Therefore as I gazed out into the future, which still conceals itself
in the foggy veil of the future and conceals the accomplishments
of the race, there appeared before my eyes an enormous temple
or festival building from which there came a confused noise,

which, however, was at times interrupted, to sound again even more loudly, mingled with a flourish of kettledrums and trumpets, and above the entrance to this building my eyes discovered with astonishment the following inscription: Clink the Glasses Here.

Yet even to write an eleventh book is still a labor and therefore already a too troublesome task for the rash hastiness of the times and the individual's rushing after absolute importance and immortal merit. To the credit of the times, one must say that it is a high goal toward which everyone strives, and to the credit of the times let it also be said that everyone achieves it. But should one not be able to take a shortcut past the eleventh book? Why not? A promise of the eleventh book is even shorter, and yet even safer, and more advantageous in every way. A promise has the splendid quality that, like courtesy, it costs nothing to the person who makes it, and yet he can coolly let it signify a work that is more noteworthy than any of the wonders of the world. For the recipient (the reading public) it exerts a mitigating and quieting influence, acts like a solvent agent to disperse every more anxious concern about making up one's mind about some matter. Every now and then one has a transient feeling that the truth should not be left standing in a doubtful form; one feels a responsibility— then one has a promise to depend on, and one is secure in cozy enjoyment. The matter does not concern one further, and now Mr. X. has promised definitely for all time to throw light on this as on everything else. What danger, then, is there? A promise is very transportable, and therefore there is nothing the couriers, on a wild-goose chase, would prefer to run with than promises. A promise, although it means everything, yet in its polite form also means no more than that it provides a splendid ingredient for tea-party gossip, inasmuch as the promise, just as in the drinking bout in the ballad,[109] is passed around the table all evening without the interference of one promiser by another. A promise is a bicarbonate of soda by which all humanity is incomparably well served.

One cannot give oneself a full enough account of this if one wants to understand correctly how to praise the philosophical optimism in which for several years we have already been inordinately comfortable, indeed blissful.[110] *Posito*,[111] I assume [*sætte*], and when I say *posito*, I have the right to assume the unlikely; therefore *posito*, I assume that Mr. A. A.,[112] whose promises supposedly have not weakened him, went to work and wrote the system. *Posito*, I assume, and when I say *posito*, I have the right to assume what is more unreasonable than the most unreasonable; therefore, *posito*, I assume that if Mr. A. A. did not write the system, then Mr. B. B.[113] wrote it—then what? Let us linger for a moment on this thought, with which, of course, we have all been familiar for several years: the thought of the prospect for the hope of the system.[114] Therefore, in order to be very brief, *posito*, I assume that the system appeared here in Copenhagen, then what? Then one would indeed have to read it, unless Mr. C. C.[115] would instantly be kind and philanthropic enough to promise a summary of the system and also position [*sætte*] us in the point of view; then we would again be saved by the promise. If this does not happen, then of course one would have to read it. How troublesome, and who would finally benefit from that? Perhaps it would not satisfy completely, and that is what the esteemed author would have for all the diligence employed, whereas with a promise he could easily benefit himself and others even more than if he had written a prodigy of a system. It is, however, common and low to keep what one promises; on the other hand, true high rank manifests itself precisely as virtuosity in promising, as the painter in Shakespeare's *Timon* says: *Vortrefflich! Versprechen ist die Sitte der Zeit, es öffnet die Augen der Erwartung: Vollziehen erscheint um so dummer, wenn es eintritt, und die einfältigen, geringen Leute ausgenommen, ist die Bethätigung des Wortes völlig aus der Mode. Versprechen ist sehr hofmännisch und guter Ton. Vollziehen ist eine Art von Testament, das von gefärlicher Krankheit des Verstandes bei dem zeugt, der es macht.* ["Good as the best. Promising is the very air o' the time; it opens the eyes of expectation: performance is ever the duller for his act; and, but in the simpler and plainer kind of people, the deed of saying is quite out of use. To promise is most courtly and fashionable: performance is a kind of will or testament which argues a great sickness in his judgment that makes it."] (See act 5, scene 1.[116]) Furthermore, if the system is read, the reading would perhaps serve to make a

V
44

distinction between those considered to have understood it and those considered to have not understood it; dissension and parties would begin, whereas now the whole generation lives in unanimity and equality in relation to the promise, to which every person is equally close.

The present book, which I herewith send out, has been written as I believe books were written in an earlier time. The one who has written it is one who has given considerable thought to the subject about which he speaks and as a consequence of this believes he knows a little more about it than is generally known. Nor is he entirely unfamiliar with what was previously written on the subject, and he strives to do justice to everyone.[117] Instead of the enormous task of understanding all human beings, he has chosen what perhaps will be called narrow-minded and fatuous, to understand himself, such as right now, why he wants to be an author, and whether the inclination in him is not what the inclination of the spirit should never be, an externally reflected inclination, lest he with great vanity decide to write a book to help others when he nevertheless knows that essentially every human being is equally sagacious, and above all that essentially every human being must help himself. If, on the other hand, the inclination is an inner and inwardly reflected inclination, then one writes a book as a bird sings its song,[118] as the tree sends forth its crown. If there is someone who enjoys it, so much the better.

Yet by wanting to understand himself in this way, a person makes slower and also rather laborious progress. What he discovers, whether gratifying or grievous, he assimilates immediately *in succum et sanguinem* [in flesh and blood].[119] For example, he does not in this way discover that all the demonstrations of the immortality of the soul that have hitherto been advanced both inside and outside Christianity are insufficient, because the true demonstration is first found in the mediation of them all; but he seeks a demonstration that convinces himself, lest the end be that the demonstration of the immortality of the soul is the only thing immortal, which one lets fly off into the sky the way children do their kites, without even having as much on it as the children have—a string. In his knowledge he does not remain indifferent like a hawker who cares only about hawking, cares about *getting rid* of his wares, cares about getting the highest price at the auction; but he continually stakes his life because he is convinced that to be able συμπαθῆσαι ταῖς ἀσθενείαις τῶν ἀνθρώπων [to sympathize with the weaknesses of human beings][120] is the true principle of knowledge, since the disposition toward everything human lies in every human being, and the clearer it is, the more profound a human being he is. He is convinced that without suffering there is no true knowledge, because suffering is the very qualification of inwardness, which acquires for a person a knowledge of his own and assures him of being able to speak the truth the same way Balaam's ass did.[121] By suffering is not meant racking one's brains and working nights in the study, but something else, an honor from which is excluded not even the simplest person, from whom the votary of scholarship differs only insofar as he suffers what he suffers more clearly and distinctly and in the form of consciousness. He is magnanimous enough to believe enthusiastically that suffering is the divine mystery of earthly existence, that only in suffering is one in covenant with God and therefore, if anyone is excluded from wisdom, it is only the fortunate one whom good fortune makes so light-minded that he suffers nothing at all, something the more earnest person will always guard himself against even if he has not been brought to suffering by externals and by the fates, because he will himself know how to acquire suffering sympathetically. He does not wish to get out of touch with everyday speech and usage and come, as sometimes happens with a scholar, like a sentinel from distant, unknown regions,[122] with the result that he continually collides with the everyday and, without being really aware of it, offends against the genius of the language and the legitimate shareholders in the common property of the language. Such a separation is grievous and only fosters the illusion that scholarship in its inaccessible distance is greater than the universal, whereas for that very reason it declines into being a finite power in the same sense as beauty and wealth, the possession of which excludes and separates but does not reconcile. The beautiful Greek scholarship understood this, and therefore it is so very beneficial to engage in it, because it did not abandon people for the purpose of sounding like a voice from the clouds but remained on the

V

45

earth, in the marketplace, among the occupations of people, something that was understood particularly by that man who gave up art, gave up the fathoming of physical things, and then began to philosophize in the workshops and in the market-place.[123] Although Greek philosophy is consequently very uplift-ing, diffused over it there is also a pensive sadness in which it is reconciled with the earthly. It knows full well its noble ancestry and does not deny it either, yet takes no vain delight in dissimi-larity and thus accommodates itself to the everyday. It is like a god who walks about in human form and at every moment works a miracle with the humble everyday phrase, although in everything he still resembles an ordinary human being except insofar as that sadness, now as a faint touch of depression, bows down his figure and now transfigures itself as a divine jest that rejuvenates his figure almost to the point of jocularity.

I have nothing more to add, unless I should for a moment busy myself with the thought that was present in the development only latently and as something extraneous, the thought of what relation I intend to have to readers. I consider this deliberation a jest, a light-minded little pastime on which one can spend a half hour when one is finished, but not before. In our day one looks at it differently and thinks that the fatuous seriousness with which an author seeks to create and acquire readers before he starts to write, that the youthful light-mindedness with which he drafts plans and initiates people into them—that this really is earnest-ness that demonstrates the maturity of the full-grown man. The one who in his consideration of life and life-relationships has not come far enough to know what can bear an earnest ordeal and what, like a thin layer of ice, can bear only the speed of a skater, can of course never achieve earnestness in himself or in his per-formance. Each being is assigned only to himself, and the one who takes care to remain here has a solid foundation to walk on that will not shame him. If he then deliberates with himself about what he wills, how far he wills, if by virtue of this delib-eration he begins slowly and silently, his earnestness will not be put to shame. If, on the other hand, it pleases a man to wax serious in the thought of what he will do for others, this demon-strates that basically he is a fool whose life is and remains a jest despite looks and gestures and powerful eloquence and careful theatrical postures, the existence of which means nothing except insofar as with the assistance of irony there can be a little amusement out of it. Whether one who wants to write a book is capable of it, time will teach him whether he will complete it, whether at the very same moment he will have an accident and upset the ink bottle over it, or mislay the manuscript, or the printer will chuck it back to him, or the messenger lose it, or the composing room burn down, or the press run be spoiled, or whether it will appear that no one cares about what he writes— no one can be informed about all this beforehand, and the one who is sagacious enough to want to presuppose all this to be in his *faveur* [favor] is certainly sagacious, but God knows what he actually can make of it and God knows what a sensible person will make of him. That which everyone can know is what he wills, what he is able to do, what he has done, all of which is suitable for earnest consideration, which in turn will regenerate his soul to new earnestness. To regard every light breeze of the times as a hint from Governance that is important for what he is to do, just as it was for the tailor's apprentice because the gust of wind was strong enough to blow him off the table, to want to parade the summer into town on a stem of chives one has grown in a flower pot,[124] to wish to conquer the holy land without even knowing where it is located on the map, to raise a hue and cry in the whole community because one has oneself made a mistake and taken a cow for a windmill, to summon all the tailors in order to explain to them that one must tie a knot in the thread,[125] to walk all day through the streets like the mail carrier and call people from their work in order to offer them a prospectus, to make out a banquet on a menu and feed the hungry on the idea of an association whose purpose is to promote the prosperity of all the poor—this is either a jest, and as such quite amusing at times, or it is earnestness, and as such a nonsensical jest, and the more nonsensical the more complete the lunacy is.

Therefore the one who is to be my reader must agree with me that, even if scholarship in our day has finished with everything, it nevertheless has unfortunately forgotten the point of the whole thing. This has nothing to do with stock companies or

v
47

with prospectuses or with circle dances around some literary idol—that is exactly the point. The one who is convinced of this, that everyone is assigned only to himself and that this is the main thing, only he is my reader, but therefore I cannot know definitely whether he is not already ahead of me. I still do believe, however, that it will in some way have importance for such a person to read what I write, although, to repeat again, it naturally could never occur to me to imagine myself into the vanity that it would be necessary for the sake of others that I write a book. Only when the inclination and need in me have determined me to write, only when I have finished, only then can it occur to me to think of a reader. With the help of this consideration, I am then also liberated from every untimely concern about the fate of the book. The present book will probably appear now; I cannot know this definitely. If it then meets a reader who derives some benefit or gratification from it, it will be to me an uncertain and uncalculated gain, and with that we are quits, to our mutual contentment and pleasure.

As for our systematicians and philosophical optimists, no doubt these will soon make sure that there is nothing for them to do here—soon, I say, yes, just as soon as I think it, as I say it, because for them everything goes like "tic tac toe." They will easily see that there is no time to waste on a laggard who has seen nothing of the world and who has undertaken only an inland journey[126] within his own consciousness and consequently gets nowhere, whereas every systematician is experienced in an altogether different way and has been "to the back of the beyond in both Trapezunt and in R—."[127] They cannot possibly find it worth the inconvenience of making a to-do over such a traveler, all the less likely since they make such a big to-do[128] over "nothing." God grant good fortune so that this may happen; then I will see one of my fondest desires fulfilled. If, however, this does not happen and if, contrary to expectation, they should desire to take an interest in me, then I ask them to be very free and easy, since I am now, as always, at their service in every way. Just one appeal, an imploring request—do with the book and with me as you will, but I beg and entreat you only this: do not with the aid of mediation put me into the systematic bric-a-brac box. I have

V
48

a fear of mediation. I cannot help it. The word has an effect on me and on my soul, not in itself but through its incessant, monotonous use, like filing a saw day in and day out, like the sound Xanthippe made with her continual carping, as Socrates tells it, the sound of pulleys (Diogenes 2, 5. 36[129]). My frame, my health, my entire constitution do not lend themselves to mediation. It may well be that this is a flaw, but when I myself confess it, surely one might humor me. When the word "mediation" is merely mentioned, everything becomes so magnificent and grandiose that I do not feel well but am oppressed and chafed. Have compassion on me in only this one respect; exempt me from mediation and, what is a necessary consequence, from becoming the innocent occasion that would cause one or another philosophical prattler to repeat, like a child at the chancel step,[130] something I indeed know well enough: the history of modern philosophy's beginning with Descartes, and the philosophical fairy tale about how being and nothing combine their deficiencies so that becoming emerges from it,[131] along with whatever other amazing things happened later in the continuation of the tale, which is very animated and moving, although it is not a tale but a purely logical movement.[132] One reads all of this in German, and when one reads it in Hegel, one reads it in such a way that one learns something from it and often turns with deference back to the master. But even if what Hegel said were as certain as that *amo* [I love] belongs to the *verbum: amavi, amatum, amare*,[133] and even if it were as evident as the demonstration of the Pythagorean theorem, it would still be just as fatuous as an adult's wanting to make himself important by publishing on this subject a book that was not intended for the young and for complete novices, and it becomes deadly boring for the one who is to receive such instruction when he really can, if some circumstance of life made it necessary, do his lesson just as well as anyone who has been confirmed at a university, even if he does not assume that it is something to write.

If what I have written should be related to some earlier work in a comparable way, whether the probability was that I diligently suppressed it or it was because of a pardonable ignorance, then if it is said with only two words without any mediation I

v
49

will certainly pay attention to it. It is not my concern in life to become an author; it is not my desire to swindle people out of their money; therefore I promise, if this is proved, to return his

^v
⁵⁰ money to every purchaser. I say with Hamann: *Nicht eine blosze* ὁρμή *sondern ein* furor uterinus *hat mich zu den meisten Aufsätzen getrieben. Anstatt Geld zu nehmen, hätte ich lieber Geld gegeben, und das Wiederspiel von andern Schriftstellern getrieben.* [No mere ὁρμή (impulse) but a *furor uterinus* (desire to give birth) has driven me to most of these essays. Instead of taking money, I would rather have given money and evoked a reaction from other authors] (7,205).[134]

VIII[135]

What I predict will either happen or it will not happen—Apollo has granted me the gift of prophecy.

TIRESIAS[136]

§ 1.

THE DIFFICULTY IN GENERAL

To start a philosophical journal in Denmark not only seems to be but truly is a dubious matter.[137] I myself have not omitted doing what perhaps even the reader most favorably disposed toward me will feel called upon to do, to shake his head, warning and reproaching to shout to me, "How did it go?"[138] . . . . . Men who with genius, with talent, with a wealth of learning, and with the unlimited confidence of the reading public are distinguished among us have made a beginning on this and sooner or later have given it up. Yes, even for Herr Professor Heiberg such an enterprise did not succeed according to expectation. Only two issues of his *Perseus, en Journal for den Speculative Idee* appeared.[139] Yet he was surely the man, if anyone in the kingdom was. When he began such a publication, he could depend upon his own power and confidently assume that contributors would flock around him, since any older person would perceive that it was an enterprise that had a worthy and imperative claim on his active assistance, and any younger person would feel flattered by the mere thought of the literary prestige of having the honor of being a contributor to Prof. Heiberg's journal, which no younger person understands better than I, who still am often reminded of how at the time the youthful mind felt intoxicated by daring to believe that a contribution would not be rejected,[140] of how no young cadet could look up more enthusiastically to the famous general under whose banner he is to fight than I did to the unforgettable editor of *Flyveposten*. Nevertheless this journal did not last long; it did not prosper with a remarkable number of subscribers, and the confluence of contributors,[141] as far as one can tell by the contents, was hardly what everyone would have expected. But if this occurred, then what probability, except the unreasonable one, is there that I will succeed in a comparable enterprise; or rather how great is the probability that something worse will happen to me? If the times have given others to understand that it could not be done, then certainly I scarcely dare to expect friendly instruction from the experience, but rather a drastic and emphatic correction that can enjoin me and my kind not to want presumptuously to venture what even the eminent abandoned.

It is indeed true that philosophical interest has spread more and more widely since that time. It is indeed true that Herr Prof. Heiberg's having made a start on this could be of great benefit to me; and on several occasions it has been seen that what the strongest were unable to do the weaker pulled off, what the rich person did not obtain the poor person won because he showed up at the lucky moment when it was time to harvest what the rich had sowed. Nevertheless I do perceive very well that the probability that my enterprise will succeed is very much less than it was for Prof. Heiberg in his time. It is easy enough to say in retrospect that weakness can be lucky enough to carry out what strength was not able to do. When one is to begin, one certainly finds no encouragement in that, since who knows the time and the opportunity? See, here I stand again at the same point: who knows the time and the opportunity? There is no man in the kingdom who knows this as Prof. Heiberg does, and yet it did not come off.

V
53

The prospects, then, are not the best; my position in no way advantageous. I am not Prof. Heiberg. Indeed, not being Prof. Heiberg, I am even less than that, I am only John Doe.[142] The older person will perhaps consider my enterprise immature or at best will have leniency enough to bide his time; in plain language, he will not support me, he will judge. The younger person will certainly not feel flattered by the literary expulsion resulting from being my contributor and will scarcely be moved by my appeals. Why do I not then give up the whole thing, why do I still nourish the hope that I will succeed? Because my *purpose* is not only good but is also one entirely different from the purpose of those who previously have attempted to publish a philosophical journal, because my *expectation* is not only lofty but is also one entirely different from the expectation of those who previously have made a beginning on it.

§2.

THE PURPOSE OF THIS JOURNAL

However satisfying it is to see philosophy spread throughout the land, so that before long no one will be found anymore who is not moved by its impulse, initiated into its blessings, for me this satisfaction has still not been able to overcome the doubt about whether the many *qui nomen philosophiæ dederunt* [who have lent their names to philosophy] have actually understood what was said and what they themselves said. I am very familiar with this doubt because it has often been my experience, although my ἐποχή [suspension of judgment] has kept me from passing myself off as a philosopher.[143] On the basis of certain observations, I once believed that I had ascertained that things were not entirely right with some of my esteemed contemporaries. In other words, when I, despite every effort, was unable to ascend to the dizzying thought of doubting everything,[144] I decided, in order nevertheless to doubt something, to concentrate my soul on the more human task of doubting whether all the philosophizers understood what they said and what was said.[145] This doubt is overcome not in the system, but in life. But if this is the case, what good is it then that philosophy overcomes all doubt if there is still doubt about whether people actually do understand philosophy? This doubt cannot be a matter of indifference either to those concerned or to philosophy—not to those concerned, because they do indeed want to understand philosophy; not to philosophy, because it does indeed want to be understood. Scholarship is not jealous of its knowledge; it desires to communicate itself to all; it desires that all people should come to knowledge of the truth.[146] It does not make great demands; it appears in a humble form; it expresses itself with the condescension of love.[147]

To take a single example, is it not again and again proclaimed by the priests of philosophy "that in our age it is a necessity for the theologian to be a philosopher in order to be able to satisfy the demand of the times?"[148] But if it is a necessity, then it must indeed also be a possibility, since even I can perceive [*indsee*] that it would be very unphilosophical of philosophy to regard [*ansee*] as necessary something that is impossible. Therefore every theologian can become a philosopher. The word "theologian" in this language cannot be taken *sensu eminentiori* [in the eminent sense] as referring to some particular highly gifted theologian, since even I can perceive that it would be unphilosophical of philosophy to think it has said something by stating a tautology, that it would be very unphilosophical of philosophy to define the supreme being within a determinate being in such a way that it is another being.

The assertion, so comforting to every theological graduate, gains in upbuilding power when one considers the following words: "in order to be able to satisfy the demand of the times." That the phrase "the times" cannot be understood here to refer to a particular individual highly gifted philosophically is easily perceived, since it would be unphilosophical of philosophy to say that this remarkable individual should seek in another or require of another what he most of all should seek in and require of himself. Nor can the phrase "the times" be understood to refer to the idea of the times, a personification of the times, because it would indeed be unphilosophical of philosophy *realiter* [actually] to distinguish between the idea of the times and that theologian κατ' ἐξοχήν [in the eminent sense] who would indeed be the idea of the times. See, philosophy is so good in these latter days, so different from that stingy old goddess who wanted to be loved and worshipped by only a few, to disclose herself to fewer. It makes every theologian into a philosopher and does it so that he can satisfy the demand of the times, which must then be philosophical, which in turn presupposes that the times, that is, the totality of individuals, are philosophical. What a lofty hope for every theological graduate! Now, if only the doubt did not re-

V
55

main about whether one actually understood what one said and what was said.

Thus all the other disciplines proclaim the same as what theology proclaims, since they all gravitate to philosophy. As a *tutti* [full orchestra] it sounds from every mouth: "Philosophy is the demand of the times." And philosophy acknowledges the times as reasonable, therefore its demand as a reasonable demand. I like to think the best of my fellow human beings, and therefore I like to think that every individual who speaks understands what he says, but for me there nevertheless always remains a residue of doubt. It is this remaining doubt that I desired to be eradicated; the purpose of the present journal is to achieve this.

If there now are others besides me who do not completely understand the very much that philosophy says in our times, especially concerning theology, then they certainly know how to conceal it; if (*posito*) [I assume] that they cannot make out philosophy, failing that they are worldly wise. I have, regrettably, always lacked this sagacity. As noted above, philosophy cannot be indifferent to whether it is actually understood or not, and yet it can learn this only through the obtuseness of the one involved, because the one who is sagacious does not let it show.

My purpose, then, is to serve philosophy; my qualification for this is that I am obtuse enough not to understand it, indeed still more obtuse—obtuse enough to betray that. And yet my enterprise can only benefit philosophy, since no harm can come to it from the fact that even the most obtuse person can make it out; it thereby wins its most complete victory and demonstrates the rightness of making all into philosophers.

Is this not a good purpose, and is it not one different from the purpose of those who previously have attempted to publish a philosophical journal, even though in it there is agreement with their purpose: to want to serve philosophy. Yet the services are different; the one serves it through his wisdom, the other through his obtuseness.

I have earnestly examined myself in terms of this purpose of mine, and in this self-examination I have found myself to be in possession of the requisite qualities. I venture to say this without committing any breach of modesty and propriety. The qualities required are: obtuseness and resignation. Surely no one will be so courteous as to argue me out of my being in possession of the first. As for the second, by making confession of the first, I provide evidence of being in possession of the latter. Moreover, I in no way want to plume myself on this as a virtue, since in all probability it will be lucrative. It may occur even to a faithful lover to wish to *test* the beloved, not so that she will thereby lose something, but so that she will appear to his infatuated gaze in heightened beauty. Philosophy I love, and philosophy I have loved from my early youth. I certainly do not need to give assurances that I feel too much respect for it to dare to allow myself to test it in the same sense as that lover tests the beloved. What he does arbitrarily, and precisely in that lies the mistake even though excusable in a lover, I do impelled by necessity. Yet the result can very well be the same—that to my loving gaze philosophy will appear more beautiful and glorious than ever. Would it then take very much resignation to acknowledge one's weakness when one dares to expect this? After all, who then would not, in the absence of something higher, gladly be the fatuous question that would give a young girl occasion to blush more beautifully than ever, the almost childish simplicity that would cause the wise man to smile more knowingly than ever, the obtuseness that would give occasion for a witticism to be uttered, the misunderstanding that would give wisdom occasion to explain itself more intelligibly than ever before! I do not then, like that lover, want to test philosophy, because I certainly have always loved it, but my love is not so happy that I would risk rash experiments. If I test it, then it is with prayer and supplication. I do not belong to the mighty who live on confidential terms with philosophy and associate with it as their equal; I am like a lowly slave in the princely palace who sees his royal majesty every day, even though a chasmic abyss separates me from him. Yet, like the slave in *Palnatoke*, I have only one wish: to see it in all its glory.[149] Could this not happen? Philosophy does not walk in the dark like Harald Bluetooth; it does not make a mistake; it does not take the shroud instead of the royal robes.[150] Would this not happen? When does philosophy appear more glorious than when

it makes itself comprehensible even to the unwise? But if no one
will admit that he is such, philosophy cannot appear in this way
either.

Is not this purpose of mine lofty; is it not different from the
purpose of those who previously attempted to publish a journal?

§3.

MY EXPECTATION

Since the reader knows my purpose, he knows my expectation
also, because my expectation is to achieve my purpose. I expect
a fortunate outcome, but two things belong to a fortunate outcome in the present instance: that my undertaking succeed in an
external and commercial sense and that it succeed in an internal
and scholarly sense.

On the external side my expectation refers to *subscribers* and
contributors.

Experience has taught that a philosophical journal dare not
expect a large following. That I, despite experience, would very
much wish such good fortune for my periodical is obvious, since
wishing is an art open to everyone. That I, despite experience,
expect a fortunate outcome may very well need an explanation.
Here it is. My journal is different from the earlier ones; therefore
I also dare to anticipate a different fate, because the difference is
of the very kind that makes a favorable fate likely.

The one who says that people are cooperative is saying neither
something new nor something untrue. They gladly support
every beneficial enterprise and above all stand by the hard-
pressed; they wish only that their benevolent work, their manifest service, be clear and unmistakable, not ambiguous and dis-
putable. Now, there is no dubiousness connected with being a
subscriber to my journal. If I were in the position of doing what
others who have attempted to publish a journal had as a purpose
and were capable of doing, to instruct or to overcome, then it
would indeed be conceivable that what the subscriber would get
from me would be more valuable than what I would receive
from him, and that in this way the one who thought to do a good

deed to me would in an odd way become my debtor. Yes, by being a subscriber he would be so far from becoming the exalted benefactor that he might seem to be making a most serious concession with regard to himself. This circumstance alone would have to make him doubtful, and a doubting man does not readily act. When, however, my subscription plan[151] comes into the hands of the reading public, the single individual will perhaps say to himself, "Let us see what it is that the author wants—he wants to be instructed—that makes sense, and if my many activities did not interfere, I would gladly instruct him myself. What does the author want—he wants to be overcome—that I can grasp, and if my position did not require all my time, I would gladly cook his goose, I who already for several years have felt myself to be a worthy, triumphant member of the congregation triumphant.[152] Since in the meantime I do not have the opportunity to do either of the two, I will nevertheless do something for him—I will subscribe." As stated, there is no ambiguity possible. My subscriber becomes my true benefactor in every sense; I can offer him nothing but a receipt and cordial thanks. The subscriber need not fear that in a subtle way I would trick him out of the claim to be called my benefactor; he is and remains that in every way, and I his debtor when he pays the bill, when he reads the journal and thinks of my welfare, even more so if he actually comes to my aid with instruction. Every sensitive person who truly wishes to do good can do scarcely anything better than to subscribe to my journal. But when I say every sensitive person, I name a countless host. See, therefore I expect many subscribers. Dare I not, dare I not expect participation? Jean Paul says somewhere, "People are always willing to help a person to bear his cross when they know it is the cross to which he will be nailed."[153]

With regard to *contributors*, I dare not, as mentioned above, expect any assistance. Yet this misfortune serves from another side only to throw light on the good fortune of my position. If I were to have many contributors, this circumstance would indeed demonstrate that many, like me, had not understood philosophy. But to the same degree that this was the case, to this same degree it would become more serious with regard to my principal expectation, my scholarly expectation to be overcome. If many

did not understand it, then that would become a dangerous argument against every philosophy, particularly against that which wants to be understood by all. If, on the other hand, I have no contributors, not a single one, then my scholarly expecta- V
tion gains probability to such a degree that it becomes almost a 59
certainty.

My *scholarly* expectation is that I may be overcome, may win by losing, or to express myself in another way that tallies exactly with my feelings, that good people may succeed in enabling me to make out philosophy.

Yet perhaps someone says, "You are too unimportant; philosophy does not find it worth the bother to overcome you." Away, loathsome thought! Would I venture to think that there is a single person among my philosophical contemporaries who could chatter so unphilosophically! Surely philosophy wants to be popular, wants to make itself understandable to all. However unimportant I may be, in all the processions through the course of time I find no place bearing a more precise designation—under the rubric "all" I do indeed fit in. The category "all" makes no petty distinction; it includes all. In addition, philosophy is certainly not a finite power, not a selfish tyrant that wants to fight, but a philanthropic genius that wants to bring all people to knowledge of the truth.[154] I do not rise in rebellion, I guard against that, I seek instruction. The more unimportant I am, the greater is the triumph for philosophy. To that end spare no means; use evil on me or the good, all accordingly as it is found serviceable; I will endure anything, suffer anything, do anything if only I may succeed in becoming initiated. Only never allow me to say yes to something I do not understand; only do not require of me that I must explain to others what I myself do not comprehend.

Perhaps someone says, "What is required of you is that you be silent and continue to listen." Ah, good Lord! Time passes. Certainly it is still unreasonable of a philosophy that is so wise about life that, by mocking those who are silent and expect something yonder, superbly knows how to explain to them so well that they are fooled; it is indeed unreasonable of such a philosophy to act as if to fool me in a similar way, or rather in a worse way, since the one who once and for all surrenders the present has hope, but I am fooled by the continual moving of the settlement date further out. Do have compassion! What good is it for me to learn ten years from now what I should have done ten years ago; then I would indeed be completely confused. Life is short; would therefore that the art not be made too long for me, above all not longer than life.[155] If it would take an entire life to understand Hegel, then this philosophy would surely contain the most profound contradiction.

But I do not need to fear this. When I consider the times, the powers of the times, and that I will get no contributors, I will certainly not seek instruction in vain. In order to strengthen myself in this thought, I will now in a few words discuss the philosophical competence of the times.

Hegelian philosophy has now thrived for several years here at home. If this philosophy, after having explained everything, now advances and explains itself, what a splendid prospect. I perhaps have not succeeded in expressing myself altogether clearly. I will try to do this and believe also that I am tolerably able to do it, because my incomprehension is not identical with a foggy intimation. There is one thing that I do know quite definitely: it is what I do not understand. There is one thing that I do desire of my contemporaries: it is an explanation. Consequently I do not deny that Hegel has explained everything; I leave that to the powerful minds who will also explain what is missing. I keep my feet on the ground and say: I have not understood Hegel's explanation. From this, in turn, I draw no other conclusion than that I have not understood him. I leave further conclusions to the powers that be who find authorization for this in their personalities. I keep my feet on the ground; I modulate into another key. I plead, I plead for an explanation, an explanation, note well, that I can understand, because it would scarcely help me if there were to be an explanation that explains everything in Hegel, but in such a way that I cannot understand it. Give me the explanation; I will take it *à tout prix* [at any price]. Toss it to me with a shrug of the shoulders; I will still give thanks for it. Since we now have many philosophers here at home who zealously and successfully have comprehended this philosophy, the consequence for me is the happy prospect of the desired instruction.

If nevertheless a difficulty remains, it is a comfort to me that there are also philosophers in my native land who have gone beyond Hegel.[156] As soon as these explain by a little telegraphic notice where they have arrived, my confidence in them will be unshakable. If I may make a request, I would request that this notice be in the form of a categorical definition in order that it can, if possible, be understandable to me, because the general explanation—I have gone beyond Hegel—is much too general for me to be able to join a thought to it; and the more precise definition, which a family name and a baptismal name contain, constitutes such a terrible contrast to that generality that everything is confused for me. At this point I will immediately admit that there have been various phenomena completely inexplicable to me. I have read philosophical treatises in which nearly every thought, almost every expression, was from Hegel. After having read through them, I have thought: Who, now, actually is the author? Hegel, I have then said to myself, is the author; the one who has written the treatise is his reporter and as such he is dependable and accurate. This I could understand. But see! This was not the way it was; the author was a man who had gone beyond Hegel.[157] Here my understanding came to a halt; the author says: I have gone beyond Hegel. If the article could speak, it would probably say: What chatter! —Hegel knew how to formulate the whole of modern philosophy in such a way that it looks as if he brought everything to an end and everything previous tended toward him. Someone else now makes a similar presentation, a presentation that to a hair is inseparable from Hegel's, that consequently is pervaded at every point by this final thought, and to this is added a concluding paragraph in which one testifies that one has gone beyond Hegel. Here my understanding again comes to a halt, and yet what is all that I need? A triviality, two words are enough, a tiny categorical definition concerning the relation to Hegel.

V
61

My scholarly expectation, then, is that I may succeed, despite my obtuseness, in becoming able to make out philosophy. If this happens, then no one has reason for complaint. Not I. I will count myself the most fortunate of all people, because the further one has been from daring to hope, the more grateful one will be. I will never forget all my benefactors, the gentleman subscribers

and all the generous people by whose aid I managed a fortunate
progress in philosophy. Philosophy cannot have reason for complaint either; it will rejoice over becoming more understandable
to more and more.

But of course something else may also occur; I may be declared to be so obtuse that philosophy cannot even have anything
to do with me. "In that case everything is indeed lost; the journal
must fold." Not at all! However obtuse I am, I can still see that
it is impossible for philosophy to reply so unphilosophically. To
reply that I am so obtuse that one cannot have anything to do
with me is to define me far more vaguely than is proper for
philosophy. If philosophy cannot define me more precisely, then
to the best of my judgment its position does not become less
unpleasant than mine and then, despite our great differences, we
have a partnership. I am so obtuse that philosophy cannot become understandable to me. The opposite of this is that philosophy is so sagacious that it cannot comprehend my obtuseness.
These opposites are mediated into a higher unity, that is, a common obtuseness. Amazingly enough, then I still slip in. Or is it
not so, does not philosophy teach that if the infinite is thought
outside the finite, then both become finitudes? Is it not repeated
again and again: *veritas est index sui et falsi* [truth is the criterion of
itself and of the false]?[158] Then if philosophy excludes something,
it renders itself finite. In order to prevent this, it must be willing
to explain itself more specifically with regard to my obtuseness
and what constitutes it. That previously I have not understood
philosophy certainly cannot be a hindrance to reaching this
point, since it would rather be a hindrance if I had understood it.
My obtuseness must then signify that I lack possibility or be an
expression of the impossibility; otherwise my obtuseness could
be an infinitely distant approximation-stipulation in relation to
philosophy. My obtuseness must then be the boundary that limits
me and thereby excludes me from philosophy. If this is assumed,
there continually remains a difficulty, because by defining my
boundary negatively I am still defined in continuity with the
other. Then I become an infinitely, infinitely, infinitely small bit
of a philosopher, but I still am included. I belong to the chaotic
mass in which "the cultured, as points of intelligence and moving

spirits,"[159] carry on their organizing work; then with their help I slip into philosophy. Now, this is said easily enough but is not so easily understood. At least I must be aided by a little middle term about how the one who is too obtuse to understand philosophy relates to the cultured person through whom he participates in the common understanding of philosophy, whether it is by understanding the cultured person or by misunderstanding him, whether he, when he understands the cultured person, understands the same thing the cultured person understands, because then he himself indeed understands philosophy or he understands something different, and then it seems not quite right to say of him that it is through the cultured person that he participates in the common understanding.

v
63

But perhaps it is for another reason that philosophy cannot have anything to do with me; perhaps the explanation of my obtuseness is the same as the explanation regarding philosophy, that is, that the one who cannot understand philosophy also cannot understand the explanation of why he cannot understand it. If this is so, then I must ask what bearing this obtuseness has on my human existence as such, whether because of it I cease to be a human being or whether in spite of it I am still in possession of that which essentially belongs to a human being in order to be a human being, that whereby he is essentially a human being. Furthermore, I must ask whether I can become blessed like other human beings, despite my obtuseness. If so, then the question is through what means do I dare hope for that. Is it through philosophy? Does it perhaps have the remarkable quality that it makes all blessed, both those who understand it and those who do not understand it? If this is denied, is it then because of my obtuseness? This does not seem reasonable, since precisely that is my unblessedness. Through what, then, do I dare to hope to become blessed? If now something else is mentioned here, then the question is whether this makes me blessed on the basis of my accidental quality, that is, on the basis of my obtuseness, since, after all, this is something accidental in me and does not essentially belong to human nature. If this is answered affirmatively, then the question is whether I do not become blessed as other human beings but only as obtuse people become blessed. If this is answered affirmatively, then the question is how I can become blessed by becoming blessed on the basis of my accidental quality, since in that case I must indeed come into contradiction with the essential in me, but such a contradiction is indeed unblessedness. If the answer to this is that my obtuseness is the essential in me, then I have ceased to be a human being, which was denied in what was said previously. If, however, I become blessed on the basis of the essential in me and this in turn is the essential to human nature, then the same thing that makes me blessed must also be able to make all other people blessed, yes, that alone that makes them blessed, because only the one who is made blessed on the basis of the essential, only that one becomes blessed. Perhaps what this was in the old days does not hold any more; in the old days it was good philosophy to say: [160]*inter accidentia sola, non autem inter formas substantiales individuorum ejusdem speciei plus et minus reperitur* [there are differences of degree only between the accidents and not between the substantial forms of individuals of the same species].[161] Therefore, when the philosopher becomes blessed through his philosophy, this is an accidental blessedness. There is, then, something higher than philosophy. It is higher in that it includes me and similar bunglers. If this is so, then the question is: will philosophy continue to be called the absolute? But if it is not the absolute, then it must be able to state its boundary. If I wanted to be a poet, the esthetician would certainly instruct me about which capacities are required for that. I would then perceive that I am not a poet and would accept my fate. If, on the other hand, poetry wanted to claim to be the absolute, then it would not dare to exclude me, because the absolute cannot be anything that is not common to all.

I do not judge, then, that it would be necessary to let my journal fold. I am, regrettably, a bit slow, and there is a lot to be learned here. My journal presumably could survive even if my expectation is not fulfilled completely in accord with my desire.

Yet something else could happen. I could be declared unfit for people to have anything to do with me, "but not so much on account of my obtuseness as on the basis of a narrow-minded defiance." "In that case, all would certainly be lost. The subscribers would presumably fall away because I would be found to

be one of the unworthy poor; the journal would have to fold."
It would truly be oppressive, especially when I take into account
the disgrace that would befall me. If I am not greatly mistaken,
however, the subscribers would very likely have a little patience
with me until philosophy had explained itself a little more precisely. Philosophy does indeed possess the truth, but the truth still
is and still remains the strongest; how then could a narrow-
minded defiance possibly stand against it? Then the result would
be certain, unless the defiant person possessed an almost dai-
monic power, and surely this cannot be the case with me, or he
was sagacious enough to conceal his defiance, sagacious enough
not to expose himself to being annihilated by the truth. This is so
far from being the case with me that I, on the contrary, desire
my annihilation, because I know that this is the prerequisite for
"my being able to ascend to a perfect existence."[162] If one were   v
nevertheless to persist in blaming my narrow-minded defiance   65
for the inability of people to have anything to do with me, then
philosophy, in order to speak as befits a scholarly discipline and
not chatter as a philistine can be expected to do, would still have
to define more precisely the character of the narrow-minded
defiance that makes communication impossible. I would then
have to ask whether this defiance is identical with obtuseness,
whether the obtuseness is based on the defiance or the defiance
on the obtuseness. If they are identical, then the matter is returned to the point we just left. If they are similar, I would have
to ask: How? And in what proportion? Does the dissimilarity
increase proportionally according to developmental law so that
the defiance expires to the same degree that the obtuseness
wanes, or are they inversely related so that when the obtuseness
has been transmuted into wisdom the defiance is potentiated to
its ultimate? I would have to inquire further about how they
relate to each other on this point, whether it is possible for the
defiance to maintain itself or whether it must succumb to wisdom's imperative. If the first is the case, then the question is
whether I, despite my defiance, can achieve wisdom; if the second is the case, then the question is whether I, despite my wisdom, can continue to defy. If the first is the case, then it must
surely be an easy matter for philosophy to bring me to wisdom,

inasmuch as it is understood that wisdom has in itself an imperative that is superior to the will's defiance. If the second is the case, then there is indeed a power superior to knowledge, a power superior to knowledge's imperative. In that case, the question is: what is this power and how does it relate to knowledge; the question is: cannot this power become the object of scholarly treatment; what is the name of the scholarly discipline that treats of this matter; what is its relation to the scholarly discipline that treats of knowledge; by becoming a scholarly discipline does it not become an object of knowledge; what relation does knowledge now have to this power that has shown itself to be superior to knowledge; must it itself be helpful in order for knowledge to be able to understand it; is it only in this instance that knowledge requires its assistance or is this always so; is there still an exception and what is this; is it not of importance that this be acknowledged before one begins to acknowledge something else; what kind of exception is this and what follows from this situation with regard to the character of that knowing; what knowing is it to which defiance is incapable of giving resistance; is all knowing necessary knowing or is all knowing to an equal degree both free and necessary; if this is the case, then this power is able to exclude me from all knowing; if this is not the case, then it is able to exclude me from only a certain kind of knowing; is the kind of knowing from which it is capable of excluding me superior for that reason or is the other kind of knowing superior for the opposite reason; if this is the case, then is philosophy indeed not the highest, but only, even at its highest, that is, in the latter kind of knowing, a knowledge of the highest?

V
66

I do not think, then, that it would be necessary to let my journal fold. I am, regrettably, a bit slow, and there is a lot to be learned here. My journal presumably could survive even if my expectation is not fulfilled completely in accord with my desire.

But there is still one situation that I want to imagine: that philosophy itself would condescend to speak to me. I do not know whether I should visualize it as a man or as a woman; therefore I think it best to imagine it as an unseen voice that sounds to one as if it were from one's inner being, although it comes from the clouds,[163] that speaks to one so humanly, al-

though its speech is divine, in such a gentle and friendly way that
it is a delight to hear it, because philosophy is always friendly and
it is only the philosophers who are "*böse* [ill-tempered]." It
would speak to me somewhat like this: "You labor under a misunderstanding. It has not been granted to you to understand me;
yet you should not for that reason be angry with me since I am
not the one who creates humanity. You are not able to comprehend me. This I do not say to affront you, even if you were the
only human being who is too limited for it; my quiet, peaceable,
blessed life affronts no one. But you are not the only one; what
is true of you is true of many others, yes, it is true of the mass of
human beings to whom you belong. I am only for the chosen
ones, for those who were marked early in their cradles, and in
order for these to belong to me, time and diligence and opportunity are required, enthusiastic love, the high-mindedness to venture to love without hope, the renunciation of much that other
people regard as beautiful and indeed is in a way. The one in
whom I find this I reward also with the kiss of the idea; I make
concept's embrace fruitful for him. I show him what the earthly
eye desires, to see the grass grow; I show it to him in a much
higher realm; there I make him understand and see how the
thoughts grow more and more luxuriantly in one another. What
is scattered in the multiplicity of languages,[164] what is universally
present in the speech of the simplest as well as in that of the most
sagacious, is gathered here and increases its quiet growth. Do not
believe it is because I am too proud that I cannot show myself to
you, that I cannot be loved by you. No! But this is part of my
nature. Farewell! Do not demand the impossible; praise the gods
that I exist, because even if you do not comprehend my nature,
there nevertheless are those who do comprehend it. Rejoice,
then, that the fortunate become happy; do that and you will not
regret it."

V
67

    This is how I perceived its address. To this I replied as follows,
as I tried out of respect for its exalted character to choose my
words as well as possible: "I have understood completely every
word you have spoken, you of exalted character, although I have
with pain also comprehended that I am not among the number
of the fortunate. Every word in your admonition has healingly

penetrated into my soul after first having purged away my earlier fatuousness. As you spoke, my heart, which had been sick and dejected, became healthy and joyful again; and as you spoke of your understanding with the loving ones, it was as if I had been transported from the noise of the world, as if I had come to a secluded place to which you always invite your votaries. I do realize that this was no place for me, but that it must be glorious to be able to go there, gratifying to contribute to preserving the tranquil abode of philosophy, lest the noise and the toil of the world disturbingly press their way in, that for this it must be a beautiful reward: to see the chosen ones radiant in the reflection of your glory. And to this you allowed everyone, also me, to make his contribution. Was it not so? Oh, but if it is so, why then do you put up with what has happened in these latter days! Why do you not send forth one of your lovers who not only has thoughts in his head but wrath in his nostrils[165] to consume the hypocritical worshipers who profane your pure character, who disquiet us who are weak by wanting to make it an imperative for us to understand you. You must not think that I by myself have hit upon such things; it was the talk and example of others that seduced me. Then the confusion will come to an end, the chosen ones will follow you, and the rest of us will not sorrow too much over our having been excluded. Is it not true, and this I dare to believe, that the dissimilarity in existence has its deepest basis in a unity in the absolute, that the possibility of making this unity manifest is not denied to any human being, that precisely through this possibility this existence points to one more perfect, where the unity will pervade everyone completely and will not be conditioned by dissimilarity as in this world? I do indeed perceive the perfection or imperfection of dissimilarity; this I perceive with pain, the fortunate with joy. But I do not comprehend that the dissimilarity is the perfection of existence. I believe, and is it not true, I dare to believe that the perfect existence will make everyone into everything and all equally much. Surely you will not deny this, you who although of divine origin yet are so human, and is being human anything else than believing this? This you will not deny, lest humanity be made unhappy—your

V
68

lovers, because they alone would become happy, the rest of us because we would not become your lovers."

If this were to happen, if philosophy in its elevated simplicity addressed me in this way, then it might seem best for me to quit, the sooner the better. To continue nevertheless to importune philosophy with my appeals would be unmanly, but although I, just as I had earlier abandoned any pretension of being a philosopher, had now also abandoned hope of becoming that, there still was a multiplicity of *deliberations* that might interest the majority of people inasmuch as they would be excluded from philosophy. My journal is titled "Philosophical Deliberations."[166] I could very well still indulge in deliberations without being a philosopher; moreover, I perhaps could nevertheless even call them "philosophical deliberations" because there must continually remain a *confinium* [border territory] between philosophy and the doctrine in which the rest of us seek refuge, and in this regard philosophy could indeed be of assistance to us, if in no other way than by thrusting away.

Whether now in our day there is a probability that philosophy will explain itself in this or in a similar but even better way, I do not know; it does no good to be on the lookout for trouble. If, however, it continues to become more and more a riddle, more and more difficult in its expression, if along this path it continues to want to achieve its lofty goal of being understood by all, then perhaps my lofty expectation can be fulfilled, my *pium desiderium* [pious wish] to become a philosopher. So I trustingly address myself to my contemporaries. I have not doubted everything; I address myself to men who have doubted everything. What a lofty hope! Have they attained certainty about everything? I do not know, but surely on some points they must have attained it. Granted that there is some exaggeration in the great amount of talk that is heard concerning the system—that it should amount to nothing at all would be too frightful a contradiction for my weak head to be able to think it. Now, if only it becomes an original Danish system, a completely domestic product, and if only I am included—even if I become nothing but a courier in this Danish system—I shall still be happy and satisfied.

So, then, for the time being I will hope, hope that my lofty expectation will be fulfilled. To that end I still have just one request to the high and mighty and the good people by whose help it will come to pass, namely, that they show a little forbearance and leniency toward me. Do not misunderstand me. It is not my idea that one is to stop speaking rigorously to me, castigating me, putting me in the corner of disgrace. Use any means when it is made necessary: a little *pereat* [let him die], a small subscription by various students and candidates who feel revolted at my obtuseness. —I shudder, but my zeal to be along is so great that I will endure everything. On the other hand, my idea is: reject every accidental victory and spare me every unnecessary humiliation, both, because they do not serve me in the principal matter. Do not dismay me with authorities, because it certainly does not serve me that others have said or understood what I cannot understand. Do not make a fool of me. I will give an example. One of my benefactors produces an explanation from Aristotle[167] to assist me to a better insight. I actually succeed in understanding it; I am already quite happy about this. But see, such an explanation is not at all in Aristotle; my benefactor only wanted to see if he could get me to believe that Aristotle would have said something like that. Well, now in itself this is utterly unimportant, because insofar as the explanation really explains something, it is indeed unimportant whether it comes from Aristotle or from a servant girl. But because of gossip and in order not to detract from my confidence in my advisors, I would still wish that people would refrain from this when it is not made absolutely necessary. Yet what would move them to do this anyway? A victory over my ignorance, that would be too poor a victory; a triumph over my not being well read, that would almost make a mockery of the victor! It would, after all, be like a teacher's wanting to rival his pupil.

V
70

In the foregoing I have tried to commend my enterprise in the best way; I have not let it lack a *captatio benevolentiæ* [procedure aimed at gaining the favorable disposition of the judge or listener] to the right and to the left; I have done what was in my power to turn every sensitive person into my benefactor: into my subscriber, my reader, my counselor. I have nothing more to add, except that I hope I have done what is necessary. In the journal itself I dare not give space to the outpourings of my heart; there I go my winding way along the path of thought.

> Dead to the many conditions here on earth,
> The multifarious, the manifold,
> The ceremonial, the everyday.
> > See Baggesen, *S.V.*, VI, p. 143.[168]

It hardly needs saying that this light reading cannot possibly, that is, without invalidating all experiences and concepts, initiate conflict and quarreling, because a word in advance [*Forord*] breaks up no quarrel,[169] and the one who strikes back begins the conflict—conflict not with "The Prefaces" [*Forordene*] but with all experiences and concepts.

WRITING SAMPLER

by A.B.C.D.E.F. Godthaab

WRITING SAMPLER
WRITING SPECIMEN
BY
A.B.C.D.E.F. ROSENBLAD
[*CHANGED TO:* GODTHAAB]
PROSPECTIVE AUTHOR

PREFACE

☞Please read the following preface, because it contains things of the utmost importance.

PREFACE

It might seem to be an excess to write a preface to a preface, but it is not that at all; on the contrary, it is only a characteristic expression for the increasing haste with which our age exerts itself, with the result that it takes a great deal to halt it for only a moment and in order to come under consideration for only a moment. In an age as agitated as ours, it no longer suffices just to be advertised in the newspaper. To be advertised in this way is the same thing as being consigned to oblivion. If one is to be noticed, one must at least appear on the first page under a hand that points to and, as it were, announces or advertises the advertisement. Alas, and soon this will not suffice either; before long there will be such a horde on the first page that the particular shout of the advertisement will in turn drown and vanish unnoticed in the multitude. Fortunate the one who is capable of inventing something new. Naturally it will not be long before the new discovery is in turn worn out, but nevertheless it may succeed the first time. For example, fortunate the lucky advertiser who first hits upon what still remains: to have his notice printed on paper that is "solely and exclusively manufactured for" and suited for reading in the privy.[1] While all the other advertisers despair—he will be noticed. He dares to have the most certain hope, he who ingeniously knew how to use the only moment that a most esteemed* but also extremely occupied public has left; he will be noticed, he will be read**—[*deleted:* absolutely *privatissime* (entirely privately) in the privy]. It is well known how

In margin: cultured

**In margin:* he has ingeniously known how to assure himself [*deleted:* if not] of a private [then at least] or privy relation to the public.

reading is done in public places, how hastily, how carelessly, but in the privy! The lucky fellow [*deleted:* not to mention the inestimable advantage of having a private relation to the public]!

But what holds for advertisements holds also for books—prefaces are no longer read. A person must hit upon something new if he wants to be noticed, like this, now, to write a preface to the preface. What stands above holds true for the present preface; it does contain things of the utmost importance—to me. To me it is truly of indescribable importance to get the public to read this preface, which will immediately place the reader in the proper point of view, and to me this is of the utmost, utmost urgent importance, that the reader be immediately placed in the proper point of view.

I hope now that I have succeeded in being noticed and may take a little more time. Therefore, if I may, I take the respectful and humble liberty of asking you [*Dem*], the most esteemed public (for far be it from me impertinently and audaciously to address a most esteemed public as Du^2), to settle down on this point of view. The situation is this. I wavered a long time before I decided on this step; I have put off the moment, but now it must be taken—and now just one request in advance: leniency, mercy, compassion, forbearance, lenient judgment by a most esteemed public.[3]

VII²
B 274:5
318

The situation is this. I am a young man in my prime; I cannot, regrettably, say more, because the trouble is simply that I am a complete unknown to you, something that one cannot be *accidentally* to a most esteemed public, which qua public knows everything noteworthy and is acquainted with everyone noteworthy—thus the real reason for this is that to date I am what is called a nobody, nothing. But from now on I hope to become something—simply and solely through your favor, the most esteemed public! My craving, my burning and urgent craving, is to become an author, which you alone are able to make happen. It is not an author who creates readers, but it is the public who creates authors—and fortunately I am a nobody, nothing. You yourself will see to it, if anyone will, that I may be able to become your creation, wholly your creation. In this connection no one will in fairness be able to deny me the grade: suitable. Usually, of course, the grade "suitable" would signify that one is something, but when it is a question of having to be created, the requirement is obviously that one be a nobody, nothing. What is it, namely, to create? It is, Pontoppidan says, "to produce from nothing or from an unsuitable material."[4] I do not need to show the esteemed public what it has long known, how concepts flip over.[5] Next to being completely nothing, which is to be suitable, it is required that one be a mediocre fellow. Also from such a one it is still possible for the public to create an author. Every competence, on the other hand, not to mention a brilliant competence, is *eo ipso* completely unsuitable. Yes, it is quite impossible for the public to *create* an author from that; therefore the public does well to despise and mock every such author, because his presence is a rebellion against the public, a limitation of its creator-omnipotence. But I, I am suitable—I am literally nothing. I have been a barber's assistant and since then a barker in the Dyrehave carnival, then an occasional waiter, a billiards scorekeeper, and am now unemployed, am in all this something that will not or cannot be a hindrance to the most esteemed public—in creating.

Therefore create me! You, the most esteemed, cultured public,* are in possession of *nervus rerum gerendarum* [the moving force in accomplishing something].[6] Just a word from you, a promise to purchase what I write, or, if it is possible, so that everything can be in order immediately, a little advance payment—and I am an author; I shall remain one as long as this favor lasts. What, indeed, is an author?[7] He is one who has something printed from which he earns money. The one who has something printed but earns no money—is not an author. This is so easy to understand that every sausage peddler can grasp it. With the concept "author" it is just the same as with being a shopkeeper. What is a shopkeeper? He is one who makes money by selling goods. If he does not earn money, then he is not a shopkeeper but is rather a

VII²
B 274:5
319

In margin: (because however great my predicament and need are, I nevertheless have firmly decided that I will apply myself only to and to write only for a "cultured" public)

fool, a benefactor, or whatever he happens to be, but a shop-keeper he is not.

What I write, then, in this book, which is not actually a book, is intended to draw your favorable attention to me. [8]In the old days, one initially wrote a work by which one sought to gain prominence, but now the task is so manifold that competence in everything is required. Just as a maid-of-all-work, who for want of being a chambermaid offers to do everything, a person does best these days by producing a sampler or a style book to qualify himself and to draw the public's attention to himself before he chooses this way of making a living and settles down as an author, or before he lets himself create or be created—not a new creation,[9] but as I through your creator-omnipotence will become that—created out of nothing.[10]

VII²
B 274:5
320

More I need not say to you, most esteemed, cultured public. You are capable of everything; it is only a matter of bringing you to a point of view, and so that you remain there it is a matter of stirring, moving, interesting, in short, winning you for the cause. [11]From the poets you must know that everything revolves around love, and from experience you know that everything revolves around money—along with love—and that the art in life is actually to get these two powers to revolve around each other in a pleasant and gentle way, something only the poets themselves experience, because only in poetry do they have enough money. [*Deleted:* Paper money, note well, is irrelevant.] In the world of actuality it is superfluous to order lieutenants not to marry without money—which is self-evident. Even if it is done ever so romantically and marriage is transformed the moment of the wedding day, without money one cannot do it, not to mention thinking further ahead and asking about the prospects. It is not marriage that is the prospect; marriage is the earnest occasion for asking about the prospects. See, it would naturally never occur to me as a solitary person to wish to be an author. I find it quite in order for a most esteemed public summarily to reject as an unworthy indigent every solitary person who wishes to become an author, and as in no way a legitimate recipient of public relief or a suitable object of the public's pity. But I simply stick to the question of the prospects (and I know

that the most esteemed public has feelings and can be moved).*
I am in love. I have the girl's Yes, and I as good as have the
father's Yes—if only there is success in making a living. Since I
myself will be your creation, so will—oh, may you be moved by
this beautiful thought—my marriage also be your work. Without
you I am nothing, through you everything.

What do I now dare to expect? As far as I am concerned, there
is, as stated, nothing in the way. I am nothing less than a genius,
but quite literally nothing. I seek consolation and hope simply in
that. [12]It is indeed assumed that the originality of a work stands
in inverse relation to the speed of its distribution and sale—what
a consolation to me, who must use the money immediately. The
consequence of that thesis is plain, that a very great genius who
is not assured of an income in any other way is bound to die of
hunger. It is good that this is not my lot; for sake of the cause one
can wait a bit for fame, but as far as income is concerned one
cannot very well wait many days and in this regard is not at all
served by any inverse relation, that wealth and abundance come
a hundred years after one's death or that one is enabled to marry
a hundred years after one is disabled for that by death. In all such
things a direct relation is the best and the most desirable.

[13]So, then, I put my writing specimen, and with it my fate, in
your hands, most esteemed public. If the work takes off by leaps
and bounds, then my fortune is made—I am an author. I throw
myself into the arms of the public or of humanity; if this more
than ordinary, although not therefore less tender, embrace is
achieved, I intend to cling more closely to my beloved. I belong
wholly to the future with my intended [*Tilkommende*], to my
intended [*tilkommende*] way of making a living, and to the wages
due [*Tilkommende*] me.[14]

[15]Finally, it should be noted that I, on a hint given by numerous subscribers or by one man who subscribes for five hundred
copies, I will write on request about everything in the name of
the century, of humanity, of our age, of the public, of the crowd,
of several, *audiatur et altera pars* [and of the other side to be heard];

VII[2]
B 274:5
321

*In margin: I know that it most graciously interests itself in helping bring
lovers together

to subscription agents who get fifty subscribers I also offer services in barbering, the brushing of clothing at certain hours of the day, the running of errands, and other attendance.

Respectfully
A.B.C.D.E.F. Rosenblad [*changed to:* Godthaab]

VII²
B 274:6
322

NO. 1

The Theater. Last evening Shakespeare's glorious masterpiece, *The School for Scandal*, was performed for the first time.[16] For every connoisseur and patron of true classical poetry, it ought to be a true classical pleasure to take part in so rare an artistic pleasure.* It is another question whether it would not have been altogether proper for someone with a loving and artistic hand to have undertaken one or two little changes, so that at least one or two expressions shocking to a cultured public would have been omitted. But we do not wish to detract from this pleasure but rather, in the name of the most esteemed public, to thank the directors of the theater for this rare pleasure while at the same time to take the liberty of suggesting that it produce a piece by Iffland[18] as soon as possible.

As for the *production*, it was so excellent in every respect that it would be difficult to find its equal outside of Copenhagen, at least not according to what the reviewer knows of scenic presentations in other cities. The reviewer recalls seeing the same piece produced in Corsøer,[19] but this performance was in no way a match for that of the Royal Theater.

Limited space unfortunately does not permit us to enter into profound or exhaustive evaluation of details; we will therefore be brief. Herr. Dir. Nielsen's[20] performance as Sir Oliver Surface was masterful and far surpassed that of his predecessor in Corsøer, Herr Rasmussen. Madame Nielsen's[21] performance was also very good and Herr Phister[22] as Snake was likewise excellent. But the

---

In margin: an artistic pleasure at the same time enhanced by the attendance at the performance of His Majesty the King and H.R.H. Prince Ferdinand.[17]

Fru Heiberg's*[24] mastery surpassed them all and every description. We would have to describe all that she did with the role if we were to give the reader a sense of the way in which she delivered her lines or of the lines she spoke. But since this would be too prolix, and moreover we do not have the script at hand, we will limit ourselves to transcribing from the *Berlingske Tidende*, which so admirably says, "We would have to transcribe the entire role if we were to give the reader a sense of the masterly performance by Herr Wiehe."[25]

VII[2]
B 274:6
323

Italian Opera. The third presentation of *Norma*[26] was on the whole well attended. Since we fancy that we know best what we owe the esteemed, cultured public and since we decry an only altogether too common negligence with regard to theatrical matters, and having obtained precise and thoroughly reliable information, we report the following: In the stalls there were 93 persons and 5 children; of these 35 were of the male sex and 58 were of the female sex. There were 60 persons in the parterre, none of the female sex. In the boxes there were 230 persons, divided as follows.

VII[2]
B 274:7
323

(to be continued)

NO. 2[27]

VII[2]
B 274:8
323

Literature. [28]These days a book has come off the press that even in Paris would create a sensation among all the bookbinders and typesetters.

The appearance of the volume is as follows. Along the margins there is a border of real gold and in every corner there is an emblem wrought in gold, somewhat as on a lady's handkerchief. In the center there is placed an extremely costly bouquet of flowers in the fashion of genuine Persian shawls. Alongside of the bouquet the title is printed in fine script, the title on one side and the author's name on the other. Therefore one must turn

---

In margin: ad se ipsum [to himself]

It could produce a droll effect if one called her *Madame* [Madam] Heiberg instead of *Fru* [Mrs.] H.[23]

the book to be able to read the title. This would be impossible if one does not take one's eyes off the bouquet of flowers that displays itself in all its splendor the very moment one picks up the book.

VII²
B 274:8
324

When one opens the book, the title page looks as follows. A luxuriant chain of arabesques winds its way around the edge, with ingenious and charming vignettes in each corner. At the same time the title page also has the remarkable feature that the title of the book and the name of the author are so artfully worked into the arabesques that only with great diligence can one make them out. *It would take too long to go through the details or to go page-by-page through this remarkable work*; we would therefore merely emphasize the absolutely matchless "A" with which page 17 begins.

In margin: When one closes the book, the other side looks as follows. Yes, it does in a certain sense look just like the front side, except that here everything is in silver, which for the one who wishes to make comparisons when he opens the book and looks at both sides of the volume at the same time is very interesting.

The contents are of course very good, something adequately guaranteed by the famous name of the author. We hope that the most esteemed, cultured public will support this fine effort in literature with strong sales.

VII²
B 274:9
324

NO. 3[29]

The Elections for the Provincial Estates are now concluded; we report the following results according to the *Berlingske Tidende*.

[*Blank space*]

We merely add the following remark. If as a result Herr Attorney Lehmann[30] had had _____ more votes, he would have beaten Herr Merchant A. Hansen; and if Herr Grocerer Øst had only had _____ votes fewer, he might have become an alternate. Regarding the election of Herr Agent Lund, it can be observed that if he had received _____ more votes, then he would, remarkably enough, have received 300 votes, which would have been very remarkable.

NO. 4

VII²
B 274:10
325

Criticism and Taste. The execution of the two notorious murderers, Ole Hansen and Hans Olsen,[31] brought a sizable most esteemed cultured crowd out to Amager.[32] Even though the weather was not at all favorable, the happiest and most loyal mood generally reigned. That worthy artist, Copenhagen's executioner, Herr Madsen, performed his difficult task with a rare virtuosity and bravado and mastery—favorably thought of earlier, he has now truly made himself deserving of the name by which he is called: the master hangman. It was therefore well-earned acknowledgment when his appearance and also his exit were greeted with loud applause. The executioner from Roskilde, who was also present to flog a third criminal,*[33] [*deleted:* possesses an unmistakable talent and gave a praiseworthy performance. In this his first attempt, he satisfactorily distinguished himself with taste and correctness in every respect.] We wish him luck in his future artistic career, while in the meantime we acknowledge how right and modest it was to make his debut with a flogging before moving on to more difficult acts.

NO. 5

VII²
B 274:12
325

VII²
B 274:12
326

[34]**News Notes**. *Merchant Marcussen* in Badstuestræde[35] had a large dinner party yesterday. At the table there occurred, however, the misfortune that the merchant knocked a gravy boat over himself and the lady next to him. This is how it happened.

In margin: performed with taste and correctness, [*deleted:* and in this his first attempt satisfactorily distinguished himself in every respect.] for which reason he was, during the presentation, rewarded with applause and finally was called to take a bow,** [*deleted:* and now displayed] a new talent, beside that of the executioner, a talent as a stump speaker, in a lecture that was more than once impossible to hear because of the thunderous "Hear, Hear" of the assembly and that concluded with his being called forward and again receiving *da capo* [an encore].

**and then received *da capo*, but when the officer of the law at the scene objected, nothing came of it, and the delinquent escaped *da capo*. The one called to take a bow displayed, however . . . . .

VII²
B 274:11
325

Just at the very moment when the servant offered the gravy boat, the merchant stood up to make a toast. With a movement of his arm, he bumped the servant and the gravy boat. This is the historical truth. We are well aware that a rumor is circulating that tells the story otherwise, namely, that with a movement of her head the lady bumped the servant. But this is only a rumor without any official standing. We have received no information as to the lady's name. Some mention Miss Lindvad; others say it was Gusta Jobbe. As soon as we learn it, we will immediately report it; the name is of enormous importance, because for the first week there will, of course, be talk of nothing else in all Copenhagen and in all Denmark.

We hope that in picking up this article the editors of other newspapers will expressly note that it comes from our paper, which always tries to be first in putting out every piece of news of universal interest.

VII²
B 274:13
326
Barber Lützov's already commendably famous and much frequented barbershop now has, on the basis of a new improvement, a new claim on the discerning acknowledgment by the most esteemed public. Herr Lützov is a well-read man who keeps up with the times and the discoveries of the times. Assured that a new era is beginning with the stethoscope, not only in the history of medicine but in the history of human life, he has decided to stethoscope everyone who comes into his barbershop, completely *gratis* and without costing anything. When one thinks back to the time when it was not the custom to be shaved, and how it is now a necessity for everyone to get a shave, one will not count Herr Lützov wrong in his opinion that someday it will be just as common to have oneself stethoscoped every day as it is now to be shaved. Someday natural scientists may discover an

VII²
B 274:13
327
instrument by which one can hear the brain beat (that it beats is certain):* [*deleted:* and Herr Lützov will again know how to keep up with the times]. To teach oneself how to do this is indeed the

---

In margin: and in turn this will become so common as it will one day to be stethoscoped.

highest of tasks, and therefore every science that helps human-kind along this way is to be praised and every man who assists the individual toward this self-knowledge is to be appreciated. We urge every male to visit Herr Lützov's barbershop in order to assure himself how beneficial and at the same time enjoyable it is to have himself stethoscoped every day in order to learn to know himself.[36]

NO. 6

VII²
B 274:14
327

Moral. Retrospective Glance at the Year 1846. According to the opinion of all the wisest and best men, New Year's Day is a supremely earnest day. Even the one who otherwise never goes to church is nevertheless accustomed to go to church on New Year's morning; even the one who otherwise never undertakes serious reflection is nevertheless accustomed to do so in earnest at the turn of the year. Even as ordinary times for the changing of servants[37] prompt us to consider a great many earnest thoughts, how much more so the changing of the year! Just as there is scarcely a single person who has not at one time in his life struck himself on the forehead and said: What is truth? and thereby thought about what truth is, so there is probably not a person, not even the most irresponsible, who on New Year's morning does not feel himself grasped by a solemn and supremely earnest mood.

But what, then, must the most earnest lover of truth say about these times when he is to speak the doughty language of candor without fear of men? Is it not religiousness in every relation that our times lack, in the relation between king and people, between master and servant, between parents and children, between public and authors? But then it is also to promote this that everyone ought to strive, each in his own way, in proportion to his gifts, according to opportunity. See, we* therefore promise our subscribers that as soon as we detect an earnest improvement and conversion we will in the future provide one third more each day

VII²
B 274:14
328

In margin: on this solemn New Year's Day, we promise

of our lubricous novel than we otherwise provide. Just as we otherwise withhold nothing,* so we ought in every way know how to open human beings to the good.

VII²
B 274:15
328

[38]*Catchpennying* [*Stüvenfængerie*[39]]. At a time when catchpennying is so frightfully and disturbingly rampant, it may certainly not be amiss again and again to warn the most esteemed cultured public not to be tricked out of its money. In a curio museum on Vesterbro, there is now on display a so-called lucky star[40] by whose help, according to the barker's pitch, everyone gets to know his full age and at the same time his future bride or bridegroom.[41] Imagine such brazen impertinence toward a most esteemed public: to take money—for telling a person how old he is! Is this not out-and-out to make a fool of the public, since one considers someone who does not even know how old he is utterly stupid? While we therefore** warn the public against giving money to such a catchpenny and for such inane instruction, we, on the other hand, permit ourselves very urgently to implore the most esteemed public not to forget its true teachers and guides, those who convey instruction that is beneficial and interesting, informative and cultivating.

VII²
B 274:16
328

NO. 7

[42]*The Swedish Students'* arrival here in the city is, as is natural, anticipated with great excitement. It is self-evident that every Scandinavian is essentially interested, but all this revolves chiefly around university graduate Jespersen.†[43] This time his motto is: Now or Never. It is already a fortnight since he had finished the speech he intends to give and on which he permitted his beloved to examine him. Not yet satisfied with it, he goes around with the manuscript, as the earnestness of the cause requires and in order to turn it into a national and common concern, and re-

VII²
B 274:16
329

In margin: do not withhold any earnest and rigorous talk

**in margin:* draw the attention of the police and the clergy to this odious practice and

†*In margin:* who, with a mind and a heart for the cause, has in his mind set himself the task of uniting the three Nordic kingdoms.

quests a passerby to listen to him. The author of this article was
fortunate enough to hear him at a gateway in Vimmelskaftet, and
it is a pleasure for me in all fairness to say that Herr Jespersen
knows his business very well, inside and out. The way in which
he said: Students, Danish and Swedish students, can never fail to
produce its effect. If in a gateway it can make such a deep impres-
sion as it made upon me, what an enormous effect will it not
have upon an assembly when it sounds forth: Students, Danish
and Swedish students—Now or Never! His facial expression and
gestures manifested a respectable effort that can be continued for
another week* [*deleted:* unless the Swedes do not come at all,
since it can then be continued even longer.]

(to be continued).

☞ *Correspondence.* We will gladly accept the submitted article,
"Prof. Madvig's[44] Latin Grammar Evaluated by an Alehouse
Keeper from a Communist Standpoint," if the author will only
see to it that a few Latin words are introduced. It looks so dull
when there is no Latin at all.

VII²
B 274:17
329

Correspondence. The editors will be pleased to accept the submitted article, "On Prof. Heiberg as Esthetician," if the author will
make up his mind to be anonymous; the article will certainly
have quite a different effect if the author's name does not appear
under it.

VII²
B 274:18
329

In margin: Correspondence. We direct the attention of all our readers, and especially of all theological students, to the currently
issued offer of a subscription to a work that should meet a deeply
felt need and long occupy a place in literature: "Clerical Phrase
Book or Handbook for Pastors," including 500 expressions arranged in alphabetical order by Esaias Strandsand, formerly a
grave-digger.[45] The author's occupation as grave-digger, all the
more since over a number of years he has been employed by

VII²
B 274:19
329

---

*In margin: unless, because either the strain of being ready long in advance,
which, as is well known, is enormously fatiguing, would weaken him to the
point of getting ill from it, or the Swedes do not come at all, since in that case
his efforts could be continued even longer.

nearly all the churches, should vouch well for the profundity and
suitability of the work; therefore we can do nothing other than
to accompany this offer with our highest commendation.

VII²
B 274:20
330

NO. 8[46]

The Association of Watchmen, founded last year,[47] held its second
ceremonial meeting yesterday at noon. Although it was noon,
according to the hosts' scheme the shutters were nevertheless
closed and the candles were lit so that it could resemble an evening party, something the watchmen enjoy very much but in
which they are actually prevented from participating. That feature gave to this festivity an enchantment all of its own that
spread through the whole festively spirited crowd in the festively
decorated hall.

The watchman from Grønnegade[48] presided. After having
proposed a toast to the police-adjutant, who was greeted with a
ninefold "Hurrah" that almost became tenfold because it almost
did not stop, the president called the meeting to order with the
sound of his whistle. Then the festive meal began. Since the program on this festive occasion called for such a great many songs[49]
that it would have been impossible to sing them all, there was at
each place a list of songs, like a wine list, so that everyone could
sing what he wished.* And because the president had been given
notice of so many speeches that it would not be possible to man-
age to give them one after the other, it was voted that they
should be given four by four at one time.

VII²
B 274:20
331

We reserve to ourselves the reporting of some of these many
speeches in several forthcoming issues.

VII²
B 274:21
331

Encouragement of public spirit is so great a good that every effort,
indeed every nod, in this direction ought not go unnoticed. The
other day one read in the obituary column in *Adresseavisen* about
the death of an eight-year-old boy; the notice concluded: "This
is announced sorrowfully to his surviving little friends." There-

---

In margin: a difficult task, which only watchmen are able to accomplish,
since they are accustomed to singing in such a fashion.

fore it may already be assumed that boys of 8 to 10 normally read their newspapers—perhaps they even write in the newspapers. What enormous progress in comparison with the patriarchal-bourgeois era when they read only their lessons. If only there are forceful efforts to press forward along this path, then the time would soon come of which the ancient prophets write, naturally as the golden age, the age—when boys would judge you.[50]

POSTSCRIPT

VII²
B 274:22
331

Without meriting any self-praise for my own competence (which would *in casu* [in this case] be a disparagement), I may assure a most esteemed cultured public that I could easily have enhanced this, my *Writing Sampler*, with still more models. I can also do the same with sketches, that is to say, as soon as the public subscribes sufficiently for me to acquire a sketch-artist and everything related to such: street-corner loafers, defamation, bandits, lies,* spies in families, kitchen snoops in households,** in short everything that might please a most esteemed, cultured public.† But no more about this, not a word about my possible competence; the main thing is that emphasis be put in the right place, upon what the public will do for me, or do through me, or make of me, by creating me as an author—from nothing and without any merit on my part.

VII²
B 274:22
332

In margin: eavesdroppers in public places and in the churches, collaborators in all clubs and societies,

**In margin:* tattletales among schoolboys, purveyors of city gossip and rumors[51]

†*In margin:* In addition, I make a sacred vow by all that is holy, for the sake of that inestimable good, the stimulation of public spirit, that I, zealous in its service, with the strictest earnestness will keep watch over clothing styles here in the city, both men's and women's, and will emphatically protest if anyone, by the difference of a bow or of a button or by lacking a button on his dress coat, seems to evade the duty-bound respect that is due a most esteemed cultured public and to betray what a person and a connoisseur of clothing easily discovers: arrogance, pride, pretension. Furthermore, on a weekly basis I will provide a list of how many courses of food each family eats ordinarily and how often each family entertains, in order that the Argus eye of publicity can keep watch on this and thereby eradicate all aristocratic pretension with regard to food and drink.

If my enterprise should succeed in spite of the many really excellent journals and books that are written, then, as soon as it pays its way, nothing will be spared to satisfy the demands of the times and the claims of the public.* As soon as there are 2000 subscribers, there will be a Christmas tree with the usual prizes for subscribers and also their wives and children.[52] When the subscribers reach 3000, **for each one, completely gratis and at absolutely no cost**,** there will be a New Year's gift as a present and likewise for each of their children, **completely gratis and at absolutely no cost**, a gingerbread cake as a present. When there are 4000 subscribers, I daresay the most esteemed public will be astounded by what will happen. But just to mention, to name the ultimate, a thought I almost wilt under, if the number of subscribers should reach 20,000—then I intend to purchase Tivoli, so that henceforth entrance to Tivoli[53] will be *solely* and *only*, and *altogether exclusively*—for my subscribers. If this happens, it is of course self-evident that I will not at that time be able to keep my promise to provide boot-shining for the subscription agents, but I will nonetheless not forget that I am and remain the creature and creation of the public[54]—from nothing and through no merit of my own. By means of a symbolic action, which corresponds to foot-washing among the Roman Catholics, I will, in order to point this out, on one Dyrehave-Sunday give a brushing for my subscribers as a token of what I am and shall remain, despite my enormous prosperity.

To achieve the goal, I shall work as hard as I can with all my powers and privately tell the public immediately what I intend to

VII²
B 274:22
333

**In margin:* First and last, care will be taken mainly to provide short stories, served like the layer cake so much enjoyed by families, so that there will continually be a layer of padding followed by a layer of story, with 3 or 4 stories used at a time.

***In margin: Note.* This phrase, incidentally, is not my invention but is owed to an experienced person. It has often happened that people came to pay dearly enough for what they have received as if it were gratis; therefore this addition of "completely" is necessary, and for the sake of further security, "at absolutely no cost." Thus one will see that this is so far from being a superfluous and vacuous accumulation that it nevertheless at times becomes rather dubious as to whether one actually receives gratis what is received "completely gratis and at absolutely no cost."

do, from which it will be seen that in a certain sense I keep more
than I promise. As soon as I have obtained 500 subscribers, I will
announce every blessed day that I have 1000; when I have obtained 1000, I will announce every blessed day: this absolutely
indispensable journal, which in so short a time already has 2000
subscribers—and in addition the third printing of no. 17 has already appeared, **which completely gratis and at absolutely
no cost** will be sent to new subscribers. Furthermore, I will write
anonymous eulogies and praise of myself in another journal. But
since this ploy has already been used very much, especially by
authors, so that it is easily suspected, I have figured out a refine-
ment. I will attack myself anonymously in another journal, but
on a point, note well, in which I am in the right, and I would
arrange the attack in such a way that it is easy to win in the
conflict, which therefore quite rightly is ended with the ashamed
withdrawal of the attacker (who is myself), who explains that he
has lost, has been unjust to me, and concludes with a panegyric
on the attacked (who is myself). In this instance my experiences
as a barker at Dyrehaven, as a waiter, and as a billiards scorekeeper have enriched me with a manifold resourcefulness. It will
help, of course, if the public will just trust me and get me underway. Yes, I can very well tell this to a most esteemed cultured
public: people are basically suckers.* The public, on the other
hand, is something so elevated and incomprehensible that no
thinker can fathom it.** One can very well speak with the public
in a city about all the people of the same city and say to the most
esteemed cultured public of this city that all the people in the
same city are suckers. As I said, but it remains *unter uns* [just
between us], esteemed public: people are basically suckers.
When one merely states that one has many subscribers and keeps
on saying it, then one gets many; just as when the one sheep goes
to water, the next one also goes, and when it is continually said
of a large flock of sheep that they go hither and yon to water,
then the rest must also go, so people believe that it must be the
demand of the times, that for the sake of use and custom—they

VII²
B 274:22
334

---

*_In margin:_ with the public it is another matter,
**_In margin:_ and that one can speak with it about everything.

must also subscribe. Thus at last it becomes a habit, a supine necessity for people to go along—and so the game is won. One already learns this from Jacob's behavior toward Laban.[55] What did Jacob do to get the white sheep to bear spotted lambs? He peeled the sticks and set them in the water troughs so that they never got to see anything else—that did the trick. So it is when it appears every day in the newspaper: I have 1000 subscribers— then I get 1000 subscribers.

Therefore, most esteemed, cultured public: create me and let me begin. You will never come to repent of this good deed. I will, esteemed cultured public, forever remain

> Your creature, creation, and nothing
> A.B.C.D.E.F. Rosenblad
> [*changed to*: Godthaab].

VII[2]
B 274:22
335

POSTSCRIPT

VII[2]
B 274:23
335

☞   Finally, please read the preface, since it contains things of the utmost importance.

The Moral

VII[2]
B 274:24
335

"As soon as it has come to the point that the crowd is to judge what is truth, it will not be long before decisions are made with the fists."

> Schelling.[56]
> *In margin:* In the preface to Steffens's
> posthumous writings[57]

SUPPLEMENT

KEY TO REFERENCES

Marginal references alongside the text are to volume and page [V 50] in *Søren Kierkegaards samlede Værker*, I-XIV, edited by A. B. Drachmann, J. L. Heiberg, and H. O. Lange (1 ed., Copenhagen: Gyldendal, 1901–06). The same marginal references are used in Sören Kierkegaard, *Gesammelte Werke, Abt.* 1–36 (Düsseldorf, Cologne: Diederichs Verlag, 1952–69).

References to Kierkegaard's works in English are to this edition, *Kierkegaard's Writings* [*KW*], I-XXVI (Princeton: Princeton University Press, 1978-). Specific references to the *Writings* are given by English title and the standard Danish pagination referred to above [*Either/Or*, I, p. 120, *KW* III (*SV* I 100)].

References to the *Papirer* [*Pap.* I A 100; note the differentiating letter A, B, or C, used only in references to the *Papirer*] are to *Søren Kierkegaards Papirer*, I-XI³, edited by P. A. Heiberg, V. Kuhr, and E. Torsting (1 ed., Copenhagen: Gyldendal, 1909–48), and 2 ed., photo-offset with two supplemental volumes, XII-XIII, edited by Niels Thulstrup (Copenhagen: Gyldendal, 1968–70), and with index, XIV-XVI (1975–1978), edited by Niels Jørgen Cappelørn. References to the *Papirer* in English [*JP* II 1500], occasionally amended, are to volume and serial entry number in *Søren Kierkegaard's Journals and Papers*, I-VI, edited and translated by Howard V. Hong and Edna H. Hong, assisted by Gregor Malantschuk, and with index, VII, by Nathaniel Hong and Charles Barker (Bloomington: Indiana University Press, 1967–78).

References to correspondence are to the serial numbers in *Breve og Aktstykker vedrørende Søren Kierkegaard*, I-II, edited by Niels Thulstrup (Copenhagen: Munksgaard, 1953–54), and to the corresponding serial numbers in *Kierkegaard: Letters and Documents*, translated by Henrik Rosenmeier, *Kierkegaard's Writings*, XXV [*Letters*, Letter 100, *KW* XXV].

References to Kierkegaard's own library [*ASKB* 100] are based on the serial numbering system of *Auktionsprotokol over*

Søren Kierkegaards Bogsamling [Auction-catalog of Søren Kierkegaard's Book-collection], edited by H. P. Rohde (Copenhagen:
Royal Library, 1967).

In the Supplement, references to page and lines in the text are
given as 100:10–20.

In the notes, internal references to the present volume are
given as p. 100.

Three spaced periods indicate an omission by the editors; five
spaced periods indicate a hiatus or fragmentariness in the text.

Forord.

Morskabslæsning for enkelte Stænder efter Tid og Leilighed

af

Nicolaus Notabene.

Kjøbenhavn, 1844.

Faaes hos Universitetsboghandler C. A. Reitzel.

Trykt i Bianco Lunos Bogtrykkeri.

Prefaces.

———————

Light Reading for People in Various Estates

According to Time and Opportunity

by

Nicolaus Notabene.

———————

Copenhagen, 1844.

Available at University Bookseller C. A. Reitzel's.

Printed by Bianco Luno Press.

SELECTED ENTRIES FROM
KIERKEGAARD'S JOURNALS AND PAPERS
PERTAINING TO
PREFACES

Preface:

Whether this preface is going to be long or short, I simply do not know at this moment. My soul is filled with but one thought, a longing, a thirsting, really to run wild in the lyrical underbrush of the preface, really to rumble about in it, for just as the poet at times must feel lyrically stirred and then again relishes the epical, so I as a prose writer feel at present an inexhaustible joy in surrendering all objective thinking and really exhausting myself in wishes and hopes, in a secret whispering with the reader, a Horatian *sussuratio* [whispering][1] in the evening hours, for the preface always ought to be conceived in twilight, which also is undeniably the most beautiful; no wonder, therefore, that we read that the Lord God walked in the cool of the evening (Genesis[2]), an evening hour when the busyness of thought is a solemn distant sound, like the laughter of the harvesters.—*JP* V 5387 (*Pap.* II A 432) May 17, 1839

See 37:17:

DISCURSIVE RAISONNEMENTS AND INCONCEIVABLE PERTINENT PROPOSALS CONCERNING THE CATEGORY OF THE HIGHER LUNACY

Preface

I believe that I would do philosophers a great service if they were to adopt a category which I myself have discovered and utilized with great profit and success to exhaust and dry up a multitude of

II
A 432
167

II
A 432
168

II
A 808
273

relations and qualifications that have so far been unwilling to resolve themselves—it is the category of higher lunacy. I ask only that it not be named after me, but that goes without saying, and besides, in analogous situations we are not accustomed to name something after the active party but after the passive one; the switch is not named after the one who switches but after the one who first gets it.

———————

It is the most concrete of all categories, the fullest, since it is closest to life and does not have its truth in a beyond, the supraterrestrial, but in a subterranean below, and thus, if it were a hypothesis, the most grandiose empirical proof of its truth could be made.

It is this category by which the transition is formed from abstract lunacy to concrete lunacy. The formula for it from one side is given by Baggesen,[3] VII, p. 195:

II
A 808
274

The Unity of Lunacy [*Galskabs*] in the Duality of all
Creation [*Alskabs*],

but expressed speculatively it is

The Unity of all Creation in the Duality of Lunacy.

All creation implies multiplicity, that is, *Quodlibet* or the loonier the better.

The duality of lunacy. We no longer can be content with discrete and partial insanities, but the concepts genus and species must have their validity here, too.—*JP* 1581 (*Pap.* II A 808) *n.d.* 1839

See 60:12–18:

For the most part Descartes has embodied his system in the first six meditations. So it is not always necessary to write systems. I want to publish "Philosophical Deliberations" in pamphlets, and into them I can put all my interim thoughts. It perhaps would not be so bad to write in Latin.[4]—*JP* V 5574 (*Pap.* IV A 2) *n.d.*, 1842

From draft of Repetition, *"A Little Contribution by Constantin Constantius, Author of* Repetition . . . *"; see 23:3:*

The book *Repetition* is accompanied by a letter to "the real reader of the book." One learns from this letter that I, "like Clement of Alexandria, have tried to write in such a way that the heretics are unable to understand it."*

**Note.* See *Repetition,* p. 147 [*SV* III 259][5]. It may very well seem curious for an author to decide to write in this manner, but it can be explained. Although literature today demonstrates that practically nothing is being done (except for the contribution by a very solitary man, who presumably belongs to Denmark, inasmuch as he is its pride and honor, but sometimes even by writing in a foreign language does what he is entitled to do, establish a European criterion for his work), one can scarcely hear a word because of the promises, trumpet blasts, subscription hawking, toasts, announcements, assurances, compliments, etc. In this simulated motion, the year marches on. At Christmas time, there is a commotion in literature, because several very sleek and elegant New Year's gifts, intended for children and Christmas trees and especially useful as gifts in good taste, compete with each other in *Adresseavisen* in order, after creating a furor for a fortnight, to be assigned by a courteous critic to a place in some anthology as inspiring models for all writers of esthetic literature in fine style. Esthetic fine style—that is the watchword. And esthetic fine style is a deadly earnest matter for which one trains oneself by abandoning ideas and thinking. In such a literary milieu it is not inexplicable that an author wishes to avoid public opinion and to let a little book, in calm consciousness of itself, go out as unnoticed and as self-contained as possible. In this respect the long Trinity season[6] is a very good time of the year if one wishes to be exempted from being whirled about in the New Year's rush of literary beggars, and if one, carefree and unconcerned, renounces the throngs of both shoppers and readers and infinitely prefers this to a very sleek and elegant cardboard-bound book to be palmed off on people at New Year's time. . . . —*Pap.* IV B 117 *n.d.,* 1843–44

IV
B 117
280

IV
B 117
281

See 1:6:

Idea:

Recollections of My Life
by
Nebuchadnezzar[7]
Formerly Emperor, Recently an Ox

Published
by
Nicolaus Notabene.[8]
      —*JP* V 5671 (*Pap.* IV A 119) *n.d.*, 1843

The journal will be divided as follows.

Praemonenda [Preface]

1. *Examinatio* [Examination]
How does a new quality emerge through a continuous quantitative determination?[9]
2. *Contemplatio* [Contemplation]
de omnibus d.[10] [On the doubting of all things]
3. *Exaedificatio* [Construction *or* Building Up]
concerning the expectancy of faith[11]

Miscellanea [Miscellany].
The question to Prof. Martensen regarding
the Aristotelian doctrine of virtue.[12]
      —*JP* V 5712 (*Pap.* V A 100) *n.d.*, 1844

From draft of "New Year's Gift"; see 1:6:

Unused

New Year's Gift[13] by
Nicolaus Notabene

If I had not more important things to do, it would have been very amusing, since it now appears that this New Year everything has become exceptionally elegant and dainty as well as banal and trivial.[14]—*JP* V 5707 (*Pap.* IV B 125) *n.d.*, 1844

From draft of "New Year's Gift"; see 1:6:

New Year's Gift
[*deleted:* edited]
by
Nicolaus Notabene
Published for the benefit of the orphanages
Copenhagen 1844

Dedicated to every purchaser of this book
—and to the orphanages
Contents
Preface
Inter et Inter[15]
—*JP* V 5708 (*Pap.* IV B 126) *n.d.,* 1844

Addition to Pap. IV B 126; *see 13:3–14:29:*

Preface

[*Essentially the same as 13:3–22.*]

My son, if you want to publish a book, you should first consider at what time of year you want to have it appear. The time
of year is everything. On this matter all the wisest and best men
agree that New Year's is the moment; what Holophernes says
about tapping on the cartridge pouch pertains to the appearance
of books around New Year's Day: without it I would not give
you a pipeful of tobacco for the whole thing.

My son, if you want to publish a book, before you write a
single line be sure of whom you will benefit. To that end you ask
a publisher or a philosophical fellow or your barber what it is that
the times actually demand. As soon as you have obtained this
information, then write with confidence; your book will do
well, because it would not be beneficial for you or for the times
if you go against what the times demand.

Fortunate the strong soul who understands what the times demand in the same way as one of those three great powers proclaims it.[*] But the one whose soul has become doubtful, because the demand of the times shows itself to be multifarious, and

IV
B 127
316

IV
B 127
317

like Maren Amme to have several voices,[**] he still ought not to lose courage. It almost happened to me. The moment had come. The New Year approached. If only I could get it out for the New Year, my fortune would be made. But to publish a book without being assured that it would do well, that was terrible. Then there awakened in my soul this thought: publish it for the benefit of the orphanages. Are not orphanages, too, one of the demands of the times? A community for the elderly and orphanages for the children.

See, therefore I no longer doubt. *My* fortune is made, because the book appears at New Year's; it will benefit, because it is published for the benefit of the orphanages and thus meets one of the demands of the times. Indeed, it will be of particular benefit, because it will give the buyer the opportunity to benefit the orphanages; it will do this unconditionally because I do not even require that the costs of printing be covered.

So go out into the world; make my fortune; bow yourself humbly before the hat of criticism (since it lacks a head); make yourself indispensable as a present on the Christmas tree.

I have nothing further to add other than that I wish, without making any distinction, a happy New Year to everyone who shares my view and to everyone who does not share my view.

Yet I had almost forgotten something. So it goes—one sometimes forgets the most important thing. In the literary world it is the custom to make a sacred vow. The ceremony is not definitely prescribed. In Scandinavia one laid a hand on Frey's boar; Hamlet swears by the fire tongs. The ceremony is unimportant, the vow alone is the main thing. Therefore, I promise to realize a long-considered plan, to publish a logical system, an ethical system, an esthetic system, a dogmatic system, in short to write it all so that generations to come will not even need to learn to write. When I have published these four systems, I hope thereby to have prepared the way for the encyclopedia I have long wished to publish.

[*]*In margin:* Sometimes one can get to know too much.
[**]*At the bottom of the page:* (Baggesen[16])
                                        —*Pap.* IV B 127 *n.d.*, 1844

Addition to Pap. IV B 126:

Inter et Inter.
Introduction.

The age of making distinctions is past.[17] Like so much else it has been vanquished by the system. In our time whoever in a scholarly way clings to making distinctions—the craving of his soul is for something that has long since vanished. The age of making distinctions is past, that productive idea of the four world-historical monarchies[18] reduces everything to the appropriate moment, whether this idea in its historical progress and immanent movement overcomes everything that rises up, or whether, more reminiscent of its first discoverer, Geert Westphaler,[19] in the pathos of conviction it assimilates everything to itself in the course of chitchat.

In margin: In our time whoever clings personally to making distinctions is an eccentric.—*Pap.* IV B 128 *n.d.*, 1844

From draft of "New Year's Gift"; see 1:6:

New Year's Gift
by
Nicolaus Notabene
published for the benefit of the orphanages
—*Pap.* IV B 129 *n.d.*, 1844

Addition to Pap. IV B 129:

Contents.

Preface.
A good deed and a good remark.
   narrated for children.

—*Pap.* IV B 130 *n.d.*, 1844

Addition to Pap. IV B 129:

Who does not know that talkative barber,[20] the tale of whose journey was in inverse relation to his journey, which was only

very short: from Haderslev to Kiel. As soon as one mentions
Geert W., one thinks immediately of that journey, but still he
knows how to tell of quite different things and, indeed, how to
carry on a political and curious conversation. But this is precisely
the great thing in Holberg's conception of G., that he has allowed him, like many a genius, to misunderstand himself and to
lay most weight on the trivial and accidental above the essential.
A genius is commonly known by this, that he makes light of what
he can do and wants instead to have one or another accidentality
stressed. Thus Nero[21] had the fixed idea that he was a zither
player. When Julius Vindex said that he was a poor emperor but
an even poorer zither player, the latter especially must have out-
raged him.[22] Thus Geert himself undoubtedly regarded that story
as for the best, and yet what is it in comparison with the ingenious notion of world history from the point of view that there
are 4 world-historical monarchies? This idea has been taken up
now in our time and one hears it everywhere, and at times it is
spoken of in such a way that one would think Geert W. to be the
source.—*Pap.* IV B 131 *n.d.*, 1844

Addition to Pap IV B 129:

His mother was a midwife, she helped herself, and from that
Socrates learned to help himself.—*Pap.* IV B 132 *n.d.*, 1844

Addition to Pap. IV B 129:

To every purchaser of this book—and to the orphans
                                    this work
                                    is dedicated.
                          —*Pap.* IV B 133 *n.d.*, 1844

Addition to Pap. IV B 129; *see 13:3–33:*

What a pleasure it is to have written a book; it is foolish talk,
which is, to be sure, also rarely heard and absolutely never has the
voice of the times in its favor—that the occupation of thinking
while the work is underway, that the beating of the heart in the
disquiet of deliberation, that the blushing and paling of the soul

in the presentiment, in the assurance of victory are supposed to
mean something. No, the significance of the book appears only
later.

What a pleasure it is to have written a book that does not owe
its origin to an unexplained inner need and therefore can never
know whether it fits into the world, but that is a fruit of mature
reflection, not of an infatuation in thought with a dreamed-of
reader, but of a marriage of convenience of publisher and public, written in such a way as the publisher wants to have it and
as the times demand, published at the opportune moment to
the benefit of all: to author, publisher, printer, bookbinder, the
reader.

> My son, if you want to publish a book, then
> you ought first to deliberate.

Promise

I can speak of all this, because I have done it.

In margin: not a sinful infatuation, but a threefold joy to and for
which criticism has already secured rooms—*Pap.* IV B 134 *n.d.*,
1844

Addition to Pap. IV B 134:

If a person wants to write a book, he ought first to deliberate
on what time of the year one will have it appear. This is of the
utmost importance; the time of year is the main thing. New
Year's is considered the best.

Before a person begins to write, he must consider who will benefit from it. To that end he inquires of one or another publisher
or of a philosophical fellow [*] what it is that the times actually
demand. As soon as he gets to know this, he writes it, and he can
be sure of being beneficial, since after all it ought to be beneficial
for the times to get what the times demanded. But he ought not
wholly sacrifice himself for the benefit of others, and he therefore
inquires about what he himself requires, and when the book
comes out by New Year's Day, then he certainly gets it.

When I had reviewed what is set forth here, I said to myself:
Now you also ought to make use of the moment: see to publish-

IV
B 135
320

IV
B 135
321

ing a beneficial book and having it appear by New Year's Day. But when I deliberated more closely on this, a difficulty arose, because what had been said about the demand of the times had been so diverse. Then my soul became doubtful, because to publish a book without any benefit would indeed be a terrible thing. In order to be certain about this, I decided to publish it for the benefit of the orphanages. Besides, orphanages are also one of the demands of the times. The community for the elderly and orphanages for the children. The same instant this thought awakened in my soul I grasped it with all passion. I am convinced that my book will be one of the most beneficial and will sell very well. I will benefit the orphanages by publishing it; the purchaser will benefit the orphanages by purchasing it, because I do not even ask that the costs of printing be covered.

I have nothing further to add, except that I wish, without making any distinction, a happy New Year to everyone who shares my view of this and everyone who does not share my view.

Yet I had almost forgotten something. In the literary world it is a time-honored custom to make a vow. Here in Scandinavia one did it by Frey's boar. This custom has passed out of use just like the keeping of one's promises. Hamlet swears on the fire tongs; I swear that I will write a logical system, an esthetic system, an ethical system, a dogmatic system, in short that I will do everything and be all things to all people, just like a missionary in Greenland[23]—at least I promise to write such a little book again—I will entreat everyone not to think more about the matter, because these are promises and I would be embarrassed if one believed in earnest that this was earnestness, but also if one believed in earnest that it was jest.

IV
B 135
322

[*]*In margin:* or of your barber.

—*Pap.* IV B 135 *n.d.*, 1844

Addition to Pap. IV B 129:

In Athens there was life and hilarity.

—*Pap.* IV B 136 *n.d.*, 1844

Addition to Pap. IV B 129:

1. The origin of making distinctions.[24]
2. The later history of making distinctions.
3. The eternal validity of making distinctions.

this is, of course, formal, but it nevertheless has eternal significance.

This must, therefore, be impressed upon the young, because they are somewhat impolite, and when one has grown older it is not so easy to tolerate their querulousness.—*Pap.* IV B 137 *n.d.*, 1844

Addition to Pap. IV B 129:

Conclusion

IV
B 138
322

Every book must have a conclusion, and every book has a conclusion. A philosophical book is in this matter different from other books in that it brings this to conscious awareness. This happens in the following way: one inscribes "Conclusion" over the last section. The philosophical conclusion must not, however, be lyrical, like the "Amen" to a sermon. In the conclusion the whole rounds itself off itself and the conclusion is therefore more invisible than a point. One must, however, hint at it; otherwise it might occur to a reader that one was not a philosophical fellow. As far as that goes, one would need merely to write the word *Conclusion* on a clean page. With the help of the gods, it may well come to that one day, but for now one must be a bit more prolix.—*Pap.* IV B 138 *n.d.*, 1844

IV
B 138
323

Addition to Pap. IV B 138:

Typographical Errors

To make use of the favorite terminology of most recent philosophy,[25] this is not the place to go into more detail about some typographical errors, which we reserve to ourselves for more complete justification and further development;* here it must suffice that we have pointed it out.

*on a more fitting occasion.

—*Pap.* IV B 139 *n.d.*, 1844

From final copy; see 1:3–5:

Light Reading for People in Various Estates According to Time and Opportunity by
Changed from: Curious Light Reading by

—*Pap.* V B 96:1 *n.d.*, 1844

From draft; see 3:1:

Preface

The well-being of the state depends on that of the family, the well-being of the family on marriage, ergo.

either/or

—*Pap.* V B 73 *n.d*, 1844

In margin of draft; see 3:9–4:3:

The Greeks actually used no prefaces at all but said immediately in the first sentence everything the book would be about.

—*Pap.* V B 74:1 *n.d.*, 1844

From draft; see 4:23–26:

Even if the most recent scholarly method first made me aware that it would have to come to a break, and even if it becomes my merit, like Feuerbach's,[26] to make the break in earnest, I still knew also how to make fate elastic and to convince myself that sooner or later it would come to this. In order to appeal in this way to something phenomenological, every—*Pap.* V B 74:5 *n.d.*, 1844

From sketch; see 5:10–6:6:

. . . . . writing a preface is like standing and gazing down into a fish tank and watching the fish move in the water[27]—*Pap.* V B 75:2 *n.d.*, 1844

From sketch; see 5:10–6:6:

. . . . . like receiving permission to be a spoiled child for a moment, to get everything one points at—*Pap.* V B 75:5 *n.d.*, 1844

From draft; see 6:30–12:21:

[*Deleted:* It is now about three months ago that I, at a quiet ceremony, was initiated into the beginning of a journey of discovery that still is and remains the most significant thing any human being can undertake,[28] although no poet will ever be able to say about him: πολλῶν δ' ἀνθρώπων ἴδεν ἄστεα καὶ νόον ἔγνω [many were the men whose city he saw and whose mind he learned],[29] since he does not move from the spot and he is only the other self, and the gloriousness is precisely that he does not become too much aware of either the former or the latter. Praised be marriage, praised be everyone who speaks in its honor.[30] If a beginner may allow himself an observation, then I will say that the reason it seems to me to be so wonderful is that everything revolves around trivialities that the divine element in marriage nevertheless transforms by a miracle into something important for the believers. For the same reason, nothing can be taken up in advance or exhausted by calculation, because it is all too trivial for that, and while the understanding stands still and the imagination goes on a wild-goose chase and calculation miscalculates and sagacity despairs, married life goes on and through the miracle of faith the transformation continually takes place. Although it would be easier for me to predict the fate of Europe] and the course of philosophy than to predict what trivialities will tomorrow fill up the day for me and my wife, nevertheless these

V
B 76
152

V
B 76
153

trivialities are in turn dearer to me, more precious, more won-
drous than the fate of Europe and the course of philosophy.

As my wife and I are sitting one day at the dinner table, I in my
thoughts and my wife busy with the serving, just when she has
taken the lid off the stew kettle, she stops suddenly, looks at the
lid in her hand, and says with a sad and plaintive countenance,
"No! This is incomprehensible. In the last two weeks a change
has taken place in you that is not at all for the better. You have
lost your cheerful spirit, your chattiness is silenced, you are lost in
a cocoon of thoughtfulness from morning til night, but it is especially obvious at the dinner table." I sit as if on the "wonder
stool,"[31] but the understanding stands still, the imagination runs
on a wild-goose chase, calculation miscalculates, sagacity despairs. She gets up from the table, she stands at my side, she puts
her arm on the back of the chair, and then hugs me while she
offers me her other hand. "I know that basically you are a gour-
met, and you have always been the friend of what tastes good,
and you know that it is my joy to place on the table what the
house and your wife are capable of and that to me it is a priceless
amusement to see you fondly on the lookout for what might
come. I know that you dote on coffee; you know it is my joy to
prepare it for you myself, to set it on the tray myself, to offer it to
you myself, and to curtsy to you while you put sugar in it. Oh,
you know perfectly well that I ask no reward, because it is too
great a pleasure to me to be of service, but when I discover that
you are distracted, absentminded, then I cannot. Your attentiveness is my sustenance; your approval, your thanks, your smile,
the jest on your lips are my inspiration. It is justly due me. Confess to me for my sake, for the sake of my joy, so that I may still
be able to do with joy what is my greatest joy."

I was in quite a pickle; I easily foresaw that I had lost. She put
her arm around my neck, held my hand tighter, and leaning over
me she said, "Explain yourself. I beg of you, tell me what it is or
confess that my guess is true—you are on the way to becoming
an author. Otherwise what are those big books for that lie open
in your study, and otherwise why do you lock up your papers
when you go out? And why your strange look and your dreamy
attitude? You perhaps do not know it yourself; sometimes you sit

V
B 76
154

and stare off into space, and when I look around the room but find nothing and then look at you again, you sit like King Nebuchadnezzar and presumably are reading invisible writing." My wife does not lack method; she knew how to soften me up first with her entreaties, and then it all would end up with a jest. In a jesting tone I would admit everything and promise everything. Meanwhile I was still all too set on becoming an author to be willing to let myself be snared so easily. With a very natural dodge, I reminded her that the food was getting cold, and as she apparently was satisfied with having cured me to this extent, the matter was put aside until later.—*Pap.* V B 76 *n.d.,* 1844

Continuation of Pap. V B 76; *see 6:30–12:21:*

At first I would not admit it, looked for excuses, since it was my intention to keep this secret from my wife. But, through those countless means a woman has at her disposal, she got a confession out of me, and then she quite calmly put the lid on the kettle and with dignity said: This is an unfaithfulness; my view of the esthetic validity of marriage is that the husband is to hold fast to his wife and he has nothing else[*] to do, which is what the pastor also said.

The pastor—my dear girl, there you probably did not hear rightly; I am afraid that I will have to see to it that you go to confirmation instruction again.[**] Marriage, you see, is a special duty, and all duties can be divided into duties toward God and toward oneself and the neighbor.

When this was all over, the food had become almost cold, but the situation was retrieved when I drew attention to this, but nevertheless she was a bit annoyed over it, because that was not what she was now talking about, something I readily conceded with the remark that I had drawn attention to it because I was afraid she had forgotten it.

She thought she had won, and yet she had only brought me to the point that I decided to go about it more carefully. Then her suspicion was again aroused.

It was on an afternoon as it grew toward dusk that she caught hold of me and again took me to confession. With kind words,

V
B 78
155

flattery, sighs, a touch of sadness, and in every way she insisted that my wanting to be an author was a kind of unfaithfulness to her. In vain I sought to open her eyes to the bright prospects when once my name would make a show in the newspaper. She did not care about this; she only insisted on keeping me as she had once accepted me, such as she had loved me, such as she would continue to love me and do everything in order to please me. But I had never intimated that I wanted to be an author. She knew how to portray all the terrible consequences for a wife whose husband became an author, how slyly she would be affronted without ever being allowed to get irate, without having anyone to become angry with, since one cannot become angry with printed books. She refused to hear anything, not a flattering word about her being the one who inspired me. She assured me that she did not believe this, and that she had never wished this, and that her marital happiness and the indescribable pastime she had promised herself would not come from this. She then returned again to her theme that the esthetic validity of marriage consisted in the husband's holding fast to the wife—more was not required.

V
B 78
156

I burst out a little impatiently: In that way I have an exceedingly poor position in life; I become only an *encliticon ornans* [decorative enclitic].[†] "Will you please say it in Danish for the sake of the unlearned?" Yes, my dearest Josephine, it cannot be translated directly. It means that in everything I become an inseparable particle. "—Yes, are we not inseparable?" —Lord, keep us, I have never considered seeking a divorce, but to be an inseparable particle is very little for a husband. —Yes, but neither did I wish to be more.†† —Then I must fervently wish that you will try to become something more than nothing, because to be an inseparable particle to nothing is rather small. This was in her opinion my usual teasing, and she knew well enough that once I had been brought to that, there was neither end nor beginning. Yet she would gladly put up with it, partly because I did it well and partly if only I would stop being an author.

When nothing helped, she at last confidentially took my arm, looked at me as ingratiatingly as possible, and said with the most lovable pathos: Dear William, I have not wanted to say this to

V
B 78
157

you so bluntly, because, without needing to do that, I hoped in another way to get you to give it up; but if you finally will not, then I will tell you quite honestly: I do not think you are cut out to be an author, but on the other hand you could be a marvel of a husband if only you would—and she added as insinuatingly as possible: You would thereby make me so indescribably happy every day, every moment, and this reward is certainly comparable to being praised in some newspaper.

Is it not as I say—marriage is a journey of discovery whose events no one can calculate beforehand? My wife had been victorious; she extracted from me the solemn promise that I would give up. She threatened war if I continued open feuding; she would burn everything. Since she had gotten her way, then—yet I reserved one thing to myself, that I would be permitted to write prefaces. I appealed to analogies, that for giving up snuff husbands had obtained permission from their wives to have as many snuffboxes as they wished. She agreed, since she probably assumed that one could not ever write a preface without writing a book, and if one were to imagine that, it could apply only to famous authors, which, to be sure is not the case with me.

[*]*In margin: præterea censeo* [Furthermore I am of the opinion]
[**]*In margin:* One would almost think that you had not been properly confirmed.
[†]*In margin:* although the husband is still to be the ruler
In margin: ††I want to be nothing at all, only that you remain with me with all your soul—*Pap.* V B 78 *n.d.*, 1844

From draft; see 17:16:

renter.*

*Note. Forgive me for betraying a knowledge in spheres where one perhaps hardly suspected it. I freely confess that I am proud of this and pattern myself in likeness to Prof. Heiberg. In *Intelligensblade*, no. 35, especially p. 244,[32] I see that he knows what every theological student knows. It is a pity that he cites his source (Winer's *Biblisches Realwörterbuch*[33]); otherwise I could swear that it was taken from the late Bröchner's notebooks,[34]

where the same passage occurs almost word for word.—*Pap.* V
B 80:2 *n.d.,* 1844

From draft; see 18:8–11:

Upon opening the book, when Reitzel's messenger brought
it to me, and sticking my nose into its pages, I read these words:
One must doubt everything; whereupon I shut the book and sent
it back, because this phrase is to me a stinking goat[35] that spoils
everything.—*Pap.* V B 80:3 *n.d.,* 1844

From draft; see 18:32–37:

. . . . . from it. Women in delivery can perhaps thank Holberg's *Barselstue* for being left in peace; why does no one write a
literary *Barselstue.*—*Pap.* V B 80:4 *n.d.,* 1844

From draft; see 20:23–36:

V
B 81
158

What in the preceding is said quite in general about the visible
reading public and reviewers does not stand in any more special
relation to the book by Christian Winther that I now have the
pleasure of reviewing.[36] I ought therefore to ask the pardon of its
author for including the preceding. What follows will demonstrate, I hope, that I am not a robber who attacks a published
book by a renowned author in order to have a place and a hearing for my comments, not a reviewer who with his customary
importance uses the appearance of a book to take the occasion to
say something himself, not a burr that sticks tightly to a famous
name. It calls for pardon; it is at least my opinion that in several
columns, although the article is headed with the title of his book,
I have as if forgotten him and my own actual role. The author
will not deny me this, I hope, when he is assured in the following
that I aspire to what is always rewarding, to lose myself in a production by Christian Winther, that I strive to be what I solely
wish to be, what a reviewer, whoever he is, qua reviewer, ought
always to stake his honor in being—a ministering spirit—*Pap.* V
B 81 *n.d.,* 1844

V
B 81
159

From draft: see 20:36–21:7:

Yet as long as we live in such an order of things, I prefer no criticism at all, because to be discussed by one of our very meritorious critics is as loathsome to me as letting a barber fumble about my face with his clammy fingers. Just as one reads in *Adresseavisen* that the mourner prefers no condolences at all because it will only increase the pain, so I prefer no criticism at all because it only causes me pain, since, thank God, I am otherwise happy and contented and secure in my loss—of all illusory faith in the reading public.—*Pap.* V B 83 *n.d.*, 1844

V
B 83
159

V
B 83
160

From draft; see 23:20–30:

Under such circumstances it surely will not surprise you, dear reader, that I choose another time of year. And this choice is easy. At every other time of the year, one is free from the publisher-art-mania that with devilish violence and force wants to have one decked out like a Haiduk with fringes and furbelows. Neither is one subjected to a collision that can occasion an unpleasant misunderstanding, since any misunderstanding is impossible. If one excepts, namely, what an altogether singular author creates, an author with whom regrettably one cannot be confused, an author who certainly belongs to Denmark, inasmuch as he is its glory, but who nonetheless in another sense does not belong to Denmark, since he with full justification applies a European standard and occasionally even uses a foreign language[37]—if one excepts the works of such a singular author, then fortunately neither can one be confused with what is otherwise achieved, which is not much more or much other than what the little black hen produces in other respects.[38] Toasts, announcements, flattery, subscription hawking, repeated assurances that "in another passage" things will be worked out more thoroughly, etc., distant cries from an anchorite who is concentrating on greater works, prophecies, promises, revelations of what is to come—all these things cannot possibly thwart any production or cause confusion but can only in a more subtle way help one come to the attention of the one by whom one wishes to be read.

V
B 85:2
160

V
B 85:2
161

Danish literature in the future will probably be only a *pium desiderium* [pious wish], because if one does not wish to be a mummer in the buffoonish New Year's literature, which is not being an author at all, then very singular qualities are required. That is, the Danish author must not only have intellect, knowledge, and the like, which have always been considered desirable, but he must also have money and above all an utterly distinctive temperament in order to find satisfaction in giving away his time, his diligence—and his money—without receiving anything but ingratitude for it. The one who gives his money to orphanages has his thanks in *Adresseavisen*; the one who uses his time to work for orphanages etc. has his thanks for it; but a Danish author receives neither the one nor the other, unless he is fortunate enough to be able to write for the theater, since there one always receives something, even when the piece is booed off the stage.

That is the way things stand, and only the one who has a decided bent for paradoxes can find it cheering, yes, even inspiring, to be an author under such circumstances. A humorous individual who derides human life can never choose any better employment than as an author in Danish literature. And even if there were no other material for amusement, the daily press writing, which actually lives from hand to mouth and in Christian fashion on shipwrecks,[39] is inexhaustible. Its politics may be feeble enough, but still it is something, but on the whole, in relation to the literature, it is, *si placet* [if you please], yes, in relation to the literature, it is all that it can be in relation to such literature. It is an echo that does not even repeat words, but like the echo in some of our churches it passes off as gossip what has been said or tacks gossip onto what has been said, which, insofar as what was said was not gossip, is a priceless amusement that makes the author's position still more interesting.* And yet this writing is critical, even authoritative, and can judge all things, is "the measure of all things"[40] and has the measure in its mouth.[41] I know of no better expression to describe how subjectively accidental everything is. The reader, however, may not know where this expression has its origin. It is not to be ascribed to me, but to an "old soldier,"[42] from whom I heard it for the first time a number of

V
B 85:2
162

years ago on Nørrefælled.[43] The troops were drawn up, the review was to begin, and his majesty was expected any minute. No soldier dared to break ranks; only officers and noncommissioned officers walked about a bit more freely. My noncommissioned officer, who probably suspected that it would be a hot day, thought it fitting to take a drink one last time before the battle. With that intention, he approaches a canteen operator's table. She has not yet unpacked but nevertheless quickly gets out the bottle of aquavit. At that very instant the call to ranks is sounded; she cannot find the measure, and the old soldier cannot do without his drink. What, then, is to be done? He takes the bottle and puts it to his mouth with these words: It is not needed, because I have the measure in my mouth. But the canteen operator was a poor woman and did not have unlimited confidence in the measure in his mouth; she took the bottle away from him. Fortunate the one who can do just as that canteen operator did!

In margin: *especially when, with the help of the improvement, he is even admired.—*Pap.* V B 85:2 *n.d.,* 1844

From draft; see 24:3:

. . . . . *Intelligensbladet. Changed from:* a half-hour's reading of *Intelligensbladet,* because even if a double number appears, even a triple number, *Intelligensbladet* is still a half-hour's reading.—*Pap.* V B 85:4 *n.d.,* 1844

From sketch:

Measure (πάντων χρημάτων μέτρον ἄνθρωπον εἶναι[44]) [man is the measure of all things]
                                 —*Pap.* V B 88:4 *n.d.,* 1844

From sketch; see 23:31:

What, I wonder, will Prof. H.[45] now say about this book—presumably one will get to know what "one" says.—*Pap.* V B 89 *n.d.,* 1844

From draft: see 26:1–5:

My dear reader, if some teacher of esthetic fine style,[46] inasmuch as this book is located in the confinium of the esthetic, should be prompted to confuse things again and make it become common knowledge that he has confused style and fine writing, you must not let yourself be disturbed by this any more than we intend to disturb him. By no means do we wish to prohibit such a person from plying his trade and also spinning out the thin thread of his chitchat, even if he were to succeed in giving his web a bit of significance by having it considered as fringes on Prof. Heiberg's *Intelligensblade*. Let him keep this good fortune, which probably inspires such a person more than the muses and the graces. When it is a question of putting a period and a comma in the right place, such a one is justified in being along, but when it is a question of ideas, of thoughts, of wild passions, of the inner movements of the soul, of the cry of despair and the deep sigh of the heart, such a one is always *outside*, even though he gives the appearance of being *at home*.[47]—*Pap.* V B 85:7 *n.d.*, 1844

From draft: see 27:34:

. . . . . The Scandinavian Association . . . . .
—*Pap.* V B 93:1 *n.d.*, 1844

From draft of Anxiety*; see 35:3–46:11:*

Preface

To write a book [*essentially the same as Preface VII*]
—*Pap.* V B 47 *n.d.*, 1844

Deleted from draft of Anxiety*; see 35:1:*

N.B. This is not to be used, because it would distract from the subject. Therefore I have written a little preface to be printed in the book.—*Pap.* V B 71 *n.d.*, 1844

Deleted from final copy; see 39:1:

. . . . . unless Professor Sibbern[48] every now and then disturbingly intervenes.

—*Pap.* V B 96:8 *n.d.*, 1844

Deleted from margin of final copy; see 39:3:

Prof. Heiberg

—*Pap.* V B 96:9 *n.d.*, 1844

Deleted from margin of final copy; see 39:8:

Prof. R. Nielsen

—*Pap.* V B 96:11 *n.d.*, 1844

Deleted from margin of final copy; see 39:14:

Herr Stilling

—*Pap.* V B 96:12 *n.d.*, 1844

Deleted from final copy; see 40:12:

He does not write in order to become self-important, still less
in order that he will become important to the whole world, as if
he decided everything or as if all generations were to be blessed
by his book. Each generation has its task and does not need to
trouble itself overmuch with being all things to those preceding
and succeeding it. Each individual member of a generation has
enough to keep himself occupied and does not therefore need to
embrace the whole age in his paternal solicitude or to make eras
and epochs begin with his book.[49]—*Pap.* V B 96:13 *n.d.*, 1844

From final copy; see 42:5:

. . . . . (see Diogenes Laertes on Socrates 2, 15, 21[50]).

—*Pap.* V B 96:14 *n.d.*, 1844

From final copy; see 44:24–25:

. . . . . an inland journey within his own consciousness [*changed from:* from his own consciousness to the presupposition of consciousness in his own consciousness].[51]—*Pap.* V B 96:15 *n.d.*, 1844

Deleted from final copy; see 47:1:

Praemonenda [Preface]
—*Pap.* V B 96:17 *n.d.*, 1844

From final copy; see 48:32:

N.N. [*changed from:* Mag. Kierkegaard.][52]
—*Pap.* V B 96:18 *n.d.*, 1844

In margin of final copy; see 60:18:

. . . . . or: νοῦς δὲ πᾶς ὅμοιος ἐστι καὶ ὁ μείζων καὶ ὁ ἐλάσσων [but every mind is the same, both the greater and the lesser].
See Tenneman, *Ges. d. Ph.* I, p. 327, note.
—*Pap.* V B 96:19 *n.d* 1844

From final copy: see 61:15:

. . . . . existence.*

*See *Perseus*. Preface.[53]
—*Pap.* V B 96:20 *n.d.*, 1844

From final copy; see 68:6:

. . . . . quarrel. Nor need it be explained why "Prefaces" did not become quite what the preface would lead one to expect.—*Pap.* V B 96:21 *n.d.*, 1844

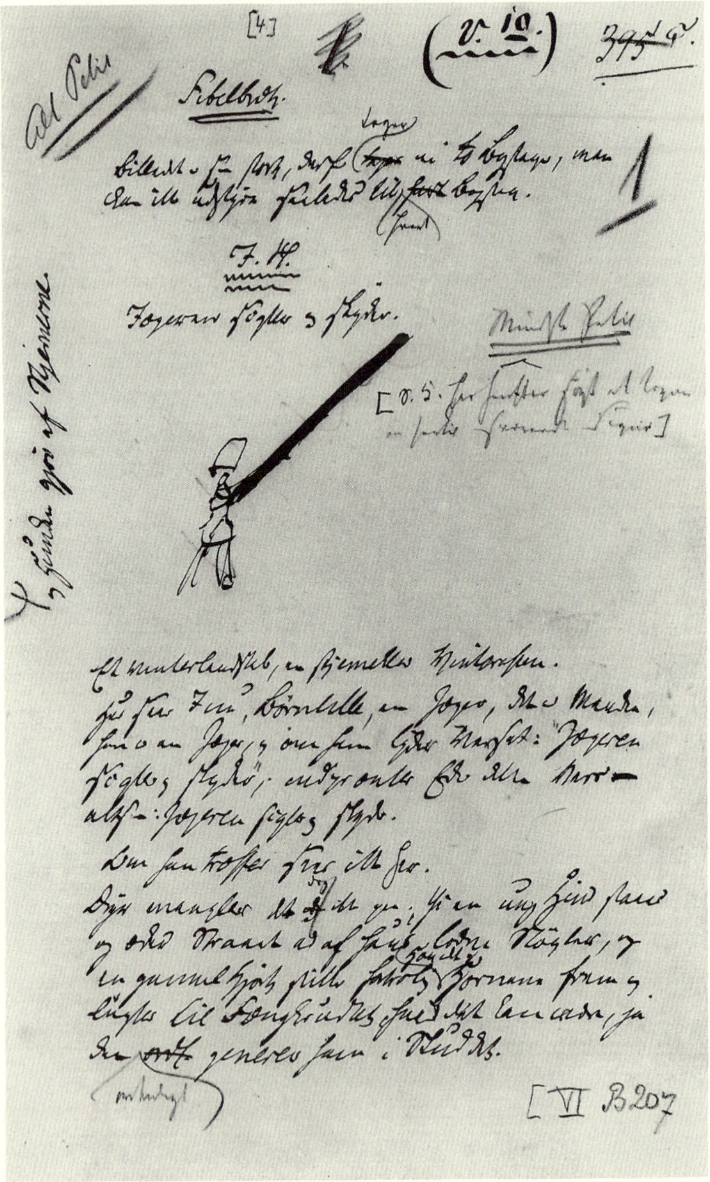
[4]
(V. 10.)
F. H.
[VI B 207

Hornbook

The picture is so large that we therefore use it for two letters; one cannot arrange such for each letter.

J. H.
The hunter aims and shoots.

[Kierkegaard's drawing of a man with a rifle.]

†, and the dog barks at the stars.

A winter landscape, a clear and starry winter evening.

Here, little children, you now see a hunter; it is a man, he is a hunter, and the verse about him goes like this: The hunter aims and shoots. You must memorize this verse. Now then: the hunter aims and shoots.

Whether he hits the mark is not seen here.

But there is no lack of animals; a young hind stands and eats straw from between its furry feet, and an old stag confidently thrusts forward its head and horns and sniffs the priming powder, whatever it is; this ordinarily tips it off at the beginning.

[Editorial marking by editors of the *Papirer* is not reproduced.]

Writing Sampler

Writing Specimen

by

A.B.C.D.E.F. Rosenblad
[*changed to:* Godthaab]
Prospective Author

NB. The book must be produced with all possible elegance: a
     border around every page (as in *Urania*), each section with
     a distinctive type, ornamental and sensational initial let-
     ters—in short, everything *à la* catchpenny books. Some
     letters in red (as in old books), others in green, blue, etc.,
     so that the book might really appeal to the public and look
     entirely like a sampler, corresponding to the motto "De-
     lightful buggy-whip ribbons, gold, green, and blue."
NB   [*Deleted:* Perhaps it could come out in serial form and be
     offered in advance as a suitable New Year's gift.]

[Editorial markings by editors of the *Papirer* is not reproduced.]

SELECTED ENTRIES FROM
KIERKEGAARD'S JOURNALS AND PAPERS
PERTAINING TO
WRITING SAMPLER

N.B. I must once again put out a little polemical piece like the *Prefaces* by Nicolaus Notabene. I am thinking it could be done under the title: Models, or Samples of Various Kinds of Writing. [*In margin:* N.B.] The particular types will be parodied. This is so the irony will also appear to better advantage.—*JP* V 5754 (*Pap.* V A 99) *n.d.*, 1844

From draft of "The Wrong and the Right"[1]

[2]Should Prof. Heiberg make a fuss on account of N. Notabene, a sentence could be inserted about one's being deterred from writing a preface by his example, and then a little malice. This provides the added advantage of H.'s acquiring a name for himself.—*Pap.* V B 192 *n.d.*, 1844

From draft; see title page:

Writing Sampler

Apprentice Test Piece
by
Willibald, Alexander, Alexius, Theodor,
Holger Rosenpind or Rosenblad[3]
Prospective Author
Apprentice Author
—*JP* V 5759 (*Pap.* VI B 194) *n.d.*, 1844–45

1. Logical Issues[4]
by
Johannes Climacus

First a preface about *Philosophical Fragments*.

2. Something about the Art of Religious Address[5]
    with some Reference to Aristotle's *Rhetoric*
    by
    Johannes de Silentio[6]
    with the motto from Aristotle's *Rhetoric*,[7] II,
    chapter 23 (in the little translation,[8] p. 197),
    about a priestess who forbade her son to become
    a public speaker.

3.   God's Judgment[9]
        A Story of Suffering
    Imaginary Psychological Construction

4.   Writing Sampler
        Apprentice Test Piece
                by
    A.W.A.H.   Rosenblad
            Apprentice Author
    —*JP* V 5786 (*Pap.* VI A 146) *n.d.*, 1845

From draft:

    by
    A.B.C.D.E.F. Rosenblad
                    —*Pap.* VII[2] B 272 *n.d.*, 1845–47

From draft:

    ab posse ad esse [from possibility to actuality]
                    —*Pap.* VII[2]B 273 *n.d.*, 1845–47

From final copy; see 69:

NB. The book must be produced with all possible elegance: a
     border around every page (as in *Urania*[10]), each section
     with a distinctive type, ornamental and sensational initial
     letters—in short, everything *à la* catchpenny books. Some

letters in red (as in old books), others in green, blue, etc.,
so that the book might really appeal to the public and look
entirely like a sampler, corresponding to the motto "Delightful buggy-whip ribbons, gold, green, and blue."

NB   [*Deleted:* Perhaps it could come out in serial form and be
offered in advance as a suitable New Year's gift.]—*Pap.*
VII² B 274:2 *n.d.*, 1845–47

From final copy; see 69:

> Delightful buggy-whip ribbons, red and blue,
> Gold, green, violet, and gray,
> Come and buy, come and buy,
> Do not let me go on so long,
> Red, gold, and gray in a bunch,
> I am a good little Jewish boy.[11]
>   —*Pap.* VII² B 274:3 *n.d.*, 1845–47

From draft; see 76:4–14:

In the old days, one wrote a first piece, by which one gained
prominence or not, but now the task is so manifold that a writer
does best by producing a sampler, a style book to qualify himself and draw attention to himself before he chooses this way of
making a living and settles down.—*Pap.* VI B 195 *n.d.*, 1844–
45

From draft; see 77:10–21:

And then it is indeed assumed that the originality of a work
stands in inverse relation to the speed of its distribution and sale,
by which the one who has to make a living from it is by no means
served; from this it must directly follow that a very great genius
who did not have a private fortune would be bound to die of
hunger; because for sake of the cause one can still wait a bit for
fame, but for daily bread one cannot wait many days and in this
regard is not served by some inverse relation, that the daily bread
came a century later.—*Pap.* VI B 196 *n.d.*, 1844–45

VI
B 196
273

VI
B 196
274

From draft; see 76:19–77:6:

Preface.

> Not only for the poets, but
> in actuality love is the wheel
> that drives all things.

A lieutenant may not marry without giving evidence of his prospects, thus with several positions. —(to be developed).

In a way this is my situation. I am in love with a girl. I as good as have her Yes, but my prospective father-in-law, of whom I otherwise have nothing but good to say, asks about my prospects, my way of making a living. I have not thought in the least about this, because I am a genius, and he has money. But he is also interested in art and scholarship, when these yield something. —Now I have risked this undertaking; if it succeeds, then he himself would decide that he is willing to invest his money in a periodical and other literary undertakings.

In the same way I place my writing specimen, and with it my fate, in the hands of the Danish reading public; if it takes off by leaps and bounds, then my luck is made, I get her, and my father-in-law risks his money on literary enterprises. —I throw myself into the arms of humanity, and if this succeeds better than ordinarily, even though it is therefore no less a tender embrace, I intend to attach myself more closely to my beloved; I belong wholly to the future with my intended [*Tilkommende*], my intended [*tilkommende*] means of making a living, and the forthcoming [*tilkommende*] periodical.

Respectfully
Rosenpind or Rosenblad
—*Pap.* VI B 197 *n.d.*, 1844–45

From draft; see 77:31–78:3:

Finally it should be recalled that I also write on request: in the name of the century, of all humanity, of our age, of the crowd, of several, just as a hint is also given at the same time that I offer services in the brushing of clothing and the shining of boots for subscription agents who get 100 subscribers.—*Pap.* VI B 198 *n.d.,* 1844–45

From draft:

No. 1

Speculative-Heralding Style

—*JP* V 5760 (*Pap.* VI B 199) *n.d.,* 1844–1845

From draft:

No. 2

Historical-Prophetic Style

of a Seer and Bard[12]

—*JP* V 5760 (*Pap.* VI B 200) *n.d.,* 1844–1845

From draft:

No. 3

Memoir-Style

VI
B 201
275

The latest assembly of the Estates or something similar from the present day, narrated by an old person under the delusion that it is fifty years ago. —I can remember Sager[13] well; he was red in the face. —First and foremost I saw Prof. Sibbern there (in the Estates) (just as Steffens saw Thorvaldsen at the coronation where he was not present.[14]) —Grundtvig,[15] especially since the time when he began to observe closing time and to see his prophecies fulfilled, because he is at your service in every way, both to weep and to cry woe, woe, woe, that he is already sacrificed—and in seeing it happen.—*Pap.* VI B 201 *n.d.,* 1844–45

VI
B 201
276

From draft:

The Hunter[16]

A Moral Tale.

—*Pap.* VI B 202 *n.d.,* 1844–45

From draft:

Historically Precise Style

The history of astronomy
in Denmark since Prof. H.
became an astronomer.

the prehistorical: hints in *Intelligensbladet*, and that H. purchased
a telescope, for which reason there is here reprinted and enclosed
the receipt as an important document.[17]—*Pap.* VI B 203 *n.d.*,
1844–45

From draft; see 24:10–26:

This event is so important in the history of Denmark that it has
been decided to use it as a principle of classification. Instead of
dividing the hist. of Denmark into the time before the House of
Oldenburg or until absolutism and the time thereafter,[18] it is now
fittingly to be divided into these 2 periods: (1) the period until
Heiberg became an astrologer,[19] (2) the period thereafter.—*Pap.*
VI B 204 *n.d.*, 1844–45

From draft:

A Venture in Ale-Norse[20]
—*Pap.* VI B 205 *n.d.*, 1844–45

From draft:

Ciceronian-Gothic.   —bold-faced brevier.
—*Pap.* VI B 206 *n.d.*, 1844–45

From draft:

VI
B 207
277

Hornbook[21]

The picture is so large that we therefore use it for two letters; one
cannot arrange such for each letter.

J. H.[22]

The hunter aims and shoots.

[*drawing*]

A winter landscape, a clear and starry winter evening.

Here, little children, you now see a hunter; it is a man, he is a hunter, and the verse about him goes like this: The hunter aims and shoots. You must memorize this verse. Now then: The hunter aims and shoots.

Whether he hits the mark is not seen here.

But there is no lack of animals; a young hind stands and eats straw from between its furry feet, and an old stag confidently thrusts forward its head and horns and sniffs the priming powder, whatever it is; this ordinarily tips it off at the beginning.

He shoots. You know well enough, little children, that one ought to be cautious with guns, and therefore he used all possible caution; this you see in his taking aim. Therefore, nothing unfortunate happened except that an old, feeble, and rather dazed crow, which had fallen asleep in a tree behind him—tumbled down and thought itself dead. When the other crows rushed forward and explained the impossibility of this, the crow answered that it had in any event felt hit and so it fell, if not because of his shot, then because his gun was fired.

The piece can also be explained otherwise: that the hunter is indeed not crazy, but that he is not shooting at the animals—but at the stars.* In that case it is quite right that he aims at them and it is not improbable that he hits them.**

VI
B 207
278

But back to the crow. All the crows laughed, because the dazed crow claimed that so it was among human beings. There was once a man who spat out of the window without hitting anyone or inconveniencing a single person. But a poor simple person, who heard about that man, that he had spat out of the window, walked a way and crept over to the place, and it finally became clear to him that it was on him that he had spat, even though the simple person had not even been in the city at the time.

Another man, made the object of an unwarranted attack, soon exalted himself on this basis; in noble self-esteem he considered his existence more meaningful than ever. He gathered his intimates and in many a moving evening hour they encouraged one another in this high-mindedness. And see! He had not used the necessary caution; it was not he but another man who was the object of the attack.

The Moral
When a shot goes off, from this it does not immediately follow that anyone has been shot, and the one who falls at the shot is a fool.

*and the dog barks at the stars.
**he indeed achieves this. When one stands on Valdby Hill, the distance, according to Professor Heiberg's calendar, will be 26 billion—2 mill. . . . . . miles, 110 and 3/4 feet.[23]
—*Pap.* VI B 207 *n.d.*, 1844–45

From draft:

Feuilleton-Style.
The Organism of the Chancellery Building[24]

A Contribution
Illuminating the Relation between the Ganglion and the Cerebral System.
—*Pap.* VI B 208 *n.d.*, 1844–45

From draft:

The difference between a peripatetic and a knight errant.
—*Pap.* VI B 209 *n.d.*, 1844–45

From draft:

*A Venture in the Especially Dainty and Elegant.
Prepared Solely as
a New Year's Gift.*[25]

To be printed in a unique typeface, with a gilded border around it, very little on each page.

The migratory birds and their laws,
a popular essay with tables. (Faber.[26])
—*Pap.* VI B 210 *n.d.*, 1844–45

Addition to Pap. VI B 210:

A preface by the publisher, in which he gives assurance in the most solemn way that it is prepared solely as a gift.—*Pap.* VI B 211 *n.d.*, 1844–45

Addition to Pap. VI B 210:

I do not assume learned or knowledgeable but only cultured readers, yet one thing, that they know Latin. I myself have spent ten years learning it. I assume that it can be learned in less time, for example, in two years. As soon as one has learned it, one can immediately proceed to read my work, and it can be read in half an hour.—*Pap.* VI B 212 *n.d.*, 1844–45

From draft:

A Venture in the Social-Civic.
—*Pap.* VI B 213 *n.d.*, 1844–45

From draft:

A Speech in the Estates.
—*Pap.* VI B 214 *n.d.*, 1844–45

From draft:

A Venture in the Project-Promoter Style.
—*Pap.* VI B 215 *n.d.*, 1844–45

From draft:

Feuilleton Article.
Von Hørensagen [On Hearsay]

or
On the Transmission of Sound.[27]
—*Pap.* VI B 216 *n.d.*, 1844–45

From draft:

A Grave Flower
respectfully
planted
by
A.W.S.H. Rosenblad.
—*Pap.* VI B 217 *n.d.*, 1844–45

From draft:

On Grave Flowers.
A Contribution to Metamorphoses of Idiom.

Life is a path, an idiom the truth of which not only people but also the idioms must comprehend, as on their journey along life's path they experience the significant transformations.—*Pap.* VI B 218 *n.d.*, 1844–45

From draft:

On the Power of the Word.[28]

(Parody of Grundtvig).

One sees the power the word has from the story[29] of the Jew who came to Holsten and when he had arrived home said: A remarkable language and land, where, when one asks for 1 shilling's worth of *Vust*, one gets 2 shilling's worth of sausage.

(he really meant *Ost* [cheese], and 1 Danish shilling, but 1 Lübecker shilling equals 2 Danish shillings, and his wrong pronunciation sounded like *Wurst* [sausage]).

At the beginning of the century, did not Grundtvig use his influence in the same way for the sake of these ideas? Which? Well, the ones now flourishing? Which ones? Well, are they the ones that Grundtvig prophesied? Which ones? How can you ask such things when you now see them fulfilled?—*Pap.* VI B 220 *n.d.*, 1844–45

From draft:

Results in Brief
the 4 world-historical monarchies
according to Geert Westphaler.[30]
—*Pap.* VI B 221 *n.d.*, 1844–45

From draft:

A venture in the especially dainty and
elegant prepared to serve solely as a
New Year's gift:

VI
B 222
281

On the Migration of Birds.
with tables and sketches.

That our age is an age of mental depression,[31] there is no doubt
and no question; the only question is what can be done about it
and what the age demands in this regard, since the age is a fashionable patient who is not given orders but is asked what he
wants. In this case it seems inadvisable to prescribe what physicians usually prescribe for depression, that is, activity, because it
most likely has motion enough, one would think, since it is an
age of ferment. As a matter of fact, the depression is the very
result of the unrest and fermentation, which will end in yeasty
bloating, because it is sick, even though some think it is too hale
and hearty. As a rule, horseback riding is the activity prescribed,
but since our age is in fact a personification and not an actual
person, it would be impossible to get it up onto an actual horse.
But riding a hobbyhorse is no activity at all, as we learn from the
experience of all ages, since every age does have its own hobbyhorse.

VI
B 222
282

Because of this need I venture to suggest a closer relationship
to nature as a provisional analgesic until we see what comes of
this ferment.* For what is as recreating as watching migratory
birds: this apparent lack of any laws and yet a perfect law. Even
watching the stars and their measured course across the sky must,
especially in this connection, be acknowledged as a significant
remedy for the depression of our age. But this is only the classical
and lacks the romantic.

Here Faber's book on our migratory
birds is to be used.

*convinced that this is what the age demands.
　　　　　—*JP* V 5761 (*Pap.* VI B 222) *n.d.*, 1844–45

From draft:

VI
B 223
282
Feuilleton style.

No. 1.

Von Hørensagen [On Hearsay] or a Contribution to
a Theory of the Transmission of Sound

VI
B 223
282
It is well enough known with what speed sound transmits itself; with regard to the law for this speed in relation to the various
media something most extraordinary has been achieved, the result of the keenest and most thorough observations: that whoever
would venture to achieve something in this regard must get up
early. I do not make so bold as to do this myself. What I am
concerned with is something else; it is the transmission of sound
through the medium that is called the crowd and that may also
be called gossip. Here one will run across oddities of the most
amazing sort; here there occurs what is otherwise unheard of,
that sound transmits itself in such a way that when one says one
thing it becomes, in transmission, something entirely different—
the only instance in which transmission departs from the rule: to
produce something resembling itself.

A fantastic description of rumor (there is undoubtedly a passage in Tertullian[32] and Cyprian[33] that could be cited).—*Pap.* VI
B 223 *n.d.* 1844–45

From draft:

*A Program of Innocent
and Inexpensive Diversions*
A Result of Many Years of Experience.

I get up in the morning—look out of the window to see if the weather is fine or just the sort of weather I happen to want. If such is the case,* I express my supreme approval with a nod and a gracious smile. As a matter of fact, my principal diversion is assuming that everything revolves around me[34] and that the whole world exists for my sake alone. This diversion is both very amusing and exceedingly innocent, for of course I do not ask that it produce results for any other human being; on the contrary, like everyone else, I am swindled by the merchants etc. A child can quarrel with another child about a horse trotting by, even come to blows, by saying: That belongs to me, and the other says: No, it belongs to me.

*If this is not the case, I divert myself by thinking about what kind of weather I would rather have and what I would have done if it had turned out that way.—*JP* V 5762 (*Pap.* VI B 224) *n.d.* 1844–45

Addition to Pap. VI B 224:

In the morning I go right away to the marketplace and find out the market prices[35]—the servant girls—Knippelsbro.[36]

The special point about my diversions is that they are varied. Here are two principal variations. I regard the whole city of Copenhagen as a great social function. But on one day I view myself as the host who walks around conversing[37] with all the many cherished guests I have invited; then the next day I assume that a great man has given the party and I am a guest. Accordingly, I dress differently, greet people differently, etc. I am sure that those who know me have frequently observed that my manner may be somewhat different, but they probably do not dream that this is the reason. —If an elegant carriage goes by with four horses engaged for the day, I assume that I am the host, give a friendly greeting, and pretend that it is I who lent them this lovely carriage.

I also vary my diversions by sometimes regarding Copenhagen as a large city and sometimes as a little one.
—*JP* V 5763 (*Pap.* VI B 225) *n.d.* 1844–45

From draft:

For
My Innocent Diversions.

in "Writing Sampler"
Sometimes I turn away from people completely and take a fancy
to the clouds;[38] this is an innocent and very legitimate infatuation, especially if one is careful to go to solitary places where one
does not encounter anyone and is painfully reminded that one
lives among people.—*JP* V 5764 (*Pap.* VI B 226) *n.d.*, 1844–45

From draft:

For the piece on: My Innocent Diversions.

————————

The Battle between the Crows and the Sea Gulls
on the Commons.
The Diversion of Fighting with the Wind.

For this I have a big umbrella with a strong frame. I go out to one
of the most gusty spots, open the umbrella, and hold it in front of
me against the wind, just as in a bayonet skirmish against the
cavalry. The grips are as follows: the one hand grasps the handle,
the thumb of the other hand is on the release button above so I
can trick the wind, if it gets too powerful, by closing the umbrella. —Now we close it.
This diversion is also a very beneficial motion,
because one must make the most curious leap.
—*JP* V 5765 (*Pap.* VI B 227) *n.d.*, 1844–45

From draft:

For: Writing Sampler

Some drawings for the spiritual peep-show
for use on Sundays by the
faithful congregation.

It is now 1800 years ago that Christianity came into the world—
what a change: we are all Christians, a whole world of Christians.

Now we are all Christians—the sign of the times in these last days is said to be that there is a decline.

> It is just as with the two professorial addresses over a deceased professor—the one concluded: Therefore be comforted and do not weep; the other began: Weep, weep. (One of the professors was Johann David Michaelis.[39])
> —*Pap.* VI B 228 *n.d.,* 1844–45

From draft:

For

Writing Sampler

Something about the night watchman's song
or about night watchmen as untaught singers

The various circumstances are to be examined.
—*JP* V 5766 (*Pap.* VI B 229) *n.d.,* 1844–45

Deleted from draft:

On the stampeding of cows
See journal[40]
—*Pap.* VI B 230 *n.d.,* 1844–45

From draft:

For Writing Sampler

What is not used about Grundtvig in *Concluding Postscript*[41] can be used here, somewhat reworked. The title will be—The Danish Pantheon:[42] Portrait of Pastor Grundtvig.—*JP* V 5767 (*Pap.* VI B 231) *n.d.,* 1844–45

From draft:

"Danish Fjanteon"[43] instead of: Danish Pantheon. It is there that we ought to have N.F.S. Grundtvig placed.—*Pap.* VI B 232 *n.d.,* 1844–45

From draft:

VI
B 233
287

A Surprising, Surprising Surprise

_____

The King of [*deleted:* Prussia[44]] has come—it is absolutely certain. We have our information from a maidservant who saw him and recognized him and from a man who has been so close to him that he could have spoken with him if His Majesty had been prepared with what he should say on such an opportunity and occasion. But on festive occasions, just as in public defense of doctoral dissertations, one is prepared with only a limited number of answers and courtesy phrases.* The whole event has something so oddly surprising about it that it must serve to excuse the editorial office staff for not having spies out and ministry reports to submit to its public. But it is certain that he has come, and since he has been seen and recognized, as far as facts are concerned it makes no difference by whom he is seen and recognized—our witnesses are not to be scorned.

The maidservant is an unusually clever chambermaid with unusually good and unusually numerous recommendations from the many places where she has worked (there has been such a demand for her). She has been engaged to be married seven times but has been very prudent about it and with none of the beloveds ever let things reach the point of ultimate assurances; she came out of it all right—a little innocent jest, and then the gifts. She is really clever. When she is supposed to do errands in the city, she does not slouch and drag along as the other maidservants do—no, she runs like the wind, but not to get home; she just wants to make sure of the time she has at her own disposal. Thus she assumes that an ordinary Wednesday or Saturday expedition to the market takes, as a rule, two to two-and-a-half hours. The days when there is so much traffic, as on Vimmelskaftet[45] and Amagertorv,[46] that a trading ship must ride at anchor more frequently, she runs through the secondary streets and counts on

VI
B 233
288

In margin: Our reporter explains that he did not get the honor of talking personally with His Majesty or of showing him about the town, which no one knows as well as he does.

having exactly two hours in which to visit someone or other. This morning she was sent out to the customs house with her master's lunch—he is a customs officer. What happens? Well, she described it, but the one who saw her excitement when she told it . . . . . She recognized the King immediately. He was a young man in a white uniform; she saw him quite clearly, so clearly that she is convinced that he also saw her, of which she is not a little proud. It amazed her no end that our King walked over and embraced someone, but a servant girl standing there, who also took the man in white to be none other than the King, explained that it must be a foreign custom, a strange way of showing courtesy, that the Chief Marshal or someone like that should represent the King so that the King himself could stand calmly as an onlooker and see how much was made of the King.

Ceremonies were hurriedly outlined (we go on with the story) for the three days the King would be Denmark's guest—but only the ceremonies for the first day are decided; we state it here and admire the wisdom of not deciding things too long in advance when one is dependent on wind and weather. Immediately after disembarking, considerable changing of clothes—that is, undressing—and then to bed to sleep. This diversion is planned to last twelve hours. Curious! Anyone who has read anything about ceremonies certainly must marvel that they are always planned as if royalty and the highest royalty did not need sleep.[47] It is the same with little people. Mr. and Mrs. Burmann's ceremony for a Sunday in Dyrehave is an excellent [example]; they ride out, eat lunch, eat dinner, spend the whole day in the bosom of the family and of nature—but no one has given any thought to sleep—and therefore Malle and Klister must seek solitude.[48]

The diversion lasts twelve hours. At eight o'clock in the evening they get up, renewed and refreshed, completely new and different people. But the visit is not an official one, nor is it purely personal, but a mixture. The ceremony has focused on this and is specifically arranged in painterly tableaus. So they get up. For a quarter of an hour, after a signal from the Chief Marshal, the two kings walk back and forth arm in arm and affectionately pat each other many times; this diversion lasts a quarter of

VI
B 233
289

an hour. Then they sit down at a great green table, for now the negotiating begins. This is the reason the Chief Marshal thought it best to provide and implement a familiar tableau. When Napoleon and Talleyrand had worked together for many days and nights, they both fell asleep. The first part of this was not painterly and cannot be depicted, only the last part. They both fell asleep, and the ceremony, which is also the program, explains that it is after many days and nights of strenuous effort. Therefore a man-in-waiting goes in and calls the King, just as in that tableau. They get up.

———————

Since the King of _____ is supposed to have the intention of getting acquainted with the Danish state, and since, in reliance on his military power, he fears only the intelligence of this country, he especially wishes to get to know this. This has been prepared for. All the male and female teachers of German have been gathered together hastily, and these are grouped in such a way that they are enough for the whole nation that is to be presented to the foreign monarch.* As if at random, our King, while walking arm in arm with the foreign King down the row, as if at random addresses one of his subjects and now another—and look, to the foreign monarch's amazement they all answer in German. They permit him to remain ignorant of the fact that they are language teachers, and our King does not get too involved with any of them for fear that one of the language teachers might betray that he was only a phrase book and not a man. Our queen, too, in passing, occasionally drops a word now to one, now to another of the women; it appears to be quite at random and yet she always chances upon a language teacher, and the foreign monarch is more surprised than ever. But it is Herr Nathanson,**[49] the wholesaler, who attracts the King's particular

VI
B 233
290

*In margin: And in order to guarantee his observations, he wishes to see them by night, has them summoned in order that they should not have time to prepare themselves.

**Everything is built around him; a nation fortunate enough to have such a man must also show him off. Our King is engaged with him somewhat longer with regard to Denmark's prosperity and also gives him the chance to shine in attention. He has offered his services as one who speaks perfect German and who is also expert in politics.[50] He is also supposed to have suggested during the time the foreign King was here that he might publish the *Berlingske Tidende*[51] in German but was refused since it was assumed that the numerous diversions would leave no time for any of the monarchs to read this paper.

—*JP* V 5831 (*Pap.* VI B 233) *n.d.,* 1845

Addition to Pap. VI B 233:

The man (the maidservant has been dealt with) has tried many occupations but has never succeeded, but when it comes to being present at a commotion or an event, he is a favorite of fortune [*Lykkens-Pamphilius*]. It never fails; when there is something afoot, he is right on the spot or just across the street.—*Pap.* VI B 234 *n.d.,* 1845

From draft; see 79:22–24:

Feuilleton Article
A Remarkable Novelty
A book has come off the press, it creates a general sensation among all the bookbinders. Its appearance is as follows:

—*Pap.* VI B 219 *n.d.,* 1844–45

From draft: see 79:21–80:23:

No. 2
Literature.

These days a book has come off the press that has created a general sensation among all the bookbinders.

---

mental arithmetic. In addition, the wholesale grocer is relied upon to use the utmost discretion in satisfying the royal visitors. The intention is to get the foreign monarch himself to enter into discussion with Nathanson, and behold, he can answer much faster than he is asked, and that is why he is given a medal that he wears around his waist—it is so heavy that it cannot be carried any other way.

The appearance of the binding is as follows.
[*Blank space*]
When one opens it, the title page looks as follows.
[*Blank space*]
When one closes it, the other side looks as follows.
[*Blank space*]

In margin: As for the quality of the contents, the author's name is sufficient guarantee.

In margin: We hope that the most esteemed, cultured public will support this fine effort in literature with strong sales.—*Pap.* VII² B 277:7 *n.d.* 1845–47

From draft: see 80:24–35:

No. 3
Politics.

The elections for the Provincial Estates.
Verbatim from the *Berlingske*, only the totals.
and quotations from the *Berlingske Tidende*.
—*Pap.* VII² B 277:8 *n.d.* 1845–47

From draft: see 81:21–82:12:

No. 5
News Notes.

Merchant Marcussen
Yesterday at dinner there was a large party at merchant Marcussen's. During the meal the Herr merchant had the misfortune to spill some soup on his waistcoat and to splash some on a lady. We hasten to report this news, about which there will be much talk, to our readers.

We hope that in picking up this article other newspaper editors will note that it is from our paper.

In margin: to knock over a gravy boat. This is how it happened—to be developed—this is the historical truth; we are well aware that a rumor is circulating, but we purvey only official information and will have nothing to do with rumor.

As always, we shall strive in this article to be the first to report all news instantaneously. We promise that, even if someone sends something to us with the request that we not break it until Saturday, we shall indeed break it on that same day.—*Pap.* VII[2] B 277:10 *n.d.* 1845–47

From draft:

Time of Scarcity

Today the price of ten eggs in the market[52] was 5 marks. One may see from this that it must be a time of scarcity—at least for eggs.—*Pap.* VII[2] B 277:11 *n.d.*, 1845–47

Deleted from draft:

News Notes.

Miss Juliane Knudsen has broken up with her beloved because he has been in a cartoon in *The Corsair.*—*Pap.* VII[2] B 277:12 *n.d.*, 1845–47

From draft: see 84:4–20:

Curiosity.

We permit ourselves to direct the attention of our readers to a remarkable combination of the natural and the supranatural on display at present out on Vesterbro. The barker explains that there is a lucky star on display from which everyone gets to know his full age and at the same time his future bride and bridegroom. The ingenuity of it is in this, that one gets to know what one knows: his age. This is not something supranatural, and for that reason we do not venture to recommend that anyone visit the panorama, because everyone knows how old he is.—*Pap.* VII[2] B 277:14 *n.d.* 1845–47

Addition to Pap. VII² B 277:14:

Catchpennying [*Stüvenfængeri*]

It would be better to do the article polemically against the shameful catchpennying that tricks money out of the country—and tells one how old one is.

———————

At a time when [*essentially the same as 84:4–13*]. Is this not making a fool of a person right to his face, since everyone certainly knows how old he is? And then to venture to permit oneself to believe that the most esteemed cultured public is so stupid that it does not know how old it is. As for the other matter, when, as I am, a man is as good as engaged, there is nothing new to know. It would be desirable that the police and the clergy would forbid such an odious practice or at any rate dissuade the public from paying money for such things.—*Pap.* VII² B 277:15 *n.d.* 1845–47

From draft; see 84:22–85:12:

The Scandinavian Idea

VI
B 235
291

Wherever there are good people they are joined by good people—the King of P.[53] is here, and now the Scandinavian Brothers arrive; I do not mean those greeted with catcalls[54] but those greeted with applause.[55]

At this point we should take the example of Sallust's story[56] of the three brothers who had themselves buried alive in order to decide boundary disputes; in like manner they express this symbolically by three of them getting drunk.

The one all revolves around here is university graduate Hans Povelsen.[57] His motto is: Now or Never. It is already a fortnight since he first permitted his beloved to examine him on the speech he intends to give, but he is not satisfied with it and with her assurance that he does it very well, and now he goes around with a copy that he hands to a passerby with the request that he stop and listen to him. The author of this article was fortunate enough to hear him at a gateway in Vimmelskaftet[58] and must testify to the fact that Mr. P. knows his business very well; his gestures perhaps could be somewhat more expert, but his voice and facial expressions were evidence of an unmistakable effort that can also be continued for three or four days yet, unless the Swedes do not come at all, since it can then be continued longer—if his strength holds out. But this is the trouble. For fourteen days and nights he has not closed his eyes, and the resulting exhaustion is evident in his alarming absentmindedness. If the Swedes do actually come and P. does actually get to give his speech,[59] there is no doubt that it will bring about a union. The danger is from another direction. It is told of a pastor that in absentmindedness he married two completely strange and incompatible people. There was nothing to object to in the act itself. The wedding discourse was unusually fine; the speaker inspired the two to be joined together uncommonly well—the trouble was that they were simply wrong for each other. There were many unpleasant consequences involved in getting separated. Thus it is not to be feared that Mr. Povelsen is likely to forget his talk on that day (although that has already happened many times in the daily practice) but that he will unite us Danes, perhaps not with the Swedes, but with another race—and it can always be difficult to become separated after having been so fervently united.

VI
B 235
292

The ceremony at this festivity is especially attached to the meaningful phrase—as Povelsen says: Now or Never. First of all 500 Swedish students will be placed vis-à-vis 500 Danish students, and they will gaze romantically at each other and then soulfully. This diversion will last a quarter of an hour.

The ceremony is planned for just one day, since in these three days the spirit will be so active that, as the prophet declares, your maidens and your young men will have visions;[60] thus one always must be prepared for a sudden marvelous proposal that would then be put into action.

In St. Peter's Church in Rome, four sermons are preached in four places at the same time; in the same way it has been resolved that four speeches should be delivered here at the same time, but since there are not as many orchestras as speakers, they must be satisfied with a common fanfare. A list of the different songs and speeches is laid at each place-setting like a menu, so each one may choose.

> (The young people's hilarity in the forest has an amusing side—which has a value of its own—but not the Ale-Norse.)

In conclusion, an apotheosis.

Grundtvig, supported by Barfoed[61] and Povelsen, appears[62] on an elevation in the forest background. He is artistically draped in a great cloak, has a staff in his hand, and his face is concealed by a mask with one eye (deep and profound so as to see into world history) and a mossy beard with birds' nests in it (he is very old—about 1,000 years); he has a hollow voice melodramatically accompanied by a few blasts on a conch (as at a town meeting); he speaks in a dithyrambic rhythm. When he has finished his speech (that is, when the committee in charge of the festivities says, "Enough," for otherwise he would never finish), a bell rings, a cord is pulled, the beard falls off, followed by the enormous cloak, and we see a slim young man with wings; it is Grundtvig as the spirit of the Scandinavian idea; he says: Ladies and Gentlemen.*

—This was Sunday. Strangely enough, Bishop Mynster preached that same Sunday. There was not a soul in church; nevertheless, just as the great congregation had inspired him to give a glorious sermon, so too the empty church inspired him. When he was finished, he gazed in front of him in silence, and if there is a transfiguration when the dead go behind the curtain, then he was transfigured in the same way—and in the same way as one who is dead.[63]—*JP* V 5832 (*Pap.* VI B 235) *n.d.*, 1845

---

*This is what I have been prophesying for half a century now. Shoemaker Mathiesen can testify that I said it to him one Sunday afternoon forty-five years ago when we met in the barber shop of district barber Biberak, now deceased. What I have suffered for the sake of this idea, how often I have been close to despair for old Denmark, how many tears it has cost me—only shoemaker Mathiesen knows this, he who first accepted my teaching, and that is why he shall also be my successor in the tyranny.

From draft: see 84:22–85:12:

Feuilleton

The arrival of the Swedish students here in the city is anticipated with great excitement. Every Scandinavian is of course interested, but essentially all this revolves around university graduate Jespersen. His [*essentially the same as 84:25–85:11*] a few days more or less, since if the Swedes do not come at all, it can then be continued as long as possible.—*Pap.* VII² B 277:16 *n.d.* 1845–47

From draft: see 86:4–27:

Humorous Feuilleton

VII²
B 287
344

The Association of Watchmen, founded last year, held its second ceremonial meeting yesterday at noon. Although it was noon, according to the hosts' scheme the shutters were nevertheless closed and the candles were lit so that it could resemble an evening party, since in actuality the watchmen are prevented from holding evening parties. That feature gives an enchantment all of its own to this performance.

The watchmen's songs were arranged in this festively decorated hall.

VII²
B 287
345

The watchman from Grønnegade presided. After having proposed a toast to the police-adjutant, who was greeted with a ninefold "Hurrah" that almost did not stop, he gave the signal with his whistle for the speeches to begin.

> Because space does not permit, we will reserve a review of the speeches for tomorrow.

Just as usual with a wine list, there lay at each place a list of songs, so that everyone might sing what he wished. It was voted—because notice had been given of an enormous number of speeches—that no more than four might speak at one time.

—*Pap.* VII² B 287 *n.d.* 1845–47

From draft; see 86:4–27:

No. 8

The Convention organized by the watchmen held its annual festive banquet yesterday at noon. The convention, which, as is well known, was organized primarily to give these official brethren from the city's various streets and neighborhoods an opportunity to get to know one another personally, to open their hearts to one another, to exchange thoughts with one another, their fears and hopes, their worries for the future, etc., in short, in order to develop and nourish the spirit of community, occupies itself for a time with "the matchless decline of the Danish watchman's song" and thus with meeting a common and long deeply felt need for a new watchman's song, for which reason there is a permanent continually singing committee that, singing, tests and selects.

The arrangements for the festive banquet were excellent. Although it was noon, according to the hosts' scheme the shutters were nevertheless closed and the candles were lit so that it could resemble an evening party—*Pap.* VII^2 B 288 *n.d.*, 1845–47

From draft:

VII^2
B 290
346

No. 9

The journalist's profession, as very few realize, is indeed so onerous that only the consciousness of what one is achieving in the service of truth for the ennobling of mankind can provide the strength to persevere. Imagine a young man in his best years— already almost an old man, almost gray-haired if he is not completely bald—to such an extent everything that he has gone through, or everything that has gone through him, has left its marks. He is sitting at his desk; we can scarcely see him—to such an extent is he so surrounded by or buried in papers, books, journals, newspapers, articles, letters, works of art. He sits at his desk, bowed under the enormous strain of bearing the weight that lies upon his shoulders—the fact that nothing, nothing, neither the most insignificant nor the most significant, nothing in the city, in the country, yes, in all of Europe, happens without going through the journalist. —Now the bell rings; it is an author with his newest work. The journalist must be in on everything. Without having once looked into the book, he must immediately be able to say what is wrong with it and suggest what direction the author should now take, what the age demands in politics, philosophy, theology, philanthropy, art, history, ethics, esthetics, pedagogy, archaeology, tactics, didactics, horoscopes, and metascopes. There is a knock at the door; it is a recently arrived artist. The journalist must be in on everything. Without ever having heard him or heard about him, he must immediately be able to pass judgment, show him what is right, serve him with counsel that reveals the art connoisseur—and then read the pile of foreign newspapers the artist carries with him, in which the artist is mentioned and which the journalist must have "lying before him." Now there is a knock at the secret door; it is one of the editor-in-chief's highly trusted associates. It is apparent in his face that something terrible has happened—but the journalist must diplomatically control himself, remain calm, or seem calm, must ask him to wait, and he continues his conversation with the artist. There is another knock. It is a note from a person in high authority who feels insulted and makes threats. The bell rings; it is an injured party. The journalist must be in on everything, must immediately, without having heard the least thing about the affair, understand it, know the law and the constitutional rights of the land better than all the lawyers. There is another knock; it is the print shop messenger who is to pick up copy.

VII[2]
B 290
347

We almost shudder when we read this; we cannot understand how a man's head can endure this. And yet the journalist has to have ever so much more in his head. Amidst all this he must readily and in every moment of the day be able to calculate mentally which of all the thousands of opinions is the public opinion, the cultured public's opinion. Day in and day out, in this tremendous crisscrossing of the most varied and contradictory opinions, day in and day out, in this shouting and complaining and clapping and clamoring and whispering confusion, in which everyone wants to have his opinion, of course without being obliged to keep it for a half hour but with the unconditional right to change it every second—to have to calculate *stante pede* [immediately] in his head which opinion is the public's, the cultured public's! How could one's head be able to endure all this without a consciousness of and faith in the significance of one's calling. We would certainly think that a person might lose his mind over this, just over this imponderable—how the journalist gets the answer out of the public after all!

And so it goes all day long. When evening comes, there are new demands on the journalist's life. He must be able to cast aside this enormous weight, completely clear his mind, so that in the party at taverner Mathiesen's he may be young, jovial, witty, charming, the ingratiating man about town, the ladies'

(to be continued)
—*Pap.* VII^2 B 290 *n.d.*, 1845–47

From draft:

For "Writing Sampler":

Advertisement.

His Reverence Pastor Madsen[64] is requested to publish the beautiful passage in about the middle of the sermon given last Sunday in Trinity Church;[65] it began thus: When from this elevation we turn our attention to the confusion of the times in order to hold fast to it etc.

Because we have with grateful discrimination remarked how for quite some time His Reverence, with a rare mobility and plasticity, enters at every moment into the movements of the moment, in order momentarily to supply calming information*—we hope that he will not omit the publication of this beautiful passage, which by being published will make it impossible for it to cost more than even the poorest beggar can afford and thus will achieve quite an extraordinary dissemination.

Several auditors

*and teach us people to stand fast

—*Pap.* VII^2 B 292 *n.d.*, 1845–47

From draft:

For "Writing Sampler":   VII²
B 294
349

Feuilleton.

A new journal. Because it may be altogether in the interest of the most esteemed cultured public to know accurately where one gets the best and cheapest wares of every sort, the best and cheapest work, where service and attention are the best and cheapest, etc., Mssrs. Grynmøller, Smidt, and Co. have begun on an enterprise to meet this need, the idea for which was actually hatched in the local lockup.

The editors oblige themselves, with the utmost honesty and conscientiousness, to put themselves in possession of the most accurate information possible about how much every tradesman, unconditionally every tradesman, earns per year. By paying 4 percent of his income to the editors, he will assure himself of the most favorable mention in the journal. If someone does not wish to give so much, he can for 2 percent assure himself of not being mentioned at all. But everyone who will not even reply will in every way be reduced to penury and misery, just as all dishonesty with regard to actual wages will be punished with fines conscientiously and honestly adjusted in relation to each one's ability.

In announcing this new journal, we know of nothing better to say in commendation than that we find the idea so excellent that we might be tempted to steal it, which would have happened if Mssrs. Grynmøller Smidt and Co. had not granted us a certain percentage.

We hope that the esteemed cultured public, by subscribing in great numbers, will promote this publication, unmistakably characterized by wanting solely to serve the public, which for a   VII²
B 294
350
long time must have had its eyes opened to the fact that the only salvation of the nations is the daily press, that neither Jesuits nor diplomats nor police informers nor courtiers were benefactors of humanity, no matter what they pretended to be, but only and solely—completely *gratis* and at absolutely no cost—the journalists, and not least those whose minds were matured to earnestness and whose characters were tempered to heroism in

the quiet solitude of the local lockup.—*Pap.* VII^2 B 292 *n.d.*, 1845–47

I would like to create a little literary mystification by, for example, publishing something I would call "The Writings of a Young Man";[66] in the preface I would appear as a young author publishing his first book.

I would call myself Felix de St. Vincent.[67] The contents would include:

1. The Crisis in the Life of an Actress
2. A Eulogy on Autumn
3. Rosenkilde as Hummer
4. Writing Sampler

—*JP* V 6060 (*Pap.* VIII^1 A 339) *n.d.* 1847

From draft of "Writings of a Young Man":

See journal JJ, pp. 216–17[68]

Eulogy on Autumn
(in the French Style)*

*NB. I think this mode of
mystification will be
effective.

Autumn is: the time of longings, the time of colors, the time of clouds, the time of sounds (sound is transmitted far more animatedly and swiftly than in the oppressive summer heat), the time of recollections.
—*JP* III 2840 (*Pap.* VII^1 B 205) *n.d.*, 1846

Addition to Pap. VII^1 B 205:

Long live autumn! There is only one glass of the champagne worth drinking, only one piece of the roast worth eating, at only one time is a girl worth loving, and there is only one girl worth this one time—and only autumn is *the season of the year.*—*JP* III 2841 (*Pap.* VII^1 B 206) *n.d.*, 1846

From draft of "Writings of a Young Man":

Eulogy on Autumn

by 5 persons

ending with a *tutti* [full orchestra].

To be used as a reply by
a humorous individual.

VII[1]
B 207
385

No. 2.

Autumn is the Time of Clouds.[69]

According to familiar Norse mythology, clouds are formed from the giant's brain.[70] And truly there is no better symbol for clouds than thoughts and no better symbol for thoughts than clouds—clouds are brain-weaving, and what else are thoughts? That is why we become weary of everything else but not of the clouds—in the autumn, which again is the time for reflecting. Long ago I wearily abandoned humankind, although I had or simply because I had made a thorough study of it. I began as a youth by loving older men—and grew bored with that. Then I loved somewhat older youth like myself and grew bored with that. Then came the young girls—and then matrons, undeniably the best, but it is sheer vanity, even when they are past their time as matrons. Weary, I turned away from humankind and humorously turned to those creatures that, unlike humankind, do not have the pretension of being the marvel of creation, but yet, perhaps for that very reason, are very entertaining because they do not pretend so much. I mean cows. And no doubt I made as many interesting acquaintances in the meadows as anywhere. I will never forget the dun-colored cow—the happy hours etc.— but yet I became bored with that.

VII[1]
B 207
386

But with the clouds—during autumn, never. They are scarcely recognizable, so changed are they, and he who never saw clouds during autumn has never seen them. In the winter it is too cold to see clouds—in the summer they are indolent and sleepy—but during autumn, dreaming (to be developed). —In the summer they stand still and are bored—in the autumn they hurry like vagabond dreams. In the summer it is as if they do not care to hang up there—in the autumn it is obvious that they support themselves in voluptuous floating. In the summer one cloud scarcely bothers to get out of the way of another. In the autumn they play with each other in jolly games, dodge each other, meet, separate, long for each other again, blend colors (as friends blend blood) with each other, become one, although the individuality of each cloud shines through.

Stand still, you who call yourself a thinker, and watch the clouds—during autumn. If you have ever thought about anything else before, then think again. Consider what you might wish to be—a human being? Such a thought could hardly occur to a human being. An angel? Tiresome! A tree? It takes too long and is too quiet. A cow? Too stolid a life. No—a cloud—in the autumn. Would I were that. The rest of the year I would stay hidden somewhere—or in nothingness, which could also be expressed in this way: I do not want to be, but every autumn I would like to live the one month.* In itself a cloud is a rather impressive thing (I would not want to be a little bitty mackerel cloud); I would like to be a large, shapely cloud. In spite of its size, a cloud is lightness itself, buoyant, and if it does not have a musical sense (but it does), it does have a sense of color—it knows how to bathe in colors.

VII[1]
B 207
387

To you, then, Autumn! With this glass I greet you, *recollecting* you, your profound and yet so fleeting thoughts, you, my best thoughts, whom we may completely appropriate without plagiarizing. When autumn comes, I leap into a carriage, pull the fur robe up over my head, put on a cap—showing only the eyes with which I can grasp at you. When the driver drives as fast as the horses can go (alas, alas, what is that compared with the clouds!), then it seems as if I had almost become a cloud.

In margin: Or I would live hidden as a thought until autumn; then I would become a cloud.

—JP III 2842 (Pap. VII[1] B 207) n.d., 1846

From draft of "Writings of a Young Man":

No. 3.

Autumn is the Time of **Sounds**.

If you imagined a trumpeter who has fallen asleep with the trumpet at his mouth, could you then say you heard anything? —How boring it must be to be an echo in the summertime. The suffocating air in the woods drives echo itself away. But in the autumn! Only then does echo hear the beloved's voice—everything is in love with echo, is only waiting to resonate. For autumn means elation. When you shout, answers come from myriads of places.—*JP* III 2843 (*Pap.* VII² B 208) *n.d.,* 1846

From draft of "Writings of a Young Man":

No. 4.

*Autumn is the Time of **Colors**.*

VII¹
B 209
388

What is color? That is, what is the meaning of color? Color is motion and disturbance made visible, just as sound is motion made audible. Everything characterized by immobility, repose, would therefore not have color. A mathematician would not color a triangle; summer is repose, serenity, is therefore colorless—the unremittingly blue heaven is certainly not color. For what is color? Color is contrast, but contrast is disturbance, movement; even if two contrasts stand ever so still directly opposite each other, the fact that they contrast is disturbance. Thus summer is repose. But then comes autumn, and with autumn come passions, and with passions disturbance, and with disturbance color, and with passion's disturbance the shifting and changing of colors. To change color is indeed the expression of disturbance, the disturbance of passions. And autumn changes colors. In contrast to summer, we may say the distinguishing feature of autumn is that it changes colors. If you say that autumn is a longer season and therefore this changing lasts some time, I reply: The contrasts during autumn are so intensely in motion every moment that it is like a continual shifting. It is impossible to see all the contrasts at once, and the change appears as one sees the same contrasts together with a new contrast and so on further.

The "dusky-hued autumn" is therefore not merely sad—it is heroic—since it is nature's doom, its battle for life. It bows under the annihilation—this is the sadness—but then again it is as if the delight of summer is momentarily remembered and echoed, but far more intensely, because the time is short.

Look—at your feet the straw withers; if you will look very carefully, you will see that every straw has its own color. Meanwhile the beech tree holds itself erect. It will not bow; it will not yield; it sadly shakes its head, but then it proudly shakes off the withered leaves again; it would rather have a few leaves that are not withered than all those withered ones. How curious it is that in the summertime no one really sees that a green leaf is green, sees what poetry there is in the green of summer, in all the green—it is almost like the greens one eats. But in the autumn! When the beech tree stands bare, with only one single green but freshly green leaf on its naked branch, then you see the color *green*, you see it by contrast.—*JP* III 2844 (*Pap.* VII[1] B 209) *n.d.*, 1846

VII[1]
B 209
389

From draft of "Writings of a Young Man":

No. 5.

Autumn is the Time of **Recollections**.

> N.B.—this discourse should be delivered in the purest and noblest spirit in order to form a contrast to the despair in others.

It is a familiar fact that the person who is an expert in the art of cooking knows how to make a delicacy out of even the most unpalatable ingredients. So it is with recollection; what it has prepared and served is delicious.

> N.B.—the tone must be raised a little or this does not come to have enough pathos.
> —*JP* III 2845 (*Pap.* VII[1] B 210) *n.d.*, 1846

From draft of "Writings of a Young Man":

> Rosenkilde as "Hummer"[71]
> A Recollection-Venture

by
A Grateful Person
—*Pap.* VIII^2 B 172 *n.d.,* 1847

Addition to Pap. VIII^2 B 172:

Introduction

I have many times thought about how thankless it is to be an actor—the mediocre criticism—to be developed.

this is a recollection-venture. It is at least 2 years since I last saw him as Hummer; during that time I have not wished to see him, lest my recollecting be disturbed by memory.[72]

—*Pap.* VIII^2 B 173 *n.d.,* 1847

Addition to Pap. VIII^2 B 172:

1. in the piece he is what one may call "the devilish" in the sense the simple person takes this word—not as the diabolical, but as a distinctive kind of plague.

   the simple person talks this way about rheumatism, that it is the devil of a bad thing.

2. his costume.

   leather breeches—umbrella—seems exaggerated—in summertime—is not. Hummer is a type, "a public figure," an eternal form, such a one must also be stereotypical in costume, designed for every season of the year because for him there is no season of the year—the glum and the comic in this—he does not have time to go home and fetch an umbrella, he everlastingly [*evigt*] goes about with an umbrella, *ad modum* [after the fashion of] the wandering [*evig*] Jew.

3. his mood.

   it is good-natured, almost obsequiously benevolent Therein lies the comic, because he himself is the arm of the law, *dira necessitas* [cruel constraint of necessity]. The contradiction in that the mood seems to betray sympathy, but he cannot; "the service is

VIII^2
B 174
273

VIII^2
B 174
274

strict." It is as if a guillotine could talk and said with good-natured benevolence: I cannot.—

Hummer is not malicious. He is roguishly sly, besides being good-natured—but is now so accustomed to being the *dira necessitas* that it has become a second nature to him. It is almost as if an executioner has become so accustomed to executing many people that he, objective as he has become, cannot understand the individual and therefore in all good nature says: It is nothing more than putting your head down on the block; then you are executed.

What can be so intensely pathos-filled, to have to be hard necessity despite all feelings and sympathies, is here superb low comedy, because Hummer is nothing short of an extraordinary man.

> His gesture in going down on his knees and parting his legs and then standing up again, a leap on his knees.[73]

—*Pap.* VIII[2] B 174 *n.d.*, 1847

X[2]
A 155
117

Prof. Martensen's Status

Well now, it is ten years since Prof. Martensen returned home from a journey abroad, brought with him the newest German philosophy,[74] and created quite a sensation with this novelty—he actually has always been more of a reporter and correspondent than a primitive thinker.

It was the philosophy of points of view—the corrupting aspect of the kind of survey—that fascinated young people and opened for them the prospect of having swallowed up everything in half a year.

He makes quite a splash, and in the meantime young students use the opportunity to inform the public in print that with Martensen begins a new era, epoch, epoch and era, etc. (*Note:* See the preface to *Philosophical Fragments*.[75]) The corrupting aspect of allowing young people to do this, thereby turning everything around.[76]

At the head of the Church there stood as its chief the man who still stands there unchanged, the admired Bishop of Sjælland[77] who, through a curious misunderstanding, is occasionally blamed for that which is his glory, because when one who is called and suited to govern actually will govern—that is something rightly praised.

Now Mynster is supposed to be weakened by opinion ("he is left standing on Jacobi"). (*Note:* See the little work *Prefaces,* no. [78])

According to opinion, Mynster also loses the battle over the principle of contradiction (*note:* see *Maanedsskrift for Litteratur*[79]) but exercises a still greater power through his personal brilliance.

Now a literary production begins: the pseudonymous works. By this time Victor Eremita[80] puts up his hand ethically with an aim at "the system." Johannes de Silentio[81] very definitely—and Mynster signals from above. Pseudonym follows pseudonym continually against the system up through Johannes Climacus.[82] The battle is in no way joined, but the terrain is surrounded. . . .

X²
A 155
118

—*Pap.* X² A 155 *n.d.,* 1849

EDITORIAL APPENDIX

ACKNOWLEDGMENTS

Preparation of manuscripts for *Kierkegaard's Writings* during the final phase is supported by a genuinely enabling grant from the National Endowment for the Humanities and gifts from the Danish Ministry of Cultural Affairs, the General Mills Foundation, Gilmore and Charlotte Schjeldahl, and the Vellux Foundation.

The translator-editor is grateful to the Board of Directors of Luther Seminary in Saint Paul, Minnesota, who authorized use of part of a sabbatical leave to complete the translation.

The learning and skill of Howard V. Hong and Edna H. Hong are evident on every page of this volume. Per Lønning, Wim R. Scholtens, and Sophia Scopetéa, members of the International Advisory Board for *Kierkegaard's Writings*, offered valuable criticism of the entire manuscript. Luther Seminary colleagues Roy A. Harrisville, Paul R. Sponheim, and Walter C. Sundberg commented on the "Historical Introduction," and Craig R. Koester gave advice on Greek and Latin passages. Nathaniel Hong, associate editor for *KW*, scrutinized the entire manuscript and prepared the electronic manuscript and index. Gretchen Oberfranc was the compositor.

Acknowledgment is made to Gyldendals Forlag for permission to absorb notes in *Søren Kierkegaards samlede Værker* and *Søren Kierkegaards Papirer*.

Inclusion in the Supplement of entries from *Søren Kierkegaard's Journals and Papers* is by arrangement with Indiana University Press.

The book collection and the microfilm collection of the Howard V. Hong and Edna H. Hong Kierkegaard Library, St. Olaf College, were used in preparation of the text, Supplement, and Editorial Appendix.

The volume was guided through the press by Marta Nussbaum Steele.

COLLATION OF *PREFACES*
IN THE DANISH EDITIONS OF
KIERKEGAARD'S COLLECTED WORKS

Vol. V Ed. 1 Pg.	Vol. V Ed. 2 Pg.	Vol. 5 Ed. 3 Pg.	Vol. V Ed. 1 Pg.	Vol. V Ed. 2 Pg.	Vol. 5 Ed. 3 Pg.
5	9	197	36	39	223
6	10	197	37	40	224
7	11	198	38	41	225
8	12	199	39	43	226
9	13	200	40	43	226
10	14	201	41	45	227
11	15	202	42	46	228
12	16	203	43	47	229
13	17	204	44	48	230
14	18	205	45	49	231
15	19	206	46	50	232
16	21	207	47	51	233
17	21	207	48	52	234
18	23	209	49	53	235
19	23	209	50	54	235
20	24	210	51	55	236
21	26	211	52	55	236
22	27	212	53	56	237
23	28	213	54	57	238
24	29	214	55	58	239
25	30	215	56	60	240
26	30	215	57	61	241
27	31	216	58	62	242
28	31	216	59	63	243
29	32	217	60	64	244
30	33	218	61	66	245
31	35	219	62	67	246
32	35	219	63	68	247
33	36	220	64	69	248
34	37	221	65	70	249
35	39	223	66	71	250

Vol. V Ed. 1 Pg.	Vol. V Ed. 2 Pg.	Vol. 5 Ed. 3 Pg.	Vol. V Ed. 1 Pg.	Vol. V Ed. 2 Pg.	Vol. 5 Ed. 3 Pg.
67	72	251	70	76	253
68	73	252	71	77	255
69	75	252			

NOTES

PREFACES

TITLE PAGE

TITLE PAGE. *"Light Reading."* In the final manuscript, the phrase was changed from "Curious Light Reading." See Supplement, p. 108 (*Pap.* V B 96:1).

Estates. The published form of the subtitle contains a reference to the traditional European concept of "estate" or "order." This may be, among other things, an echo of the subtitle of the *Haustafel* [Table of Duties] often appended to Martin Luther's *Small Catechism*: "consisting of certain passages of the Scriptures, selected for various estates and conditions of men [*pro omnibus sanctis ordinibus ac statibus* and *für allerlei heilige Orden und Stände*], by which they may be admonished to their respective duties." See *Catechismus Minor*, in *Libri Symbolici*, ed. Karl August v. Hase (Leipzig: 1837; *ASKB* 624), pp. 385–89; *Kleiner Katechismus*, in *Die Bekenntnisschriften der evangelisch-lutherischen Kirche*, 9 ed. (Göttingen: Vandenhoeck & Ruprecht, 1982), pp. 523–27; *Small Catechism*, in *The Book of Concord: The Confessions of the Evangelical Lutheran Church*, tr. and ed. Theodore G. Tappert et al. (Philadelphia: Fortress Press, 1959), pp. 354–56. Although not certainly but likely written by Luther himself, this *Haustafel* was early appended to the *Small Catechism* of 1530. Appended to the catechism's description of the privileges and duties of Christians in general, this collation of passages of Scripture described the duties of Christians in various estates or orders. In the generations after Luther, the *Haustafeln* were often greatly expanded. Kierkegaard, for example, knew this aspect of the Lutheran catechetical tradition as it appeared in Nikolai E. Balle, *Lærebog i den evangelisk-christelige Religion* (Copenhagen: 1824; *ASKB* 183), pp. 56–94, especially pages 87–88, which discuss the specific duties of husbands and wives. For mention of Balle's primer and illustration of its importance in the Christian nurture of Danish children in Kierkegaard's day, see *From the Papers of One Still Living*, p. 92, *KW* I (*SV* XIII 83); *Either/Or*, II, pp. 266–67, 270, 323, *KW* IV (*SV* II 239–40, 242, 290); *Stages*, p. 444, *KW* XI (*SV* VI 414); *Letters*, 195, p. 278, *KW* XXV. For an indication that in the period he worked on *Prefaces* Kierkegaard was pondering the relation of the "estates" or "orders" traditionally recognized in Lutheran theology and in European social thought of the day, see Supplement, p. 108 (*Pap.* V B 73), and p. 135 (*Pap.* VI B 213–14).

In Kierkegaard's Denmark, the term and concept "estate" also referred to the four consultative bodies or "Estates" (named for the cities where they met:

Itzehoe, Slesvig, Viborg, Roskilde) established by law in 1834 to advise the king and his government. The first estates were elected and appointed in 1835.

Nicolaus Notabene. The pseudonym is based on the scholar's marginal notation *NB* or *Notabene* [Note well]. Kierkegaard first considered this as a pseudonym for a project labeled simply "Idea" but did not develop it. See Supplement, p. 100 (*Pap.* IV A 119). Kierkegaard later considered Nicolaus Notabene as a pseudonym for the unfinished "New Year's Gift" and the unpublished "Writing Sampler." See Supplement, pp. 100–08, 127 (*Pap.* IV B 125–39; V A 99).

1. See Supplement, p. 108 (*Pap.* V B 73).

2. With reference to the remainder of the paragraph, see Supplement, p. 108 (*Pap.* V B 74:1).

3. The reference to beginning a system with nothing is an allusion to Georg Wilhelm Friedrich Hegel (1770–1831), who, in order to avoid starting his philosophy at an arbitrary point, attempted to reach behind all intellectual assumptions and arrive at what he claimed was a presuppositionless point of departure for philosophy. He saw this in the concept of being (*Sein*)—being, stripped of all intellectual definitions or conceptual distinguishing marks, hence pure and abstract and therefore also describable as "nothing" (*Nichts*). See, for example, *Postscript*, pp. 111–12, 113–15, *KW* XII.1 (*SV* VII 91, 93–94); *JP* III 3306 (*Pap.* VI A 145).

4. With reference to the following three sentences, see Supplement, p. 108 (*Pap.* V B 74:5).

5. See Horace, *Odes*, I, 9, 19. *Q. Horatii Flacci opera* (Leipzig, 1828; *ASKB* 1248), p. 11. *Horace the Odes and Epodes*, tr. C. E. Bennett (Loeb, New York: Putnam, 1930), pp. 28–29. The freely quoted text reads: "*lenesque sub noctem susurri* [low whispers at the trysting-hour as night draws on]." See *JP* V 5387 (*Pap.* II A 432).

6. See Supplement, p. 109 (*Pap.* V B 75:2, 5).

7. See Corsair *Affair*, Supplement, pp. 117–23, *KW* XIII, for an article in *Corsaren*, 278, January 16, 1846, col. 2–8, with a caustic commentary on Kierkegaard as a horseman and lampoons of Kierkegaard on horseback and of Kierkegaard on the shoulders of a woman with the caption "how you trained your girl" by cartoonist Peter Klæstrup.

8. Now a suburb of Copenhagen, Valby was then a rural area to the south and west of the city.

9. See, for example, *Johannes Climacus*, p. 148, *KW* VII (*Pap.* IV B 1 130); *JP* III 3065–67 (*Pap.* XI^1 A 195–96; XI^2 A 210).

10. "Snowdrop and winter fool [*Sommergæk og Vinternar*]" was the first line of one form of a verse sent anonymously to a friend before Easter. The letter (*Gækkebrev*, letter that fools or deceives) also contained a snowdrop and was clipped or pricked and folded in various patterns. The receiver had to guess the name of the sender before Easter. The custom continues to the present day. See

"Another Defense," *Early Polemical Writings*, p. 5, *KW* I (*SV* XIII 8). In *Prefaces* (*en gjæk i Vinteren og en Nar i Sommeren*), the terms, in their separate elemental meanings, are reversed.

11. With reference to the following eight paragraphs, see Supplement, pp. 109–13 (*Pap.* V B 76, 78).

12. A reference to the official form of the royal censor's permission to publish a book.

13. Jens Baggesen, "*Kallundborgs Krønike eller Censurens Oprindelse,*" *Danske Værker*, I–XII (Copenhagen 1827–32; *ASKB* 1509–20), I, p. 245. The poem includes the line: "Because the course of justice is very long."

14. Cf. Luke 15:11–32.

15. Belshazzar, son of Nebuchadnezzar. See Daniel 4:5 and 5:5–24.

16. The elder Cato (234–149 B.C.) was accustomed to conclude his speeches in the Roman senate with "*Ceterum* [or *Præterea censeo*] *Carthaginem esse delendam* [Furthermore I am of the opinion that Carthage must be destroyed]. See Plutarch, "Marcus Cato," *Lives*, II, 27; *Plutarks Levnetsbeskrivelser*, I–IV, tr. Stephan Tetens (Copenhagen: 1800–11; *ASKB* 1197–1200), II, p. 458; *Plutarch's Lives*, I–XI, tr. Bernadotte Perrin (Loeb, Cambridge: Harvard University Press, 1914–26), II, 27, p. 383.

17. See Ludvig Holberg, *Jacob von Tyboe*, III, 4, *Den Danske Skue-Plads*, I–VII (Copenhagen: 1788; *ASKB* 1566–67), II, no pagination. *Ubi predicamentale* [the where predicative] and *ubi transcendentale* [the where transcendental] are logical categories referring respectively to particular places and to places in empty space or beyond the known world. In Holberg's play the character Magister Stygotius ridicules academics who are unable to distinguish these categories.

18. For centuries prior to the Second Vatican Council (1962–65), the Roman Catholic mass was normally recited in Latin.

19. See Genesis 2:24. The official liturgy for the marriage service in the Church of Denmark prescribed the use of Matthew 19:3–6 for weddings taking place on weekdays. See *Forordnet Alterbog for Danmark* (Copenhagen: 1830; *ASKB* 381), pp. 262–63.

20. See note 1 above.

21. An enclitic is a word that usually loses its accent in being attached closely to another word and hence is pronounced in rapid succession, as "not" in "cannot."

22. See Ecclesiastes 12:13.

23. See Terence, *Andria*, 555; *Andria Selvplageren og Formio; tre latinske Skuespil af Publius Terentsius Aser*, tr. and ed. Mathias Rathje (Copenhagen: 1797; *ASKB* 1295), p. 63; *The Lady of Andros, Terence*, I–II, tr. J. Sargeaunt (Loeb, Cambridge: Harvard University Press, 1936), I, pp. 60–61. The freely quoted text reads *amantium ira amoris integratiost* [lovers' quarrels are love renewed].

24. Cf. I Thessalonians 5:18.

25. With reference to the following five paragraphs, Supplement, pp. 101–02, 104–06 (*Pap.* IV B 127, 134, 135).

26. Elaborate New Year's annuals were often produced and purchased for

presentation as Christmas gifts in nineteenth-century Denmark. See *Two Ages*, p. 17, *KW* XIV (*SV* VIII 16).

27. Holberg, *Ulysses von Ithaca*, II, 3, *Danske Skue-Plads*, III, no pagination. Holophernes in this play teaches soldiers to march in step by beating time on their cartridge pouches.

28. See, for example, *Either/Or*, I, p. 140, *KW* III (*SV* I 119); *Stages*, pp. 11, 340, 493, *KW* XI (*SV* VI 17, 318, 458).

29. Holberg, *Barselstuen*, III, 5, *Danske Skue-Plads*, II, no pagination. Holberg's character Maren Amme can produce two voices at once.

30. Kierkegaard here uses the word to refer to New Year's books purchased to be given as gifts. In Kierkegaard's polemical mode, the term *nitid* often implies an allusion to J. L. Heiberg.

Urania: Aarbog for 1844 was printed on good paper stock, with each page surrounded by a black border; its binding was ornamented with gilt decoration. It included a "Star Calendar for 1844" and an essay on the astronomical year by J. L. Heiberg, along with contributions by such Danish notables as theologian Hans Lassen Martensen, poet Christian Winther, and writer Thomasine Christine Gyllembourg-Ehrensvärd.

31. In Norse mythology Frey was the god of crops, fruitfulness, and prosperity. Frey possessed a golden bristled boar, Gullin-bursti, given to him by the dwarfs to draw his chariot.

32. See *Hamlet*, III, 3; *Shakspeare's dramatische Werke*, I–XII, tr. August Wilhelm v. Schlegel and Johann Ludvig Tieck (Berlin: 1839–41; *ASKB* 1883–88), VI, p. 79; *The Complete Works of Shakespeare*, ed. George Lyman Kittredge (Boston: Ginn, 1936), p. 1172. Schlegel and Tieck translated "these pickers and stealers" as *Diebeszangen*. See *Postscript*, p. 514, *KW* XII.1 (*SV* VII 447).

33. See Genesis 24:9; 47:29.

34. Johan Ludvig Heiberg, in *Perseus, Journal for den speculative Idee*, II, 1838 (*ASKB* 569), p. 3 (without page number), speaks of "the first contribution to the execution of a long held plan," the first twenty-three paragraphs of "The Logical System," and of his "intention, on the basis of this presentation and its continuation, to prepare the way for the Esthetics that it has long been his wish to present." See *Repetition*, Supplement, pp. 283–300, *KW* VI (*Pap.* IV B 110–11, 116).

35. See *Two Ages*, p. 70, *KW* XIV (*SV* VIII 67).

36. In Danish, a *Præsenteer-Bakke* is a serving platter; the word can also be used to mean "in public view." In its former sense it establishes the context for the reference to a "plate" [*Tallerken*] that occurs later in the paragraph.

37. A conflation of the account in Plutarch of the barber who spread the word of the defeat in Sicily (413 B.C.) and the legend of the runner who fell dead after bringing the news to Athens of the victory at Marathon (490 B.C.). See Plutarch, "Nicias," 30, *Lives*; Loeb, III, pp. 309–11. See also *Fragments*, p. 106, *KW* VII (*SV* IV 268).

38. Kierkegaard knew of the newly constructed synagogue on *Krystalgade* in

Copenhagen. The reference here, however, is more likely to a popular restaurant favored by the intelligentsia, Mimi's Cafe.

39. Carl Andreas Reitzel (1789–1853) operated a bookstore and was the publisher of many of Kierkegaard's books. The bookstore and publishing house under his name continue to the present day.

40. In controversy with the Donatist sect, Augustine of Hippo (354–430) drew a distinction between the visible and the invisible Church. The visible Church, Augustine taught, always remains a mixed body (*corpus permixtum*) of sinners and saints. The invisible Church includes only the saints, the justified elect who truly belong to Christ and are his body.

41. See Supplement, pp. 113–14 (*Pap.* V B 80:2).

42. A street in Copenhagen.

43. The reference to Anacharsis appears in Diogenes Laertius, *Lives of Eminent Philosophers*, I, 103; *Diogenis Lærtii de vitis philosophorum*, I–II (Leipzig: 1833; *ASKB* 1109), I, pp. 49–59; *Diogen Laërtses filosofiske Historie*, I–II, tr. Børge Riisbrigh (Copenhagen: 1812; *ASKB* 1110–11), I, pp. 46–47; Diogenes Laertius, *Lives of Eminent Philosophers*, I–II, tr. R. D. Hicks (Loeb, New York: Putnam, 1925), I, pp. 104–11.

44. Danish orthography of the period varied for this sound.

45. With reference to the following two sentences, see Supplement, p. 114 (*Pap.* V B 80:3). The allusion is to the method described by René Descartes and current in the philosophy of the day that truth can be achieved only by beginning with doubt. In Kierkegaard's view, doubt cannot be conquered by knowledge, since reflection is an infinite process unless broken off by an act of the will. Against the misuse of the Cartesian *de omnibus dubitandum est*, Kierkegaard also wrote *Johannes Climacus*, *KW* VII (*Pap.* IV B 1–17).

46. It was a Shrovetide custom for riders on horseback to tilt at a suspended barrel containing a cat. See *Two Ages*, p. 110, *KW* XIV (*SV* VIII 102).

47. With reference to the remainder of the sentence and the following sentence, see Supplement, p. 114 (*Pap.* V B 80:4).

48. One Morten Frederiksen, the Danish "master thief," while imprisoned in Roskilde fashioned a leg out of cloth and straw, and the guards, thinking it was his leg, put a chain around it, whereupon he escaped (November 23, 1812).

49. Holberg, *Barselstuen*, *Danske Skue-Plads*, II, no pagination.

50. The woman confined for delivery in *Barselstuen* was originally played by a male actor.

51. A reference to cultural arbiter Johan Ludvig Heiberg (1791–1860). Heiberg's diverse interests included, among other things, literary criticism, the theater, poetry, philosophy, politics, and astronomy.

52. See Luke 15:11–32. J. L. Heiberg reviewed *Either/Or* rather critically in "*Literaire Vintersæd*," *Intelligensblade*, 24, March 1, 1843. Kierkegaard replied in *Fædrelandet*, 1168, March 5, 1843. See "A Word of Thanks to Professor Heiberg," *Corsair Affair*, pp. 17–21, *KW* XIII (*SV* XIII 411–15). See also *Either/Or*, Supplement, II, pp. 406–07, *KW* IV (*Pap.* IV B 54).

53. J. L. Heiberg edited *Kjøbenhavns flyvende Post* from 1827 to 1830 and from 1834 to 1837 (*Interimsblade*).

54. "The Rope Is Burning" is a Danish version of "Hunt the Thimble." The object hunted is a piece of rope. Whether the hunter is "warm" or "cold" is reported by the other players. In this context Kierkegaard also plays on the double meaning of "rope" as "lash."

55. See *Hamlet*, III, 1, Schlegel and Tieck, VI, pp. 61–67; Kittredge, p. 1172.

56. Herr Klatterup is a figure in Heiberg's *Recentsen og Dyret, Skuespil af Johan Ludvig Heiberg*, I-VII (Copenhagen: 1833–36; *ASKB* 1553–59), III, 27, pp. 274–85.

57. With reference to the following four sentences, see Supplement, p. 114 (*Pap.* V B 81).

58. See J. L. Heiberg's New Year's book, *Urania: Aarbog for 1844* (Copenhagen: 1843; *ASKB U* 57), pp. 94–102, in which the author discusses for his own purposes passages and concepts from Kierkegaard's *Repetition*. Kierkegaard wrote replies to Heiberg but did not publish them. See *Repetition*, Supplement, pp. 283–319 (*Pap.* IV B 110–117), and pp. 379–83, note 14, *KW* VI.

59. With reference to the remainder of the paragraph, see Supplement, p. 115 (*Pap.* V B 83).

60. See Supplement, p. 114 (*Pap.* V B 81) and *Either/Or*, Supplement, II, p. 412, *KW* IV (*Pap.* IV A 167).

61. In *Intelligensblade*, 44, February 1, 1844, p. 231, J. L. Heiberg designated his *Urania* as a "New Year's gift intended for the esthetically cultured public." The same article (p. 236) thanks "the reading public" for its kind reception of *Urania: Aarbog for 1844*.

62. In the currency of the day, one *Rigsdaler* was equivalent to 16 marks or 96 shillings.

63. With reference to the following paragraph, see Supplement, p. 99 (*Pap.* IV B 117, p. 281).

64. See note 30 above.

65. *Kjøbenhavns Kgl. Adressecomptoirs alene privilegerede Efterretninger* [*Adresseavisen*], the oldest Danish advertising paper, dating back to the eighteenth century.

66. This is a reference to Hans Peter Holst (1811–1893), teacher of Danish in the *Efterslægtskabets Skole*, editor of *Ny Portefeuille* until April 1, 1843, and author of *Ude og Hjemme. Reise-Erindringer* (Copenhagen: 1842; *ASKB* 1569). See *Either/Or*, Supplement, II, pp. 405–06, *KW* IV (*Pap.* IV B 48, 51).

67. J. L. Heiberg, *Kong Salomon og Jørgen Hattemager, Skuespil*, II, 13, pp. 345–51. In Heiberg's play, Salomon Goldkalb, a Jewish merchant, is mistaken for the Baron Goldkalb. See *Fragments*, p. 6, *KW* VII (*SV* IV 176). See Matthew 6:29.

68. See Supplement, p. 117 (*Pap.* V B 89); *Either/Or*, Supplement, II, pp. 403–04 *KW* IV (*Pap.* IV B 45, 46).

69. See Supplement, p. 117 (*Pap.* V B 85:4). See J. L. Heiberg, "*Litteraire Vintersæd*," *Intelligensblade*, 24, March 1, 1843, pp. 288–92, for comments on

how "one" will evaluate *Either/Or*. See also *Either/Or*, Supplement, II, p. 406, *KW* IV (*Pap.* IV B 51).

70. See Mark 9:2–8; Matthew 17:1–8; Luke 9:28–36.

71. See Supplement, p. 132 (*Pap.* VI B 204).

72. An allusion to the character of Oldfux in Holberg, *Den Stundesløse*, II, 10, *Danske Skue-Plads*, V, no pagination; *The Fussy Man, Four Plays by Holberg*, tr. Henry Alexander (Princeton: Princeton University Press for the American Scandinavian Foundation, 1946), p. 26. See also *Either/Or*, Supplement, II, p. 406, *KW* IV (*Pap.* IV B 53).

73. J. L. Heiberg, in *Urania: Aarbog for 1844*, p. 122, speaks of the age as "depressed." Prior to this (p. 119) Heiberg recommends consorting with nature, and especially the stars, as a remedy against this depression. See p. 137.

74. Probably a reference to and play on the name of councilor Rasmus Stiernholm, a representative of *Det forenede Velgjørenhedsselskab* [The United Welfare Association]. See *Repetition*, Supplement, pp. 284–85, notes 33 and 41, *KW* VI (*Pap.* IV B 110).

75. Regarding J. L. Heiberg's long-contemplated plans, see note 34 above.

76. J. L. Heiberg was a devoted amateur astronomer with an observatory in his home on Christianshavn. See Heiberg, *Urania: Aarbog for 1844*, pp. 129–60, for discussion of whether stars and planets are inhabited. See also *Stages*, p. 172, *KW* XI (*SV* VI 164).

77. A reference to Nikolai Frederik Severin Grundtvig (1738–1872), Danish pastor, bishop, hymnist, poet, historian, educator, politician, and advocate of folk traditions. In seeking to defend the Christian faith against rationalist attack, Grundtvig claimed to have discovered that the Living Word of God, as distinct from the written word of Scripture, speaks through the Church in the Apostles' Creed when used in the baptismal liturgy. Later Grundtvig amplified his claim for this "matchless discovery" by contending that Jesus had delivered the words of the Apostles' Creed to the disciples in the forty days after the Resurrection and before the Ascension. For the hyperbolic use of the term "matchless," see, for example, Grundtvig's review of Jakob Peter Mynster's *Om Begrebet af den christelige Dogmatik* in *Maanedsskrift for Christendom og Historie*, ed. Jacob Christian Lindberg, I, 1831, p. 609 (ed. tr.):

> What I nevertheless in the most urgent way must and will *request* of him, as well as of all *Christian* pastors and theologians in Denmark and Norway, is only that they will give my explication of the independent universal validity of the expression of faith the keen and kindly disposed attention undeniably deserved by a discovery that promises to Christ's kingdom on earth an amendment of its bonds and opens the brightest prospects, not only of victory over all enemies but of an increasing enlightenment and free development of powers the world will be compelled to call matchless.

For another use of "matchless," see Grundtvig, "*Blik paa Kirken i det første Aarhundrede*," *Theologisk Maanedsskrift*, ed. Andreas Gottlob Rudelbach, X, 1827, pp. 2–4. See also *Postscript*, pp. 34–46, *KW* XII.1 (*SV* VII 23–34).

78. In *Urania: Aarbog for 1844*, p. 147, J. L. Heiberg asserted that the earth occupied a "very respectable position" among the planets.

79. A reference to J. L. Heiberg's *En Sjæl efter Døden*, in *Nye Digte* (Copenhagen: 1841; *ASKB* 1562), pp. 29–158, and to Hans Lassen Martensen (1808–1884), who reviewed Heiberg's poem ("a divine comedy in miniature") in *Fædrelandet*, 398, January 10, 1841, col. 3217. See also *Postscript*, p. 171, *KW* XII.1 (*SV* VII 142).

80. A reference to J. L. Heiberg's review of Waldemar Henrik Rothe's work of 1836 on the Trinity and the Atonement, *Læren om Treenighed og Forsoning: Et spekulativt Forsøg i Anledning af Reformationsfesten* (Copenhagen: 1836; *ASKB* 746). See *"Recension over Hr. Dr. Rothe's Treenigheds- og Forsoningslære,"* *Perseus*, I, 1837, pp. 1–89. In his review, Heiberg argues the necessity of a philosophical approach to theology.

81. See Holberg, *Den Stundesløse*, I, 9, *Danske Skue-Plads*, V, no pagination; Alexander, pp. 16–21. Pernille, the maid of the principal character Vielgeschrey [*den Stundesløse*, the busy trifler], plays on his absentmindedness and busy trifling to permit the marriage of his daughter to her lover rather than to the bookkeeper Vielgeschrey has chosen for her.

82. A play that originally appeared in 1817 and was later published in *Skuespil*, I, pp. 197–376.

83. With reference to the following paragraph, see Supplement, p. 118 (*Pap.* V B 85:7).

84. The *Maadeholds Forening* of Copenhagen was founded on October 8, 1843, after the issuance of a public declaration of its purposes. On January 6, 1844, the newspaper *Fædrelandet* carried a bombastic article, "A Few Words about the Opponents of the Temperance Cause. Open letter to the members of the Temperance and Abstinence Union." The article spoke of "our intention, through *united* power, through *association*, to influence others," of "our lofty endeavor to restore, if possible, an errant unfortunate to society and to the family, a lost soul to God and to virtue," and of "the great and extremely important influence of the spirit of association," etc. On the principle of association, see *Two Ages*, pp. 106–08, *KW* XIV (*SV* VIII 99–100).

85. See Revelation 3:16.

86. See Supplement, p. 118 (*Pap.* V B 93:1). The text gives *skandinaviske Samfund*, but Kierkegaard probably has in mind *Det skandinaviske Selskab*, organized in 1843 as the successor to *Det skandinaviske Samfund*, which had been banned by the government.

87. Cf. Matthew 5:46–47; Luke 6:32–34.

88. See Luke 17:10.

89. See Matthew 11:12.

90. See Psalm 104:15.

91. See Horace, *Odes*, III, 25, 1; *Opera*, p. 96; Loeb, pp. 258–59.

92. A reference to a literary controversy between Hans Peter Kofoed-Hansen and Jakob Peter Mynster. In a review of *Either/Or*, Kofoed-Hansen had accused the Danish Church of alienating the cultured by its lack of philosophical

sophistication. See *Fyenske Fierdingsaarsskrivt for Literatur og Kritik*, IV, I, 1843, pp. 384–85. Mynster replied, citing works of Kierkegaard as examples of philosophically sophisticated presentations of Christian faith. See Kts, "*Kirkelig Polemik*," *Intelligensblade*, ed. J. L. Heiberg, IV, 41–42, January 1, 1844, pp. 97–114. "Kts" was Mynster's pseudonym, formed from the initial consonant of the second syllable of each name (Ja*k*ob Pe*t*er Myn*s*ter).

The phrase "the cultured" [*de dannede*] also has a broader reference. It was a slogan claimed by both liberal reformers and the politically conservative during the period of revolution and constitutional reform in Denmark.

93. Jakob Peter Mynster (1775–1854) was a leading Danish pastor and, from 1834 until his death, Bishop of Sjælland and primate of the Danish Church. An ardent advocate of the established order and of the legal establishment of the Danish Lutheran Church, Mynster was renowned as a preacher and revered by many as an example of convinced, personal Christianity. As a youth, Kierkegaard often went with his family to hear Mynster's sermons and heard them read aloud in their home by his father. As an adult, Kierkegaard continued to be among Mynster's auditors and readers. Kierkegaard here refers to Mynster's *Prædikener paa alle Søn- og Hellig-Dage i Aaret*, I–II (Copenhagen: 1837; *ASKB* 229–30). For Kierkegaard's reflections on Mynster's sermons in the late 1840s, see, for example, *JP* V 6064, 6070, 6073 (*Pap.* VIII^1 A 366, 388, 397).

94. See Supplement, pp. 162–63 (*Pap.* X^2 A 155, *n.d.*, 1849) for later mention of J. P. Mynster with reference to this section of *Prefaces*.

95. Mynster, "*Andagtstimernes Bestemmelse og Værd*," and "*At vi ikke skulle forarges*," *Prædikener*, I, pp. 1–14, and II, pp. 416–29.

96. An untranslatable play on *oplægge paa ny*, which means both "to lay up again" and "to reprint."

97. Popular literature of the day often bore the inscription "Printed this year!"

98. See *For Self-Examination*, p. 36, *KW* XXI (*SV* XII 324).

99. In his programmatic essay, *Om Philosophiens Betydning for den nuværende Tid* (Copenhagen:'1833; *ASKB* 568), p. 16, J. L. Heiberg asserts, "We must confess that in our time religion is for the most part a matter for those without culture, while for the cultured it belongs in the realm of the past and the by-gone." See also "Another Defense of Woman's Great Abilities," *Early Polemical Writings*, p. 4, *KW* I (*SV* XIII 7), and note 15, pp. 230–31.

100. See J. L. Heiberg, *En Sjæl efter Døden*, *Nye Digte*, p. 113, in which "The Poet" speaks of an unbelief tearing him from the breast of the Church and of a longing for the congregation that thus resonates through his work.

101. Historians of religion often associate early Christianity with urban centers and resistant paganism with rural areas. The term *pagan* itself referred originally to the "villager" or "rustic."

102. With reference to "Preface VII," see Supplement, p. 118 (*Pap.* V B 47, 71). This section of *Prefaces* was originally intended to serve as the preface for *The Concept of Anxiety*. It was written on a different kind of paper than the rest of the manuscript of *Prefaces* and paginated with Roman numerals I–XI.

103. See Holberg, *Hexerie Eller Blind Alarm*, III, 3, *Danske Skue-Plads*, I, no pagination. The specific phrase does not occur.

104. "Mediation" is the Latin, Danish, and English version of the German *Vermittlung*. See, for example, Hegel's *Wissenschaft der Logik*, *Werke*, III, pp. 100, 105, 110; IV, p. 75; *Jubiläumsausgabe* [*J.A.*], I-XXVI, ed. Hermann Glockner (Stuttgart: Frommann, 1927–40), IV, pp. 110, 115, 120, 553; *Hegel's Science of Logic* (tr. of *W. L.*, Lasson ed., 1923; Kierkegaard had 2 ed., 1833), tr. A. V. Miller (London: Allen and Unwin; New York: Humanities Press, 1969), pp. 99, 103, 107, 445; *Encyclopädie der philosophischen Wissenschaften, Erster Theil, Die Logik*, para. 65, 70, *Werke*, VI, pp. 133–34, 138; *J.A.*, VIII, pp. 171–72, 176; *Hegel's Logic* (tr. of *E. W.*, 3 ed., 1830; Kierkegaard's ed., 1840, had the same text), tr. William Wallace (Oxford: Clarendon Press, 1975), pp. 101, 105; *Anxiety*, pp. 81–93, *KW* VIII (*SV* IV 350–63). See *JP* II 1578; III 3072, 3294 (*Pap.* II A 454; III A 108; IV A 54).

105. An area in Dyrehaven or Deer Park, north of Copenhagen, known as Dyrehavsbakken, was and still is the site of a carnival-like amusement park.

106. See Supplement, pp. 97–98 (*Pap.* II A 808); "Literary Quicksilver or A Venture in the Higher Lunacy," Corsair *Affair*, pp. 73–74, *KW* XIII (*SV* XIII 471–72).

107. See Genesis 6–10:1. Noah is a "bifrontal" character as the sole survivor of the flood and progenitor of succeeding generations.

108. The phrase is borrowed from medieval sacramental theology. The *opus operatum*, a sacramental act efficient in and of itself, is contrasted with the *opus operans* [act in doing] and the *opus operantis* [act of the doer]. Roman Catholic theology thus argues that the sacrament is effective *ex opere operato*, as an act properly intended and done, without respect to the qualities of the administrant or recipient.

109. A drinking song in a collection by the Danish pastor and historian of literature, Albert Thura, *Adskillige Betænkninger og Indfald paa Vers* (Copenhagen: 1726), 32, includes the chorus: "Round, round, round as decently and joyfully we put the glass to our mouths." The song was intended to be sung "at the request of a good friend, in pleasant company, with a glass of wine." A similar phrase occurs in Holberg, *Jacob von Tyboe*, IV, 5, *Danske Skue-Plads*, III, no pagination.

110. See Supplement, p. 119 (*Pap.* V B 96:8).

111. See *Either/Or*, II, p. 99, *KW* IV (*SV* II 91).

112. See Supplement, p. 119 (*Pap.* V B 96:9). The reference is to J. L. Heiberg.

113. See Supplement, p. 119 (*Pap.* V B 96:11). The reference here is to Rasmus Nielsen, *Den speculative Logik i dens Grundtræk*, I-IV (Copenhagen: 1841–42), I, p. 35, in which Nielsen describes his effort as a "fragment of a philosophical methodology."

114. See *Two Ages*, p. 70, *KW* XIV (*SV* VIII 67).

115. See Supplement, p. 119 (*Pap.* V B 96:12). The reference is to Peter Michael Stilling, *Philosophiske Betragtninger over den speculative Logiks Betydning for*

Videnskaben, i Anledning af Prof. R. Nielsens: "Den spekulative Logik i dens Grundtræk" (Copenhagen: 1842), in which Stilling describes Nielsen's effort as introductory and propaedeutic.

116. *Timon of Athens*, V, 1. See Schlegel and Tieck, VII, p. 373; Kittredge, p. 1073. Schlegel and Tieck render the phrase *"ist die That des Wortes"* rather than *"ist die Bethätigung des Wortes."*

117. For continuation of the text, see Supplement, p. 119 (*Pap.* V B 96:13).

118. See *Anxiety*, p. 7, *KW* VIII (*SV* IV 279).

119. See Cicero, *Letters to Atticus*, IV, 18; *M. Tullii Ciceronis opera omnia*, ed. J. A. Ernesti, 2 ed., I–IV (Halle: 1756–57; *ASKB* 1224–29), *Epist. ad Atticum*, III, p. 601; *Letters to Atticus*, tr. E. O. Winstedt, I–III (Loeb, New York: Putnam, 1920–25), I, pp. 327–39. The freely quoted text reads *succum ac sanguinem.*

120. Cf. Hebrews 4:15. The Greek text of Hebrews has ἡμῶν [our] instead of τῶν νθρώπων [of humans].

121. See Numbers 22:28–30.

122. Perhaps a reference to Achim v. Arnim, *Bertholds Erstes und Zweites Lebens* (Berlin: 1817).

123. Socrates. See Supplement, p. 119 (*Pap.* V B 96:14). See also Diogenes Laertius, *Lives*, II, 21; *Vitis*, I, pp. 70–71; Riisbrigh, I, pp. 66; Loeb, I, pp. 150–51.

124. It was the custom in rural Denmark for young people to begin May celebrations by marching a green tree into town.

125. Perhaps a reference to Til Eulenspiegel, a peasant clown in northern Germany in the fourteenth or fifteenth century. See, for example, *Irony*, p. 34, *KW* II (*SV* XIII 130); *JP* V 5082, 5110 (*Pap.* I A 51, C 61). Kierkegaard's library also contained *En ganske ny og lystig Historie om Ulspils Overmand Eller Robertus von Agerkaal* (Copenhagen: 1724; *ASKB* 1467); *Underlig og selsom Historie, Om Tiile Ugelspegel* (Copenhagen: 1701; *ASKB* 1469). For the analogy of the knot, see, for example, *Sickness Unto Death*, p. 93, *KW* XIX (*SV* XI 204); *For Self-Examination*, p. 196, *KW* XXI (*SV* XII 464).

126. See *JP* II 1451; V 5726 (*Pap.* XI² A 171; V B 47:13) for this crucial metaphor, an epitomization of Kierkegaard's authorship.

127. An allusion to Holberg, *Gert Westphaler*, 7 ("*Trapezund eller Catte-zund*"); *Gert Westphaler* (original version), II, 3: "*Bordeus* [Bordeaux] *og Røven* [Rouen] . . . *Trapezund eller Catesund.*" See *Postscript*, p. 287, *KW* XII.1 (*SV* VII 246).

128. The Danish term *Ophævelse* is a play on G.W.F. Hegel's use of *Aufhebung* and *aufheben* (the dialectic of contradiction and mediation). The Danish *Ophævelse* together with the verb *gøre* [to make] means to make much ado, a to-do, a fuss, a disturbance, a commotion. See *Irony*, pp. 257–58, *KW* II (*SV* XIII 332); *Repetition*, p. 186, *KW* VI (*SV* III 121); *Postscript*, pp. 51, 89, 364, *KW* XII.1 (*SV* VII 38, 69, 315); "That Single Individual," *Point of View*, *KW* XXII (*SV* XIII 609); *JP* II 1574 (*Pap.* II A 766).

129. Diogenes Laertius, *Lives*, II, 5; *Vitis*, I, p. 77; Riisbrigh, I, p. 73; Loeb, I, pp. 166–67.

130. In the Dano-Norwegian Lutheran tradition in the nineteenth century, children were catechized while standing on the floor of the nave before the gates to the chancel.

131. This is probably a reference to Danish Hegelians, notably J. L. Heiberg and Hans Lassen Martensen. Heiberg had aligned himself with this movement through his *Om Philosophiens Betydning for den nuværende Tid* in *Perseus, Journal for den speculative Idee*; *Intelligensblade*, 1–48 (1842–44). Martensen reviewed Heiberg's *Indlednings Foredrag til det i Novbr. 1834 begyndte logiske Kursus* in *Maanedsskrift for Litteratur*, XVI, 1836, pp. 515–28. During a two-year European study tour (1832–34), Martensen read Hegel's works and studied with the foremost Hegelian speculative theologian, Carl Daub.

132. See J. L. Heiberg, "*Recension over Hr. Dr. Rothes Treenigheds- og Forsoningslære*," *Perseus*, I, 1837, pp. 35–41.

133. *Amo* is the first person present indicative of the verb *amare* [to love]; *amavi* is the first person perfect indicative; *amatum* is the perfect passive participle. This word is traditionally used to teach the verbal forms of the first Latin conjugation. See *Repetition*, Supplement, p. 319, *KW* VI (*Pap.* IV B 117).

134. From a letter of Johann Georg Hamann to Johan Gottfried Herder, February 6, 1785, *Hamann's Schriften*, I-VIII, ed. Friedrich Roth and G. A. Wiener (Berlin, Leipzig: 1821–43; *ASKB* 536–44), VII, p. 205.

135. See Supplement, p. 120 (*Pap.* V B 96:17).

136. Horace, *Satires*, II, 5, 59–60; *Q. Horatii Flacci opera* (Leipzig: 1828; *ASKB* 1248), p. 211; *Satires, Epistles and Ars Poetica*, tr. H. Rushton Fairclough (Loeb, New York: Putnam, 1929), pp. 202–03. The freely quoted text reads: "Whatever I say will or will not be; for prophecy is great Apollo's gift to me." See *Two Ages*, p. 106, *KW* XIV (*SV* VIII 98–99).

137. Kierkegaard appears to have seriously considered publishing such a journal. For a preliminary sketch, see Supplement, p. 100 (*Pap.* V A 100).

138. See Holberg, *Mester Gert Westphaler i fem Acter*, I, 3, *L. Holbergs Comedier*, I-VII, ed. A. E. Boye (Copenhagen: 1824–32), VII, p. 25, in which Gert says, "How did it go with Arius when he set himself up against his bishop?" Arius (d. 336), a priest of Alexandria, propounded a heretical Christology and was deposed by his bishop, Alexander of Alexandria.

139. I of *Perseus* appeared in June 1837 and II in August 1838.

140. In 1834 and 1836, the young Kierkegaard occasionally wrote for Heiberg's *Kjøbenhavns flyvende Post*. See "Another Defense of Woman's Great Abilities," in *Early Polemical Writings*, pp. 3–5, *KW* I (*SV* XIII 5–8); "The Morning Observations," pp. 6–11, *KW* I (*SV* XIII 9–15); "On the Polemic of *Fædrelandet*," pp. 12–23, *KW* I (*SV* XIII 16–27); "To Mr. Orla Lehmann," pp. 24–34, *KW* I (*SV* XIII 28–39).

141. See *Perseus*, II, 1838, pp. v-viii, for a list of its 133 subscribers, including Søren Kierkegaard. The only two issues of the journal to appear included six articles, four by Heiberg himself, one by Hans Lassen Martensen, and one by Carl Weis.

142. See Supplement, p. 120 (*Pap.* V B 96:18).

143. See Diogenes Laertius, *Lives*, IX, 69–70 and 74–75; *Vitis*, II, pp. 163–64, 166; Riisbrigh, I, pp. 432–33, 435; Loeb, II, 482–83, 488–89. See also, for example, *Fragments*, pp. 82–85, *KW* VII (*SV* IV 245–48). See also *JP* I 777 (*Pap.* IV B 13:21).

144. This is the theme of Kierkegaard's *Johannes Climacus, KW* VII (*Pap.* IV B 1–17).

145. See, for example, *Johannes Climacus*, pp. 133–36, *KW* VII (*Pap.* IV B 1, pp. 116–19).

146. See I Timothy 2:4.

147. See Philippians 2:5–9.

148. J. L. Heiberg, "*Recension over Hr. Dr. Rothes Treenigheds- og Forsoningslære,*" *Perseus*, I, 1837, p. 11, had called the development of a "speculative theology an unavoidable necessity."

149. See Adam Gottlob Oehlenschläger, *Palnatoke,* IV, *Oehlenschlägers Tragødier*, I–X (Copenhagen: 1841–49; *ASKB* 1601–05), II, pp. 271–72.

150. Ibid. The page of King Harald Bluetooth asks to see the king clothed in his coronation robes before he agrees to commit a murder for the king. The king, whose royal garments hang side by side with his burial garments in his chamber and who claims to be able to find his royal garb in the dark, intends to comply with the wish of the page but emerges from his chamber mistakenly dressed in his burial clothing. Later he is murdered by Palnatoke.

151. For a more earnest discussion of a subscription plan, see *Practice in Christianity*, Supplement, pp. 297–304, *KW* XX (*Pap.* X⁵ B 35, pp. 254–55; 38, pp. 256–57; 39, pp. 257–58; 40, pp. 258–62).

152. An allusion to the *ecclesia triumphans* [the Church Triumphant] as distinct from the *ecclesia militans* [the Church Militant] or the earthly Church engaged in warfare against sin, death, and the devil. The *ecclesia triumphans* is the Church of the blessed in the present and the future, the Church at rest.

153. The source of the quotation from Johann Paul Friedrich Richter (1763–1825), writing under the pseudonym Jean Paul, has not been located. See Matthew 10:38 and 16:24.

154. See I Timothy 2:4.

155. Perhaps a reference to Hippocrates, *Aphorisms*, I, 1; Hippocrates, I-IV, tr. W.H.S. Jones (Loeb, New York: Putnam, 1923–31), IV, pp. 98–99. This may also refer to Seneca, *De Brevitate Vitæ*, I, 1; *Seneca Moral Essays*, I-III, tr. John W. Basore (Loeb; Cambridge, Harvard University Press, 1913–15), "On the Shortness of Life," II, pp. 286–87.

156. An ironic reference to the attempt of Hegelians to "go beyond" or "go further" by extending or building a philosophical system along the lines of Hegel's *Encyclopädie der philosophischen Wissenschaften* (titled *System der Philosophie* in *Jubilæums Ausgabe*). See, for example, *Fragments*, pp. 20–21, 24, *KW* VII (*SV* IV 190, 193).

157. J. L. Heiberg's essay "Det logiske System," *Perseus*, II, August 1838, p. 44, concludes: "In passing it can be noted . . . how far the previous presentation differs from the Hegelian etc." On p. 5 there is a discussion of the Hegelian

system's "imperfections in detail." In his review of this issue of *Perseus* in *Maa-nedsskrift for Litteratur*, XIX (1838), p. 92, F. C. Sibbern stresses that Heiberg is beginning to "go beyond Hegel."

158. Freely quoted from Benedict de Spinoza, *Ethics*, II, *Scholium* to *Proposi-tio* 43; *Opera philosophica omnia*, ed. A Gfroerer (Stuttgart: 1830; *ASKB* 788), II, pp. 331–32; *Ethics*, tr. Samuel Shirley and ed. Seymour Feldman (Indianapolis: Hackett, 1982), p. 92. See *Sickness unto Death*, p. 42, *KW* XIX (*SV* XI 155); *Fragments*, p. 50, *KW* VII (*SV* IV 217).

159. The source of the quotation has not been identified.

160. See Descartes, *Discourse on Method, Opera philosophica* (Amsterdam: 1685; *ASKB* 473 [1678]), I, p. 1; *Discourse on Method, The Philosophical Writings of Descartes*, I-III, tr. John Cottingham, Robert Stoothoff, Dugald Murdoch (Cambridge: Cambridge University Press, 1985–91), I, p. 112.

161. For continuation of the sentence, see Supplement, p. 120 (*Pap.* V B 96:19).

162. See Supplement, p. 120 (*Pap.* V B 96:20). The phrase is probably a reference to p. xiv of *Perseus*, I, 1837: "In Danish, to be sure, Perseus means 'the destroyer,' but the destruction was not the absolute negation of time and death, but rather the heroic, out of which something new and more noble proceeds."

163. Perhaps a contrast of the daimon of Socrates with biblical allusions to the voice of God coming from above.

164. See Genesis 11:1–9.

165. Cf. Job 4:9.

166. See Supplement, p. 98 (*Pap.* IV A 2). Kierkegaard actually considered publication of a series of pamphlets under the title *Philosophical Deliberations*.

167. A reference to *Urania . . . 1844*, p. 98, in which J. L. Heiberg had criticized Kierkegaard for a confusion of natural and spiritual categories in *Rep-etition*. For a more extended response to Heiberg, see *Repetition*, Supplement, pp. 283–319, especially p. 308, *KW* VI (*Pap.* IV B 110–11, 116–17).

168. Baggesen, "*Min Gienganger-Spøg eller den søde Kniv*," *Danske Værker*, VI, p. 143.

169. With reference to the remainder of the sentence, see Supplement, p. 120 (*Pap.* V B 96:21). *Forord bryder ingen Trætte.* This Danish proverb has developed out of different sayings and in this instance means that a word given in advance—an agreement—prevents a quarrel later. Kierkegaard indulges here in wordplay with this proverb: *Forord* [preface] and *Forord* [word in advance]. See also *From the Papers of One Still Living, Early Writings*, p. 55, *KW* I (*SV* XIII 45).

WRITING SAMPLER

TITLE PAGE

TITLE PAGE. See Supplement, pp. 127–28 (*Pap.* VI A 146, B 194). The pseudonyms, literally "Roseleaf" and "Goodhope," do not appear among the published pseudonyms. See Supplement, pp. 128–29 (*Pap.* VII² B 272, 274:2,3).

1. See *Adler, KW* XXIV (*Pap.* VII² B 235, p. 83) and *JP* II 2143–44 (*Pap.* VII¹ A 24–25).

2. 4. In Danish *Dem* is the accusative of the second-person plural pronoun. *Du* is the informal form of the second-person singular, corresponding to the archaic English "thou" and the German *du*.

3. See *Adler, KW* XXIV (*Pap.* VII² B 235, p. 13).

4. Erik Pontoppidan, *Sandhed til Gudfrygtighed, udi en eenfoldig og efter Mulighed kort dog tilstrækkelig Forklaring over . . . Dr. M. Luthers liden Catechismo* (Stavanger: 1849, *ASKB* 190), Question 351; *Epitome of Rev. Dr. Erick Pontoppidan's Explanation of Martin Luther's Small Catechism,* tr. Edmund Belfour (Chicago: Anderson & Lawson, 1878), p. 48, includes this passage as Question 240 with the following translation: "*What is it to create?* It is to make something out of nothing, or out of chaotic matter. Heb. 11:3."

5. See, for example, *Fragments,* p. 6, *KW* VII (*SV* IV 177); *Postscript,* p. 115, *KW* XII.1 (*SV* VII 94).

6. See *Either/Or,* II, p. 277, *KW* IV (*SV* II 248).

7. See *Adler, KW* XXIV (*Pap.* VII² B 235, pp. 12–16). See also *JP* I 156 (*Pap.* VII¹ A 51).

8. With reference to the remainder of the paragraph, see Supplement, p. 129 (*Pap.* VI B 195).

9. See II Corinthians 5:17.

10. Cf. *JP* II 1251 (*Pap.* VII¹ A 181).

11. With reference to the remainder of the paragraph, see Supplement, p. 130 (*Pap.* VI B 197).

12. With reference to the remainder of the paragraph, see Supplement, p. 129 (*Pap.* VI B 196).

13. With reference to the following paragraph, see Supplement, p. 130 (*Pap.* VI B 197).

14. The sentence includes a pun that cannot be reproduced in English. Among other things, *Tilkommende* can refer to the wages due one and to one's fiancé. The word can also refer to something forthcoming or expected.

15. With reference to the following paragraph, see Supplement, pp. 130–31 (*Pap.* VI B 198).

16. Kierkegaard mismatches author and play. This appears to be intentional burlesque with Kierkegaard using a heavy hand on ignorance and fake literacy. Kierkegaard knew Shakespeare intimately and owned an edition of Richard

Brinsley Sheridan's *The School for Scandal* in Danish: *Bagtalelsens Skole. Komedie i fem Acter*, tr. N. V. Dorph (Copenhagen: 1841; *ASKB U* 104), *Royal Theater Repertoire*, 126. *The School for Scandal* was first produced in London on May 8, 1777. After a long period in which it did not appear in the repertoire of the Royal Theater in Copenhagen, it was performed there on December 14, 1846, and frequently thereafter.

17. King Christian VIII (1786–1848), who reigned from 1839 to 1848, and his brother, Crown Prince Ferdinand (1792–1863).

18. August Wilhelm Iffland (1759–1814), German playwright and theater director in Gotha, Mannheim, and Berlin.

19. Korsør is a town on the southwest shore of Sjælland.

20. Nicolai Peter Nielsen (1795–1860), a well-known Danish actor of the day, was appointed drama director at the Royal Theater in Copenhagen in 1829. J. L. Heiberg, director of the theater, dismissed him from this post in 1849. Nielsen was widely thought to have been the prototype for Heiberg's figure of an actor in *En Sjæl efter Døden*, *Nye Digte* (Copenhagen: 1841; *ASKB* 1562).

21. Anna Helene Dorothea Nielsen (1803–1856) was a member of the Royal Theater company from 1821 until her death. A great favorite of the critics, she was especially noted for her portrayal of women at various stages in their lives. See *Stages*, pp. 131–32, *KW* XI (*SV* VI 126–27); Supplement, pp. 562–64 (*Pap.* VI B 2–3). See also *Letters*, Letter 170, Dedication 15 (b), p. 435, *KW* XXV.

22. Joachim Ludvig Phister (1807–1896), a prominent actor admired by Kierkegaard. See "Herr Phister as Captain Scipio," in *Christian Discourses* and *Crisis*, pp. 327–44, *KW* XVII (*Pap.* IX B 68, pp. 383–400). See also *Either/Or*, I, pp. 239, 279, *KW* III (*SV* I 213, 250), and *JP* VI 6807 (*Pap.* X⁴ A 568).

23. Perhaps a comparative reference to Anna Helene Dorothea Nielsen, who early in her career was billed as *Madame* and later preferred *Fru* [Mrs.].

24. Johanne Luise Heiberg (1812–1890), the actress whom Kierkegaard discusses at length in *Crisis* (*KW* XVII).

25. Probably a reference to Michael Rosing Wiehe (1820–1864), the eldest of three brothers famous as actors on the Danish stage of the day.

26. The opera *Norma*, composed by the Italian Vincenzo Bellini (1801–1835) and first produced at La Scala in Milan during the Carnival season of 1831–32, was played three times in Copenhagen during the 1846–47 season.

27. With reference to No. 2, see Supplement, pp. 145–46 (*Pap.* VII² B 277:7).

28. With reference to the following paragraph, see Supplement, p. 145 (*Pap.* VI B 219).

29. With reference to No. 3, see Supplement, p. 146 (*Pap.* VII² B 277:8).

30. Peter Martin Orla Lehmann (1810–1870), who had previously represented another district, was first elected to represent Copenhagen in the Roskilde Estates on December 22, 1846. See *Fædrelandet*, 308, December 29, 1846.

31. See J. V. Neegaard, *Morderne Ole P. Kollerøds, Ole Hansens, Peder Chris-*

tian Knudsens og flere andre Forbryderes Criminalsag (Copenhagen: 1838). See also *JP* I 83 (*Pap.* XI¹ A 358).

32. Amager is an island separated from Sjælland by harbor waters and connected by bridge. See also *JP* II 2145 (*Pap.* VII¹ A 37). In 1842 Copenhagen's executioner conducted an execution in such an unseemly manner that he was suspended from office and charged as a criminal. As a result of these events, a decision was made to secure a guillotine and a commission was charged with constructing this device. Nothing came of these plans, however, and in 1846 a new executioner was appointed to serve all of Sjælland.

33. Although public whippings were by this time infrequent, the city owned a whip and required its executioner to administer floggings.

34. With reference to the following paragraph, see Supplement, pp. 146–47 (*Pap.* VII² B 277:10).

35. A street in central Copenhagen.

36. See *JP* III 2811 (*Pap.* VII¹ A 189).

37. The usual times when servants were hired or left a job were May 1 and November 1.

38. With reference to the following paragraph, see Supplement, pp. 147–48 (*Pap.* VII² B 277:14,15).

39. A German word with a Danish ending. See *Stages*, p. 491, *KW* XI (*SV* VI 456).

40. *Kjøbenhavns Flyveposten*, 224, September 26, 1846, reported of a panorama displayed at Vesterbro 9 (now 49) that it was "provided with the following new equipment . . . the mechanical peepshow or lucky star, where everyone gets a temperament chart." See *JP* V 5932 (*Pap.* VII¹ A 95).

41. See also *JP* V 5932 (*Pap.* VII¹ 95).

42. With reference to the following paragraph, see Supplement, pp. 148–51 (*Pap.* VI B 235; VII² B 277:16).

43. A fictional reference to the Danish student Hans Frederik Poulsen (1815–1869).

44. Possibly a reference to philologist Johan Nicolai Madvig (1804–1886), whose critical writings on classical literature had won acclaim in Denmark and abroad, and to his critic Professor Torkel Baden (1765–1849). See *Repetition*, Supplement, p. 301, *KW* VI (*Pap.* IV B 117); *Postscript*, p. 622, *KW* XII.1 (*SV* VII 542). See also *JP* V 5926 (*Pap.* VII¹ A 55).

45. See *JP* V 6065–66 (*Pap.* VIII¹ A 383–84).

46. With reference to No. 8, see Supplement, pp. 141, 151–52 (*Pap.* VI B 229, VII² B 287, 288).

47. In the 1840s there were nearly two hundred night watchmen in Copenhagen; some walked the streets and tended the lamps, while others were posted in church steeples.

48. A street in Copenhagen.

49. The Copenhagen watchmen were famed and long remembered for their songs marking the hours of the night.

50. See Isaiah 3:4; Ecclesiastes 10:16ff. See *Point of View, KW* XXII (*SV* XIII 551). See also *JP* II 1162 (*Pap.* VII¹ A 58).

51. See Corsair *Affair*, Supplement, p. 176, *KW* XIII (*Pap.* VII¹ B 42). Presumably an allusion to F. L. Høedt (1820–1885), a part-time teacher at Borgerdyds School, Christianshavn, 1844–1845. References to him appear in *Corsaren* 208, 209, 211, September 6, 13, 27, 1844.

52. See *JP* V 5887–88 (*Pap.* VII¹ A 98–99). See also *Corsaren*, 270, November 21, 1845; Meïr Goldschmidt, *Livs Erindringer og Resultater*, I-II (Copenhagen: 1877), I, p. 264.

53. Copenhagen's now world-famous amusement park opened on August 15, 1843.

54. See *Adler, KW* XXIV (*Pap.* VII² B 235, p. 14).

55. See Genesis 30:25–43.

56. Friedrich Wilhelm Joseph von Schelling (1775–1854), German idealist philosopher.

57. F.W.J. Schelling (see note 56 above) provided a preface to the posthumous works of the Norwegian-born Henrik Steffens. See Heinrich Steffens, *Nachgelassene Schriften. Mit einem Vorworte von Schelling* (Berlin: 1846; *ASKB* 799), p. xvii. See also *JP* IV 4112 (*Pap.* VII¹ A 63). Kierkegaard's Danish rendering of Schelling's German differs in these entries.

SUPPLEMENT

PREFACES

1. See p. 5 and note 5.

2. See Genesis 3:8.

3. J. I. Baggesen, *Asenutidens Abracadabra*, in *Danske Værker*, I–XII (Copenhagen: 1827–32), VII, pp. 195 ff. See Kierkegaard's parallel in *Pap.* II B 1–21.

4. See *Johannes Climacus, KW* VII (*Pap.* IV B 103–50).

5. See *Repetition*, p. 225, *KW* VI.

6. In the Lutheran liturgical calendar of the era, the Trinity season was the longest section of the church year, falling in the spring, summer, and autumn seasons between Trinity Sunday and Advent.

7. See *Stages*, pp. 360–63, *KW* XI (*SV* VI 336–39).

8. The first proposed use of the pseudonym eventually employed for *Prefaces*.

9. See *Anxiety*, p. 30, *KW* VIII (*SV* IV 303).

10. See *Johannes Climacus, KW* VII (*Pap.* IV B 103–50).

11. See *Eighteen Upbuilding Discourses*, pp. 7–29, *KW* V (*SV* III 13–34), 205–26 (IV 95–113), 253–73 (139–56).

12. H. L. Martensen's *Grundrids til Moralphilosophiens System* had been published in 1841. From 1842 Kierkegaard did considerable reading of Aristotle and about Aristotle in W. G. Tennemann, *Geschichte der Philosophie*, I–VIII$^{1-2}$–XI (Leipzig: 1798–1819; *ASKB* 815–26).

13. Kierkegaard here had in mind a parody of Johan Ludvig Heiberg's *Urania: Aarbog for 1844* (Copenhagen: 1843; *ASKB U* 57).

14. This is a reference to J. L. Heiberg's treatment of *Repetition* in *Urania: Aarbog for 1844*. See also *Repetition*, Supplement, pp. 281, 283–98, *KW* VI (*Pap.* IV B 101, 110–11); *Anxiety*, pp. 18–19, *KW* VIII (*SV* IV 291).

15. The proposed pseudonym, Inter et Inter, is mystifying. Literally the Latin phrase means "Between and Between." It may refer to a location between (*inter*) parts of the series of pseudonymous works and (*et*) to a position between (*inter*) the pseudonymous works and the signed works. This would account for its association with *Prefaces* and the published use of the pseudonym for the later work, *Crisis, KW* XVII (*SV* X 344). It may also allude to the proverb *Distinguendum est inter et inter* [It is necessary to distinguish between notions that need to be distinguished]. In this instance the pseudonym might refer to the need to distinguish between logical confusions.

16. Jens Baggesen (1764–1826), Danish poet.

17. See Supplement, p. 107 (*Pap.* IV B 137). See *Anxiety*, p. 3, *KW* VIII (*SV* IV 276).

18. See Hegel, *Philosophie der Geschichte, Werke*, IX, pp. 129–135; *Jubiläumsausgabe* [*J.A.*], I–XXVI, ed. Hermann Glockner (Stuttgart: 1927–40), XI, pp. 151–57; *The Philosophy of History* (tr. of P. G., 2 ed., 1840; Kierkegaard had

1 ed., 1837), tr. J. Sibree (New York: Dover, 1956), pp. 105–10, in which the phases of the expression of the Absolute Mind in history are outlined: the Orient as unreflected consciousness; the Greek world, the period of adolescence; the Roman state, the manhood of history, the reality of abstract universality; and the fourth phase of world history, old age as perfect maturity and strength. Danish jurist Carl Mettus Weis (1809–1872) published in J. L. Heiberg's *Perseus, Journal for den speculative Idee*, II, August 1838 (*ASKB* 569), pp. 47–99, an article, "*Om Statens historiske Udvikling*," based on Hegel's idea of the four phases of world history. See also *Fragments*, p. 78 *KW* VII (*SV* IV 242).

19. A reference to the talkative main character in Ludvig Holberg's *Mester Gert Westphaler Eller den meget talende Barbeer*, I, *Danske Skue-Plads*, I-VII (Copenhagen: 1788; *ASKB* 1566–67), no pagination. See Supplement, p. 137 (*Pap.* VI B 221), pp. 103–04 (*Pap.* IV B 131).

20. See Holberg, *Mester Gert Westphaler Eller den meget talende Barbeer*, Scene 8, *Danske Skue-Plads*, I, no pagination.

21. Nero Claudius Caesar, emperor of Rome (54–68).

22. Gaius Julius Vindex incited a rebellion against Nero. Philostratus records that Vindex stirred his soldiers for battle with a speech in which he declared that "Nero was anything rather than a harpist, and a harpist rather than a sovereign." See Philostratus, *The Life of Apollonius of Tyana*, V, 10; *Flavius Philostratus de Aeltern, Werke*, tr. F. Jakobs, Books I-IV in one vol. (Stuttgart: 1821–32; *ASKB* 1143), p. 430; *The Life of Apollonius of Tyana, the Epistles of Apollonius and the Treatises of Eusebius*, I-II, tr. F. C. Conybeare (Loeb, Cambridge: Harvard University Press, 1912), I, pp. 486–87. See also *JP* IV 4105 (*Pap.* IV A 13).

23. Danish Lutheran missionary efforts were begun in Greenland in 1721 by Hans Povelsen Egede (1686–1758).

24. See note 17 above.

25. Presumably a reference to J. L. Heiberg. See *Pap.* IV B 33.

26. Ludwig Andreas Feuerbach (1804–1872), a student of G.W.F. Hegel, abandoned Hegel's idealism and argued that Christian beliefs in God, heaven, eternal life, etc. are merely projections of human desires. See also *Fragments*, Supplement, pp. 217–18, *KW* VII (*Pap.* V B 1:10).

27. See *JP* V 5564, 5678 (*Pap.* III A 245; IV A 132).

28. See *Stages*, p. 89, *KW* XI (*SV* VI 87).

29. Homer, *Odyssey*, I, 3; *Homers Odyssee*, tr. Christian Wilster (Copenhagen: 1837), p. 3; *Homer The Odyssey*, I-II, tr. A. T. Murray (Loeb, Cambridge: Harvard University Press, 1976–80), I, p. 3.

30. See *Stages*, pp. 89–90, *KW* XI (*SV* VI 88).

31. A game (*Forundringsstolen*, also sometimes named *Beundringsstolen*), the wonder stool, in which one person sits in the middle of a circle of players, while another, using the formula "What are you wondering?" asks the others what they want to know about the sitter. The questioner then repeats the whispered question to the sitter, who tries to guess the author of each question. The first correct guess places a new victim on the chair. This game is referred to also in *Fragments*, p. 52, *KW* VII (*SV* IV 219); *Sickness unto Death*, p. 5, *KW* XIX (*SV*

XI 117); "To Mr. Orla Lehmann," *Early Polemical Writings*, p. 24, *KW* I (*SV* XIII 28); *JP* V 5100 (*Pap*. I A 75, p. 57).

32. J. L. Heiberg, "*Om Principet for Historiens Begyndelse*," *Intelligensblade*, 35–36, September 1, 1843, pp. 241–83.

33. Georg B. Winer, *Biblisches Realwörterbuch zum Handgebrauch für Studierende, Kandidaten, Gymnasiallehrer und Prediger ausgearbeitet*, I-II (Leipzig: 1833–38; *ASKB* 70–71).

34. Presumably the tutorial materials of Hans Brøchner (1796–1843), who upon graduation (1817) tutored in theology at the University of Copenhagen.

35. Perhaps a reference to Horace, *Epodes*, XII, 5. Q. *Horatii Flacci opera* (Leipzig: 1828; *ASKB* 1248), p. 143. *Horace The Odes and Epodes*, tr. C. E. Bennett (Loeb, New York: Putnam, 1930), pp. 398–99. The text to which Kierkegaard may refer reads: *polypus an gravis hirsutis cubet hircus in alis* ["a polyp or a goaty stench is bedded in the armpits"].

36. Presumably Christian Winther, *Fire Noveller* (Copenhagen: 1843), which had been announced in *Berlingske Tidende*, 238, September 5, 1843, as appearing "these days," or *Digtninger* (Copenhagen: 1843), reviewed in *Berlingske Tidende*, 311, November 22, 1842), as appearing "these days."

37. See p. 85 and note 44.

38. See Holberg, *Den Stundesløse*, II, 1, *Danske Skue-Plads*, V, no pagination; *The Fussy Man, Four Plays by Holberg*, tr. Henry Alexander (Princeton: Princeton University Press, for the American Scandinavian Foundation, 1946), p. 26. In response to Vielgeschrey's boast about his little black hen, Christoffer, reading the record book, says: "It's just as you say, Sir, forty eggs. What else she has given is not put down." See also *Stages*, p. 53, *KW* XI (*SV* VI 54).

39. See Holberg, *Peder Paars et heroiskcomisk Digt*, ed. K. H. Seidelin (Copenhagen: 1798), I, Song 2, pp. 24–51. The reference is to the island of Anholt, whose inhabitants lived from wrecks of ships. Holberg implies that the inhabitants of the island may by means of lights lure ships onto the rocks.

40. See Supplement p. 117 (*Pap*. V B 88:4). Protagoras (481–411 B.C.) was a leading Greek Sophist. His famous formulation, based on the privacy of experience, is given in Plato *Theaetetus*, 152 a (see also *Cratylus*, 386 a); *Platonis quæ exstant opera*, I-XI, ed. Friedrich Ast (Leipzig: 1819–32; *ASKB* 1144–54), II, pp. 30–31; *The Collected Dialogues of Plato*, ed. Edith Hamilton and Huntingdon Cairns (Princeton: Princeton University Press, 1963), p. 856: "'man is the measure of all things—alike of the being of things that are and of the not-being of things that are not.'"

41. Kierkegaard had previously applied this phrase directly to J. L. Heiberg: "Prof. Heiberg has 'the measure in his mouth.'" See *Either/Or*, Supplement, II, p. 407, *KW* IV (*Pap*. IV B 55). The Danish word *Maal* is ambiguous. On the one hand, it designates a measure, a measuring device, a criterion. On the other hand, it designates a goal, a final end. The latter meaning is synonymous with *Formaal* [purpose] and *Hensigt* [aim]. See also *Irony*, p. 207, *KW* II (*SV* XIII 287); *Postscript*, p. 312, *KW* XII.1 (*SV* VII 268); *Sickness unto Death*, pp. 79–80, *KW* XIX (*SV* XI 191–92).

42. In the play *Guldkorset*, the character Corporal Remi frequently alludes to sayings from "an old soldier." *Guldkorset: Lystspil i to Acter efter det Franske ved J. L. Heiberg, Det Kongelige Theaters Repertoire*, 79 (Copenhagen: 1836). See, for example, I, 4, p. 3. A two-act French comedy by Melesville and Brazier, *Cathérine ou la croix d'or*, was translated into Danish as *Guldkorset* by J. L. Heiberg and appeared eight times its first season with Louise Heiberg playing the role of Catherine. The play occasioned a well-known controversy between Heiberg and the Danish playwright Thomas Overskou. See *Early Writings*, Supplement, p. 177, *KW* I.

43. The north commons of Copenhagen.

44. See p. 116 and note 40 above.

45. A reference to J. L. Heiberg.

46. Presumably Hans Peter Holst (1811–1893). See "Preface IV" note 66.

47. A play on the title of a work by Hans Peter Holst, *Ude og Hjemme: Reise-Erindringer* (Copenhagen: 1842; *ASKB* 1569).

48. Frederik Christian Sibbern (1785–1872) was professor of philosophy at the University of Copenhagen when Kierkegaard was a student.

49. See *Anxiety*, p. 7, *KW* VIII (*SV* IV 279).

50. The reference appears to be inaccurate. See rather Diogenes Laertius, *Lives*, II, 5, 21; *Vitis*, II, pp. 79–80; Riisbrigh, I, p. 66; Loeb, II, pp. 150–53.

51. This phrase was probably deleted from *Prefaces* because it moved specifically toward themes under consideration in *The Concept of Anxiety*. See *Anxiety*, Supplement, p. 179, *KW* VIII (*Pap.* V B 47). This latter formulation with its accent on hereditary sin clearly places these lines within the scope of *Anxiety* rather than within the satirical sphere of *Prefaces*. The final satirical formulation in *Prefaces* aptly characterizes Kierkegaard's own approach to the task of his authorship. See also *JP* V 5092 (*Pap.* I A 72).

52. "Mag." is an abbreviation for *Magister* [master]. The degree of *Magister Artium* (*Liberalium*) [Master of the Liberal Arts] was conferred by the philosophical faculty of the University of Copenhagen. The degree was equivalent to that of Doctor of Philosophy, the degree conferred by the other faculties. In 1854 the philosophy faculty's degree *Magister Artium* was replaced by Doctor of Philosophy, and all persons holding the degree *Magister Artium* were declared to be *Doctores Philosophiæ*. Kierkegaard had received the degree of *Magister Artium* upon completion of his dissertation, *The Concept of Irony, with Continual Reference to Socrates* (*KW* II) in 1841.

53. J. L. Heiberg was editor of the short-lived *Perseus, Journal for den speculative Idee* (Copenhagen: 1837–38; *ASKB* 569).

WRITING SAMPLER

1. "The Wrong and the Right" (*Pap.* V B 155–92) contains drafts of parts of *Stages*.

2. See *Stages*, p. 6, *KW* XI (*SV* VI 11).

3. See Supplement, p. 128 (*Pap.* VI A 146). Literally translated, the pseudo-

nyms are "Rosestick" and "Roseleaf." Willibald had already appeared as a character in *The Battle between the Old and the New Soap-Cellars, Early Writings,* pp. 103–24, *KW* I (*Pap.* II B 1, 7–22).

4. The entire entry is a listing of titles or possible titles of works on which Kierkegaard was engaged during 1844–45. "Logical Issues" refers to *Postscript.* See *Postscript,* Supplement, pp. 7–8, *KW* XII.2 (*Pap.* VI B 13, A 146, B 89).

5. At the time Kierkegaard was considering writing something on religious address. See *JP* I 627, 635; V 5785 (*Pap.* VI A 17, B 129, 132). The theme of the art of Christian speaking or religious address was of live concern to Kierkegaard throughout his life; this involved the use of Aristotle's *Rhetoric* and the making of crucial distinctions between it and his projected work. He began a series of lectures, "The Dialectic of Ethical and Religious Communication," which he did not finish or deliver or publish. The substance, however, appears throughout the authorship. See *JP* I 648–57 (*Pap.* VIII² 79–89).

6. Pseudonymous author of *Fear and Trembling* (*KW* VI).

7. See Aristotle, *Rhetoric,* II, 23, para. 14, 1399 a 20–25; *The Complete Works of Aristotle;* I–II, ed. Jonathan Barnes (rev. Oxford tr.; Princeton: Princeton University Press, 1984), II, pp. 2229–30.

8. *Aristoteles Rhetorik,* tr. K. L. Roth (Stuttgart: 1833; *ASKB* 1092).

9. See *JP* V 5801, 5813 (*Pap.* VI A 31, 55).

10. A reference to J. L. Heiberg's lavishly produced volume, *Urania: Aarbog for 1844* (Copenhagen: 1843; *ASKB* U 57).

11. See *Adler, KW* XXIV (*Pap.* VII² B 235, p. 13); *JP* III 2766 (*Pap.* VII¹ A 67).

12. A reference to N.F.S. Grundtvig. See *Postscript,* Supplement, p. 16, *KW* XII.2 (*Pap.* VI B 21:8).

13. Hans Carl Sager (1808–1885), master baker and a director of poor relief in Copenhagen. Sager also served in the Roskilde Estates in 1844.

14. See Heinrich Steffens, *Was Ich erlebte. Aus der Erinnerung niedergeschrieben,* I–X (Breslau, 1843; *ASKB* 1834–43), X, p. 369, and *Berlingske Tidende,* 8, January 9, 1845. Bertel Albert Thorvaldsen (1768–1844), Denmark's foremost sculptor, was not in fact present at the coronation of King Christian VIII. Steffens did, however, visit with Thorvaldsen in conjunction with the occasion. See J. M. Thiele, *Thorvaldsen i Kiøbenhavn, 1839–1844* (Copenhagen: 1856), pp. 116–18. See also Rigmor Stampe, ed., *Baronesse Stampes Erindringer om Thorvaldsen* (Copenhagen: 1912), p. 66, note 346.

15. See *Postscript,* Supplement, p. 26, *KW* XII.2 (*Pap.* VI B 29, p. 111); p. 27 (*Pap.* VI B 30, p. 113); pp. 27–29 (*Pap.* VI B 33).

16. See Supplement, pp. 132–34 (*Pap.* VI B 207).

17. See *Either/Or,* Supplement, II, pp. 418–19, *KW* IV (*Pap.* IV B 59, p. 215); *Repetition,* Supplement, pp. 283–85, *KW* VI (*Pap.* IV B 110).

18. Count Christian of Denmark was elected King Christian I of Denmark in 1448. All subsequent Danish monarchs have been descendants of Christian I.

19. See p. 24.

20. *Ølnordiske* [Ale-Norse] is a pun on the Danish *Old nordiske* [Old Norse], which refers to N.F.S. Grundtvig's well-known interest in Norse mythology. See Supplement, pp. 148–50 (*Pap.* VI B 235). See also *Stages*, Supplement, p. 535, *KW* XI (*Pap.* V B 187:8); *Postscript*, Supplement, p. 27, *KW* XII.2 (*Pap.* VI B 30, p. 113); *JP* V 5819 (*Pap.* VI A 73).

21. A reference to J. L. Heiberg, *Ny A-B-C Bog i en Times Underviisning til Ære, Nytte, og Fornøielse for den unge Grundtvig. Et pedagogisk Forsøg* (Copenhagen: 1817), p. 21.

22. Johan Ludvig Heiberg.

23. See *Repetition*, Supplement, p. 284, *KW* VI (*Pap.* IV B 110, p. 259).

24. The so-called *Røde-Bygning* [Red Building] on Slotsholmgade in Copenhagen, built in the time of Frederik VI (1671–1730), now housing ministerial offices, was in Kierkegaard's time called the *Kancellibygning* [Chancellery Building].

25. See, for example, *Repetition*, Supplement, p. 281, *KW* VI (*Pap.* IV B 101).

26. A reference to Friederich Faber, *Über das Leben der hochnordischen Vögel. Mit vier Tabellen* (Leipzig: 1826). The first chapter of this work treats the range and migratory patterns of boreal birds. Faber (d. 1828) was from 1825 married to Anne Kirstine Elisabeth Kierkegaard, a daughter of Michael Anderson Kierkegaard, cousin of Søren Kierkegaard's father. See Supplement, pp. 137–38 (*Pap.* VI B 222).

Kierkegaard later pursued the theme of migratory birds. A letter to him from Henrik Lund of April 12, 1850, is a reply to "the extensive task you assigned me in your last letter" concerning the arrival times of migratory birds. See *Letters and Documents*, Letter 262, *KW* XXV. Birds provide a thematic metaphor in "What We Learn from the Lilies in the Field and from the Birds of the Air," *Part Two, Upbuilding Discourses in Various Spirits*, pp. 155–212, *KW* XV (*SV* VIII 245–96), and in *The Lily in the Field and the Bird of the Air*, in *Without Authority*, pp. 1–45, *KW* XVIII (*SV* XI 3–46).

27. See Supplement, p. 138 (*Pap.* VI B 223).

28. See *Stages*, pp. 24, 463–65, *KW* XI (*SV* VI 28, 431–33).

29. See Steen Steenen Blicher and E. Bindestouw, *Fortællinger og Digte i jydske Mundarter* (Randers: 1842), p. 30.

30. See p. 103 and note 19.

31. See p. 24.

32. An African church father (160?–230?). For this purpose, Kierkegaard may have used Q. *Sept. Flor. Tertulliani Opera*, ed. E. F. Leopold, I–IV (Leipzig: 1839; *ASKB* 147–50), or Q. *Sept. Flor. Tertullians sämmtliche Schriften*, ed. and tr. Frants Anton von Besnard (Augsburg: 1837; *ASKB* 151).

33. Bishop of Carthage (248–258) and martyr (200?–258). For this purpose Kierkegaard may have used *Th. C. Cypriani Opera genuina*, ed. D.J.H. Goldhorn (Leipzig: 1838–39; *ASKB* 139–40).

34. Ironically, the most widely known and now the best known of the cartoons of Kierkegaard to appear in *The Corsair* has a text akin to this phrase. See

"The Great Philosopher," in Corsair *Affair*, Supplement, p. 133, *KW* XIII (*Corsaren*, 285, March 6, 1846, col. 8–11). Gyldendal Forlag, on a poster using the cartoon in connection with the publication of the third edition of the *Samlede Værker* (Copenhagen: 1962), stated: "What was then malicious caricature is today literally true."

35. See Supplement, p. 147 (*Pap.* VII² B 277:11).

36. A bridge across the harbor channel between Copenhagen proper and Christianshavn. Larger ships quite frequently required and still require the drawbridge to be raised. See *Either/Or*, I, p. 25, *KW* III (*SV* I 9); *Letters*, Letter 17, *KW* XXV.

37. Kierkegaard was Copenhagen's foremost peripatetic and street observer and conversationalist. See, for example, Andrew Hamilton, *Sixteen Months in the Danish Isles*, I-II (London: 1852), II, p. 269: "The fact is *he walks about town all day*, and generally in some person's company. . . . When walking he is very communicative."

38. See Supplement, pp. 157–58 (*Pap.* VII¹ B 207).

39. Johann David Michaelis (1717–1791), professor of philosophy (1746–50) and Oriental languages (1750–91) at the University of Halle.

40. *JP* V 5841 (*Pap.* VI A 104).

41. See especially *Postscript*, pp. 34–46, *KW* XII.1 (*SV* VII 24–34).

42. A reference to *Dansk-Pantheon: et Portraitgallerie for Samtiden, ledsaget af biographiske Notitser* (Copenhagen: 1845–51). The twenty-second installment (1844) included a portrait of Grundtvig with a biography by P. L. Møller.

43. Kierkegaard indulges in wordplay here. *Fjant* is "silliness, foolery."

44. "Prussia" is deleted in the manuscript. King Frederick William IV of Prussia arrived in Copenhagen on June 18, 1845, and departed on June 22. See *Berlingske Tidende*, 143–49, June 17–23, 1845.

45. A narrow, winding street in central Copenhagen, now part of a *Gaagade* [walking street] stretching from the Royal Theater to the Town Hall.

46. A small square connected with Vimmelskaftet. See note 45.

47. Kierkegaard may here be thinking of a description of these events in *Berlingske Tidende*, 147, June 21, 1845, which described the events as occurring continuously.

48. A reference to characters in J. L. Heiberg, *De Uadskillige, Skuespil af Johan Ludvig Heiberg*, I-VII (Copenhagen: 1833–41; *ASKB* 1553–59), IV, pp. 235–38. The action of the entire play occurs in the context of a family outing in Dyrehaven.

49. Mendel Levin Nathanson (1780–1868), merchant, writer on trade and finance, and editor of *Berlingske Tidende* 1838–56 and 1865–66.

50. See *Berlingske Tidende*, 143, June 17, 1845.

51. Denmark's oldest regularly published newspaper, founded in 1749 by an immigrant from Mecklenburg, Ernst H. Berling. Neither the family name nor the name of the newspaper has any connection with the city of Berlin.

52. See Supplement, p. 139 (*Pap.* VI B 225).

53. Prussia.

54. M. W. Brun's play in five acts, *De skandinaviske Brødre*, had a disastrous premiere performance on June 13, 1844.

55. The Scandinavian Student Congress met in Denmark on June 23–28, 1845, and met a warm welcome.

56. See Sallust, *The War with Jugurtha*, 79; *C. Sallustii Crispi Opera quae supersunt . . .* , I-II, ed. F. Kritzius (Leipzig: 1828–34; *ASKB* 1269–70), II, pp. 413–20; *The War with Jugurtha*, Sallust, tr. J. C. Rolfe (Loeb, Cambridge: Harvard University Press, 1921), pp. 298–301. Kierkegaard also owned *Opera omnia*, ed. Guil. Lange (Halle: 1833; *ASKB* 1271) and *Opera* (ed. stereot., Leipzig: 1829; *ASKB* 1272).

57. Danish student, Hans Frederik Poulsen.

58. See note 45. Kierkegaard presumably refers here to the place where Peder Madsens Gang [Alley] entered Vimmelskaftet, part of the present-day Strøget, a series of streets creating a pedestrian thoroughfare through the center of the city. In Kierkegaard's day this alley was notorious for prostitution. See also "Public Confession," *Corsair Affair*, p. 7, *KW* XIII (*SV* XIII 401).

59. Poulsen delivered his address on the evening of June 24, 1844, in the *Ridehus* of Christiansborg Palace. The speech resulted in legal charges by Orla Lehmann, but Poulsen was acquitted. See *Fædrelandet*, 1922–24, June 25–28, 1845.

60. See Joel 2:28–29.

61. Poul Frederik Barfod (1811–1896), politician, poet, and historian, not to be confused with H. P. Barfod, editor of the first edition of Kierkegaard's journals and papers, *Efterladte Papirer*.

62. On June 25, 1845, the Scandinavian Association had a festival day in Dyrehaven with a program including a song and two talks, one improvised, by N.F.S. Grundtvig.

63. The final two paragraphs of this entry appear to be largely ironical and fictive, including most likely the episode of the empty church. Although they remained unpublished, these comments on Mynster are among the earliest intimations of Kierkegaard's later criticism of this cherished friend of his father and the pastor of his own youth.

64. Possibly a reference to W. H. Rothe (1777–1857), curate of Trinity Church in Copenhagen, 1822–30, and pastor, 1830–57.

65. Kierkegaard preached his probational sermon in this church on March 24, 1844.

66. Kierkegaard did not publish this work. Part 1 of this projected work appeared separately in *Fædrelandet*, June 24–27, 1848, under the title *The Crisis and a Crisis in the Life of an Actress* (*KW* XVII). Portions of Part 2 were completed but remained unpublished. See Supplement, pp. 156–60 (*Pap.* VII^1 B 205–10). Part 3 on Christen Niemann Rosenkilde in the part of Hummer in J. L. Heiberg's *De Uadskillige*, in *Skuespil af J. L. Heiberg*, I-VII (Copenhagen: 1833–41; *ASKB* 1553–59), IV, pp. 223–348, was left unfinished (*Pap.* VIII^2 B 172–74). Part 4 is *Writing Sampler*.

67. The pseudonym might literally be translated "The happy one from St. Victor." The pseudonym was not used in a published work.

68. Kierkegaard developed this theme in a journal entry:

In Praise of Autumn

poetic . . . . .

When the autumn comes with its brisk, invigorating coolness, when the remnant of summer heat in the atmosphere is like a possibility, a motherly solicitude lest the indulger be chilled, when one always has, so to speak, a light coat at hand while the autumn winds increase—when autumn comes and the transitoriness of life elicits craving, when the forest does not stand secure as if it would stand thus to all eternity but changes color even as one is looking at it, because change inflames desire. When a woman remains secure and quiet, she does not excite, but when she changes colors, the change signifies: hurry, hurry! It is the same with autumn. In the summer the clouds never float as hurriedly as in the autumn. And in the autumn the echo never thinks of pausing to relax in the warm air of the woods—no, it rushes by without pausing.—*JP* III 2833 (*Pap.* VI A 89) *n.d.*, 1845

Addition to Pap. VI A 89:

Everything that is present prompts criticism, but recollection disarms and allows one to use ideality not to reject but to embellish the past.—*JP* III 2834 (*Pap.* VI A 90) *n.d.*, 1845

In margin of Pap. VI A 89:

Everything during autumn indeed reminds us of decline—and yet it strikes me as being the most beautiful of seasons. When I begin to decline, would that someone might think as well of me as I do of autumn!—*JP* III 2835 (*Pap.* VI A 91) *n.d.*, 1845

69. See Supplement, p. 140 (*Pap.* VI B 226); *JP* V 5746 (*Pap.* V A 84).

70. The giant Ymer, slain by Bor's sons (Odin, Vili, and Ve), who then made the universe out of Ymer's body. His flesh became the earth, his bones mountains and stones, his hair trees and grass, his skull the heavens, his blood the seas and rivers, his brains the clouds, and his marrow the dwarfs who live under the earth and under stones. From his eyebrows the gods are said later to have made a fortress, Midgaard, a defense against the giants.

Kierkegaard's library was richly stocked with works on mythology and folklore, including N.F.S. Grundtvig, *Nordens Mytologie eller Udsigt over Eddalæren* (Copenhagen: 1808; *ASKB* 1948); *Nordens Mythologi eller Sind-billedsprog* (Copenhagen: 1832; *ASKB* 1949); Thomas Crofton Croker, *Irische Elfenmärchen*, tr. Brothers Grimm (Leipzig: 1826; *ASKB* 1423); K. P. Moritz, *Guderlære* (Copenhagen: 1847; *ASKB* 1946); Paul Friedrich A. Nitsch, *Neues mythologisches Wörterbuch*, I–II (Leipzig, Sorau: 1821; *ASKB* 1944–45); W. Vollmer,

Vollständiges Wörterbuch der Mythologie aller Nationen (Stuttgart: 1836; *ASKB* 1942–43).

71. Christen Niemann Rosenkilde (1786–1861), a Danish actor famed for comic roles. Rosenkilde played the part of Hummer in J. L. Heiberg's *De Uadskillige, Skuespil*, IV, pp. 223–348. See also *Postscript*, Supplement, p. 130, *KW* XII.2 (*Pap.* VII¹ B 88, p. 290).

72. On memory and recollection, see *Stages*, pp. 9–14, *KW* XI (*SV* VI 15–20).

73. Perhaps a reference to J. L. Heiberg, *De Uadskillige, Skuespil*, IV, p. 303.

74. Hans Lassen Martensen (1808–1884), professor of theology at the University of Copenhagen and successor to Jakob Peter Mynster as Bishop of Sjælland, returned to Denmark in the autumn of 1836 after a two-year period of study and travel. In Berlin he studied with Henrich Steffens and Philipp Marheineke and read Hegel's works. In Heidelberg he studied with Carl Daub. He visited David Friedrich Strauss in Tübingen and Franz Baader in Munich, where he also heard Friedrich Wilhelm Joseph v. Schelling lecture. See *JP* II 1570; V 5200 (*Pap.* II A 52, 7); *Fragments*, pp. 6–7 and note 10, *KW* VII (*SV* IV 176–77).

75. See *Fragments*, pp. 5–8, *KW* VII (*SV* IV 175–79).

76. See *Fragments*, Supplement, pp. 226–27, *KW* VII (*Pap.* X² A 155, p. 117).

77. A reference to Jakob Peter Mynster.

78. "Preface VI." See pp. 31–34. Jakob Peter Mynster had in an earlier reference to *Fear and Trembling* related it to an expression by the German philosopher Friedrich Heinrich Jacobi (1743–1819): "*Ja, ich bin der Atheist und Gottlose, der . . . lügen will, wie Desdemona sterbend log* [Yes, I am the atheist and non-believer who . . . wants to lie, as Desdemona dying lied]." See *Jacobi an Fichte, Friedrich Heinrich Jacobi's Werke*, I–VI (Leipzig: 1812–25; *ASKB* 1722–28) III, p. 37. For Mynster's comment, see Kts, "*Kirkelig Polemik*," *Intelligensblade*, ed. J. L. Heiberg, IV, 41–42, January 1, 1844, p. 105. "Kts" was Mynster's pseudonym, formed from the initial consonant of the second syllable of each of his name (Ja*k*ober Pe*t*er Myn*s*ter). See also *Postscript*, p. 262, *KW* XII.1 (*SV* VII 221).

79. Mynster, J. L. Heiberg, and H. L. Martensen were parties to an extended debate over the principle of contradiction. The exchange took place in a series of articles in *Tidsskrift for Litteratur og Kritik*, 1839–45.

80. The pseudonymous editor of the first volume of *Either/Or*. See *KW* III (*SV* I).

81. The pseudonymous author of *Fear and Trembling*. See *KW* VI (*SV* III).

82. The pseudonymous author of *Fragments* and *Postscript*. See *KW* VII, XII (*SV* IV, VII).

BIBLIOGRAPHICAL NOTE

For general bibliographies of Kierkegaard studies, see:

Jens Himmelstrup, *Søren Kierkegaard International Bibliografi*. Copenhagen: Nyt Nordisk Forlag Arnold Busck, 1962.

International Kierkegaard Newsletter, ed. Julia Watkin. Launceton, Tasmania, Australia, 1979–.

Aage Jørgensen, *Søren Kierkegaard-litteratur 1961–1970*. Aarhus: Akademisk Boghandel, 1971. *Søren Kierkegaard-litteratur 1971–1980*. Aarhus: privately published, 1983.

Kierkegaard: A Collection of Critical Essays, ed. Josiah Thompson. New York: Doubleday (Anchor Books), 1972.

Kierkegaardiana, XII, 1982; XIII, 1984; XIV, 1988; XVI, 1993; XVII, 1994; XVIII, 1996.

Bruce H. Kirmmse, *Kierkegaard in Golden Age Denmark*. Bloomington: Indiana University Press, 1990.

François H. Lapointe, *Sören Kierkegaard and His Critics: An International Bibliography of Criticism*. Westport, Connecticut: Greenwood Press, 1980.

Søren Kierkegaard's Journals and Papers, I, ed. and tr. Howard V. Hong and Edna H. Hong, assisted by Gregor Malantschuk. Bloomington, Indiana: Indiana University Press, 1967.

For topical bibliographies of Kierkegaard studies, see *Søren Kierkegaard's Journals and Papers*, I-IV, 1967–75.

INDEX

address: public, 27; religious, 128, 193

Adresseavisen, 23, 37, 86, 99, 115, 116, 176

advertisement, 154; novelty and attention to, 73–74

age: of ferment, 137; of making distinctions, 103; of mental depression, 137, 177. *See also* times, demands of the

Ale-Norse, 132, 194

Amme, Maren, 102

analogy: black hen, 115; cat in barrel, 18, 20, 175; examination, 19; Harald Bluetooth, 52; knot, 181; layer cake, 88; Marathon messenger, 15; marriage, 149; peep show, 36–37; preface writing, 5–6; renter, 17, 113; shopkeeper, 75–76; spitting story, 133; tailor's apprentice, 43; teacher and pupil, 66; testing lover, 52; tic tac toe, 44; unwarranted attack story, 133–34; wastewater drain, 19

Anholt Island, 191

aquavit, 117

Aristotle, 66, 189; *Rhetoric*, xvii, 128, 193; on virtue, 100

Arnim, Achim von: *Bertholds Erstes und Zweites Lebens*, 181

association: and membership, 28–29; and moral power, 29–30, 178; of watchman, 86, 151–52

association-idea, 37, 43

astrology, xi, 24

astronomy, 24, 132–34, 137, 177, 178

Athens: life in, 106

attack, unwarranted. *See* analogy

Augustine of Hippo, 175

author: anonymous, 85, 89; and criticism, 66; Danish, 115–16; definition of, 75; public's creation of, 74–77, 87–88, 90; relation to public, 19; relation to reader, xiv, 18, 42, 44. *See also* book; preface; writing

autumn, 156–60, 197

Baader, Franz, 198

Bacchus, 30

Baden, Torkel, 187

Baggesen, Jens Immanuel, 67, 98, 102, 189; *Asenutidens Abracadabra*, 189; *Danske Værker*, 173; *Kallundborgs Krønike eller Censurens Oprindelse*, 173

Balaam's ass, 41

Balle, Nikolai E.: *Lærebog i den evangelisk-christelige Religion*, 171

barber, 174; in Plutarch's "Nicias," 174–75; talkative, 103–04

barber Biberak, 150

barber Lützov, 82–83

Barfod, Poul Frederik, 150, 196

Bellini, Vincenzo: *Norma*, 186

Belshazzar, 173

Berling, Ernst H., 195

Berlingske Tidende, 79, 80, 146, 191, 193, 195

BIBLE

New Testament

II Corinthians: 5:17, 185

Hebrews: 4:15, 181; 11:3, 185

Luke: 6:32–34, 178; 9:28–36, 177; 15:11–32, 173; 17:10, 178

ADVISORY BOARD